Praise for
Journeys to the Other Side of the World

'Abundantly good'
TLS

'A wondrous reminder of Attenborough's pioneering
role and the often hilarious difficulties he faced . . .
full of delightful tales'
Daily Express

'Engaging and evocative but ultimately poignant . . .
Attenborough is a fine writer and storyteller'
Irish Times

'An adventure that sparked a lifetime's
commitment to the planet'
The Lady

'With his usual charm and generosity,
Attenborough allows us along for the ride'
Irish Examiner

'Fascinating'
OK!

Praise for the *Sunday Times* bestseller
Adventures of a Young Naturalist

'A marvellous book . . . utterly engaging'
Daily Telegraph

'An elegant and gently funny writer'
The Times

'Immensely colourful and dramatic'
Daily Mail

'Full of Attenborough's trademark enthusiasm,
wit and intelligence'
Sunday Express

'As impressive and as enjoyable as his TV programmes
and there can be no higher praise'
Daily Express

'This is a great book for anyone who wants to vicariously
travel like an old-fashioned adventurer and seeks to
understand how far we have come in developing
a protective attitude to wildlife'
New York Times

Journeys to the Other Side of the World

Journeys to the Other Side of the World

Further Adventures of a Young Naturalist

DAVID ATTENBOROUGH

www.tworoadsbooks.com

First published in Great Britain in 1981 by Lutterworth Press as
Journeys to the Past: Travels in New Guinea, Madagascar, and the Northern Territory of Australia

This edition first published in Great Britain in 2018 by Two Roads
An imprint of John Murray Press
An Hachette UK company

This paperback edition first published in 2019

1

Original publications © David Attenborough 1960, 1961, 1963
This abridged combined volume © David Attenborough 1981
This edition of *Journeys to the Past* is published
by arrangement with *The Lutterworth Press*.
Introduction © David Attenborough 2018

Photographs © David Attenborough

The right of David Attenborough to be identified as the
Author of the Work has been asserted by him in accordance
with the Copyright, Designs and Patents Act 1988.

A CIP catalogue record for this title is available from the British Library

Paperback ISBN 9781473666672
eBook ISBN 9781473666665

Typeset in Bembo by Palimpsest Book Production Ltd, Falkirk, Stirlingshire

Printed and bound by Clays Ltd, Elcograf S.p.A.

Hodder & Stoughton policy is to use papers that are natural, renewable
and recyclable products and made from wood grown in sustainable forests.
The logging and manufacturing processes are expected to conform to
the environmental regulations of the country of origin.

Hodder & Stoughton Ltd
Carmelite House
50 Victoria Embankment
London EC4Y 0DZ

www.hodder.co.uk

Contents

BOOK THREE: Quest Under Capricorn

Introctuction

Every year for a decade, between 1954 and 1964, it was my great luck to go to the tropics and make natural history films. Initially, our expeditions were organized jointly by BBC Television and the London Zoo and our aim was not only to film animals but to catch some of them. The television programmes, in consequence, were given the overall name of *Zoo Quest*. Very sadly, however, ill health prevented the Zoo's representative, Jack

Lester, from taking part in the third trip. Thereafter, the Zoo's involvement was reduced to receiving such creatures as those of us from television managed to bring back. Filming animals in the wild, rather than capturing them, therefore, became our first priority. As time passed our interests also broadened and the tribal people we met on our journeys began to figure with increasing prominence in the films, so the name *Zoo Quest* seemed inappropriate as the title of this volume. The first three books I wrote about these journeys were republished in a slightly condensed form in 1980 and then once more in 2017 with some additional revision and the title *Adventures of a Young Naturalist*. Here are the second three, similarly slightly revised.

Catching a boa in Madagascar

It is over sixty years since we returned from the last of these journeys. Hardly surprisingly, a great deal has changed. The eastern half of New Guinea, then administered by Australia, has become independent as Papua New Guinea, and the Jimi Valley, which then was only beginning to be explored, now not only has roads along it, but also its own Member of Parliament. Queen Salote, who ruled Tonga at the time of our visit, died in 1965 and was succeeded by the Crown Prince as King Taufa'ahau Tupou IV, and he in turn by George Tupou V. The New Hebrides, once governed by that strange and unique form of colonial administration, an Anglo-French condominium, has become the independent state of Vanuatu. In Australia the tiny town of Darwin has become a city and the land around Nourlangie the National Park of Kakadu, complete with hotels and roads suited for such a role. The Asian water buffalo that at the time of our visit were still running wild in great numbers have now been exterminated to allow that wonderful but fragile ecosystem to return to something approximating its original condition. The rock paintings at Nourlangie that we were the first to photograph have now become internationally famous and have featured on Australian postage stamps. Barks painted by Magani, the artist who told us so much about how he worked, are now in the collections of the Australian National Gallery, and the men who painted the rocks near Yuendumu have been succeeded by artists who do indeed use modern paints and whose canvases now sell for hundreds of thousands if not millions of dollars. Some of the details of Aboriginal ceremonial practices that appeared in the original edition have been shortened in order not to offend current Aboriginal sensitivities.

Television techniques, of course, have changed beyond recognition. Sound recorders no longer use tape and do not refuse to work in the tropical sun. Television cameras are electronic and tiny compared with the monsters we used and no longer need to be swathed by special padding to keep them quiet. What is more, they can now replay their pictures immediately so that we no longer have to wait for months before we know whether or not we have the pictures we hoped we had.

Nonetheless, I have left the accounts of these places and events essentially as I wrote them.

David Attenborough, May 2018

BOOK ONE

Quest in Paradise

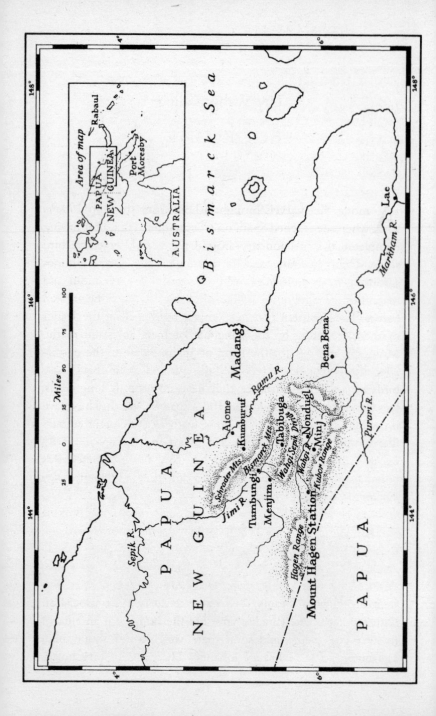

I

The Wahgi Valley

Among the marvels brought ashore from the ship *Vittoria* when she reached Spain on 6 September 1522, after having completed the first journey around the world, were five bird skins. Their feathers, and in particular the gauzy plumes sprouting from their sides, were of a matchless splendour and magnificence and quite unlike anything that had been seen before. Two of them had been given to Magellan, the leader of the expedition, by the King of Batchian, an island in the Moluccas, as a gift for the King of Spain. Pigafetti, the chronicler of the expedition, recorded the gift and wrote that 'These birds are as large as thrushes; they have small heads, long beaks, legs slender like a writing pen and a span in length. They have no wings but instead of them, long feathers of different colours like plumes: their tail is like that of a thrush. They never fly except when the wind blows. They told us that these birds come from the terrestrial Paradise, and they call them *bolon dinata*, that is divine birds.'

Thus these gorgeous creatures became known as Birds of Paradise. They were the first recorded specimens ever to come to Europe. Pigafetti's account of them was relatively unsensational. No doubt they had been shorn of their wings by the native skinners in order to emphasize the glory of their plumes. But their breathtaking beauty, their extreme rarity, their association with the 'terrestrial Paradise' invested the birds with an aura of mystery and magic, and soon there were stories about them as fantastic as their beauty. Johannes Huygen van Linschoten, describing his own voyage in the Moluccas seventy years later, wrote that 'In these Islands onlie is found the bird which the Portingales call passeros de sol, that is Fowle of the Sunne, the Italians call it Manu codiatas and the Latinists, Paradiseas, and by us called Paradice-birdes, for ye beauty of their feathers which passe al other birdes; these birdes are never seene alive, but being dead they fall on the Ilands: they flie, as it is said alwaies into the sunne, and keep themselves continually in the ayre, without lighting on the earth for they have neither feet nor wings, but onlie head and body and for the most part tayle.'

The lack of legs described by Linschoten is easily explained, for even today the local people habitually remove the legs of the birds to make the task of skinning easier. The fact that Pigafetti had stated that birds of paradise possessed legs was either conveniently forgotten or else forcefully contradicted by later writers in their anxiety to sustain the romance of the stories surrounding the birds. However, Linschoten's descriptions of their mode of life posed a number of problems to a thoughtful naturalist. If the birds were always in flight, how did they nest and incubate their eggs, and what did they eat? Soon answers were devised, answers that were as irrational as the fancies they sought to rationalize.

One writer described how 'there is in the back of the male a certain cavity, in which the female, whose belly is also hollow, lays her eggs and so by the help of both cavities, they are sitten upon and hatched'. Another, after explaining that the birds, during their perpetual flight, fed only on dew and air, added that instead of a stomach and intestines, which would have been useless to so extraordinary a feeder, the cavity of the abdomen is filled with fat. A third, hoping to add credibility to the story of their feet-lessness, and having noticed that pairs of curling wiry quills are found among the plumes of some species, wrote that 'They sit not upon the ground, but hang upon boughs by strings or feathers which they have and so rest themselves, like flies or aierie things.'

Even two hundred years after the first skins had come to

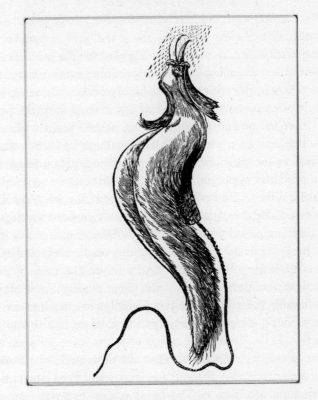

A bird of paradise as illustrated by Aldrovandus, 1599

Europe, the exact identity of the birds' home, the 'terrestrial Paradise', was still unknown. It was not until the eighteenth century that it was discovered that they lived in New Guinea and its offshore islands. When European naturalists saw the living birds in their natural surroundings for the first time, most of the myths surrounding them were dispelled. Nevertheless, the air of romance which surrounded the birds ever since Pigafetti's time has never quite been forgotten and when Carl Linnaeus, the great Swedish naturalist, gave a scientific name to the species most likely to have been described by Pigafetti, he called it *Paradisea apoda*, the Legless Bird of Paradise.

But the scientific discoveries of the last two hundred years have revealed that the true facts about the birds of paradise are almost as fantastic as the earlier legends, for the birds possess some of the most splendid and improbable feather adornments to be found in the entire bird world. Over fifty different species are now recognized which differ widely in shape and size. Some, like *Paradisea apoda*, have cascades of filigree plumes growing from beneath their wings. Others bear huge iridescent shields of feathers on their chests. Some have long, glossy black tails glinting shades of purple. In others the tail feathers are reduced to quills. Wilson's Bird is bald with a bright blue scalp, the King of Saxony's Bird has two head plumes twice the length of its body, each adorned with enamel-like plates of pale pearly blue. The biggest are the size of crows; the smallest, the red King Bird of Paradise, is little larger than a robin. The birds of paradise, in fact, are alike only in that their plumage is of almost unbelievable extravagance and they indulge in ecstatic courtship dances during which they display their glorious plumes to their drab hens.

Such beautiful and romantic creatures were surely worth going thousands of miles to see, and for years I had been obsessed by the thought of doing so. The London Zoo had not exhibited specimens for several years, and at the time that I was pondering on an expedition to go in search of them, it possessed none at all. Furthermore, no film had ever been shown, in Britain at least, of the wild birds performing their display dances. I decided that I would go to New Guinea, make an attempt to film them; and bring some back alive to London.

New Guinea is immense. It is the largest non-continental island in the world, over a thousand miles from end to end. It is ridged by chains of mountains as high as the Alps, the upper slopes of which are mantled not with snowfields and glaciers, but with forests of giant trees hung with sodden moss. Between these ranges run huge valleys clogged with jungle, many of them then virtually unexplored. Towards the coast spread vast mosquito-ridden swamps hundreds of square miles in extent.

Politically the island is divided into two almost equal parts. At the time of our journey the western half was governed by Holland and the eastern by Australia. In the highlands of this last territory, close to the centre of the whole island, lies an upland valley where at a small settlement called Nondugl, an Australian millionaire-philanthropist, Sir Edward Hallstrom, had established an Experimental Farm and Fauna Station. He had built great aviaries which contained more birds of paradise than all the zoos of the world put together, and living there was one of the greatest of all animal collectors and an expert on the Paradisea, Fred Shaw Mayer. Nondugl, therefore, was the ideal place for us to visit, if we could get permission to do so.

Sir Edward had for many years been a friend and benefactor of the London Zoo, and when I wrote to him and told him of our ambitions he replied suggesting that we should use the station as our base for our four-month expedition.

Charles Lagus and I had already tackled three animal collecting and filming trips in the tropics together. As we sat in an airliner being rushed eastwards towards our fourth, both of us were immersed in the worries which unfailingly troubled us at the beginning of a new journey – he mentally checking his photographic equipment, fearful that he had left some vital item behind, I trying to anticipate all the bureaucratic obstacles with which we should be faced before we reached Nondugl and attempting to reassure myself that we had anticipated and prepared for most of them.

Within three days we had reached Australia. From Sydney we flew northwards to New Guinea. In Lae, on the north-east coast of the island, we disembarked from a comfortable four-engined aircraft and boarded a less luxurious plane which each week flew up with supplies to the Wahgi valley in the central highlands.

We sat on aluminium, shelf-like seats which had been set up along half the length of one of the sides. In front of us lay a long mound of cargo running the length of the cabin and lashed with ropes to rings in the deck. It contained mail bags, armchairs, massive cast-iron parts of a diesel engine, cardboard boxes full of day-old chicks, a great number of loaves of bread and, somewhere among it all, sixteen pieces of our own baggage and equipment.

Our fellow passengers were seven half-naked Papuans who sat rigid and tense, with tight lips and set expressions, staring with unseeing eyes at the pile of cargo stacked a few inches in front of them. For some of them at least, this was their first flight – before we took off I had had to show them how to fasten their seat belts – and their skins glistened with little beads of perspiration.

Rain spattered against the small windows, its sound drowned by the roar of the engines. I could see nothing outside but greyness. The plane rocked and shuddered as we rose higher and higher over invisible mountains. I shivered slightly for it was cold and my skin was still clammy with the sweat which had poured from me in the muggy heat of Lae.

The plane climbed steadily until the grey cloud outside began to disintegrate into racing wraiths of mist. Suddenly the cabin brightened as though an electric light had been switched on. I looked out of one of the windows. The sun was sparkling on the polished, quivering wings of the aircraft. Several miles away, dark peaks, like islands, jutted through the immobile billows of clouds. Soon, rents appeared in the white shroud beneath us, each an oddly unreal vignette revealing sometimes the serpentine twist of a silver river, sometimes a few minute huts, but, most often, featureless green corduroy. These glimpses of the land beneath grew in size and number until at last they fitted together into a continuous picture of range after range of razor-backed hills rising in succession, some thickly forested, some naked but for uniform brown grass. One after the other, their crests passed beneath us until abruptly they dropped and we were no longer flying over savage escarpments but along a wide green valley. This was the Wahgi.

At intervals the land had been cleared for airstrips. One of these landing grounds was the experimental farm at Nondugl. Our plane dipped low over the station buildings. A tiny truck emerged from one of the sheds and moved slowly down the thin red line which scarred the landscape connecting the houses to the airstrip. We landed bumpily and, as Charles and I climbed stiffly out, the truck raced round the bend, on to the grassy strip and squealed to a halt beneath the plane's wing. Two men jumped out. One, a stocky, burly man wearing a broad-brimmed, sweat-stained hat and khaki overalls, introduced himself as Frank Pemble-Smith, the manager of the station. The other, an older, thinner man, was Fred Shaw Mayer.

Together we unloaded our goods from the plane. Frank swore mildly when he discovered that some spare parts for his farm machinery were not in the cargo and spent a few minutes exchanging gossip with the pilot. Then the plane's engines restarted, it roared down the strip, heaved itself into the air and headed for the next station which, in flying time, was only four minutes away. Frank arranged for his Papuan station hands to load our gear on to the trailer of a tractor which had been waiting close by, and then he whirled us off in his truck to meet his wife and have tea in his house.

As we sat eating scones in his neat living room, I could see standing motionless outside the startling figure of a tall, heavily bearded and semi-naked man. His brown arms and hairy chest had been blackened by soot and his face was painted with dots and stripes of red, yellow and green. His waist was encircled by a broad stiff cummerbund, made from woven fibre, over the front of which hung a narrow length of woolly fabric reaching down to his shins. Behind, like a bustle, he had tucked a bushy

9

spray of leaves. He was decked with a wealth of pearl-shell jewellery: a belt of small pieces hung from a string around his waist; a huge pearly breastplate was suspended from a cord round his neck; a broad crescent encircled his chin, partially concealing his beard; and he had inserted a long slender sickle, cut from the rim of a pearl shell, through the pierced septum of his nose. His most dazzling and resplendent personal adornment, however, was neither his pearl shells nor his paint, but his gigantic feather headdress. It contained the plumes from at least thirty individual birds of paradise belonging to five different species. Ruby, emerald, velvet black and enamel blue, these marvellous feathers formed a crown of unbelievable splendour.

His magnificence seemed the more startling because of his setting, for he was standing on a freshly mown lawn and had, for his background, the wire-netting fence of a tennis court. Parked by his side was a bright red tractor. I found myself looking at him as I would view a circus exhibit or a tourist attraction. Yet when I glanced higher up at the wild mountains behind, it was the tennis court, the tractor and the china teacup from which I was drinking which struck the jarring, intrusive note. It was I who was in the circus, and the man outside, together with thousands of his compatriots in the forests beyond, who was the audience.

Frank saw me staring. 'That,' he said, 'is the local head-man – the *luluai*. His name is Garai and he's one of the wealthiest and most amiable of all the local men. I told him that you two fellows were coming to look for birds of paradise and I expect he's waiting about to be the first one to tackle you in case there's any trade to be done.'

When we had finished tea, we went out to meet him. He shook hands with us enthusiastically, but with the indefinable awkwardness of someone to whom such action is unfamiliar, and grinned broadly, exposing a perfect set of massive white teeth.

'Arpi-noon,' he said.

'Arpi-noon,' I replied, pleased to be able to use almost the only words of pidgin English I knew. Unfortunately, I was unable to add anything else, for you cannot speak pidgin merely by adding 'um' or 'ee' to the end of normal English words. It is a language in its own right, with its own syntax, grammar and vocabulary. It had been created comparatively recently, largely by the people of New Guinea themselves, to enable them to communicate, and therefore to trade, not only with the white foreigners who came to their country but also with one another, for in New Guinea there are several hundred different native languages.

Pidgin has taken its vocabulary from many sources. Some words come from Malay – *susu* for milk, and *binatang*, which I had learned in Indonesia a year earlier as meaning animal but which here meant more narrowly, insect. There are also German words, for this part of New Guinea was once a German colony – *raus*, clear out; *mark*, which is still often used to mean a shilling; and *kiap* which seems to be a corruption of *kapitan* and is now used to mean a government officer. There are also, of course, many Melanesian words. But the bulk of the vocabulary is derived from English. In the transition from one language to another many of these words are run together and have had their consonants softened to suit the native tongue so that, when written with their official spelling, a little imagination is needed to divine their origin – *kisim*, give him, *pluwa*, the floor, *solwara*, the sea, *motaka*, a car, for instance. This spelling can be so confusing that for the pidgin conversations here, I have adopted a less accurate but more easily understandable version. Some words have taken on a new meaning – *stop* means to be present not to finish, and *fella* is added to many words to indicate an entity. Some expressions have had their meaning so transformed that it is unwise to try to improvise recklessly lest some of your remarks take on a highly indelicate and totally unintended meaning.

Frank told Garai why we had come to Nondugl.

'You lookim,' he said. 'Dis two-fella masta e stop long Nondugl.

E like findim all kind pidgin, na all kind binatang. Garai, you e savvy place belong altogether pidgin, na you e showim dis place, na masta e givim Garai plenty mark.'

Garai grinned and nodded enthusiastically. I mentioned to Frank that we were also hoping to make a film about the local people and their ceremonies.

'Suppose you fella like makim big-fella sing-sing,' Frank continued. 'Dis two-fella masta e givim picture long dis-fella sing-sing.'

Garai replied with a torrent of pidgin, spoken so rapidly and with such an unfamiliar intonation that I could not understand. Frank translated.

'Tomorrow night,' he said, 'a courtship ceremony called a *kanana* is going to be held down in Garai's settlement. Do you want to go?'

It was our turn to nod enthusiastically.

'Na two-fella masta e like talk "thank you too much",' said Frank. 'Behind, long dark e come up tomorrow, e like come place belong you an lookim dis-fella kanana.'

The next night Garai arrived at Frank's bungalow to escort us to the kanana as he had promised. We followed him through banana groves and past thickets of bamboo, creaking in the breeze. The air was cold and vibrant with insect noise. It was near midnight but we had no need of our torches to help us find our way for the moon was full and the sky clear.

After a quarter of an hour, we reached Garai's hamlet surrounded by casuarina and banana trees. He led us past several low, circular, thatched huts. Through chinks between the stakes which formed the walls came the glimmer of fires and the subdued murmur of conversation. We stopped in front of a hut which was larger than the rest and of a different shape. It was about forty feet long and through the thatch at either end projected the ends of a pair of poles. One of each pair was shaped as a female symbol, the other as a male. Banana trees loomed black above it, silhouettes against the starry sky.

Garai pointed to the low entrance.

'Na you two-fella masta go lookim, one-fella someting e stop inside,' he said.

The kanana *ceremony*

We crawled in on our hands and knees. Immediately I was assailed by stifling heat and choking, acrid smoke. I could see nothing for my eyes were smarting so much that I was unable to open them. When, after a few seconds, I forced myself to do so, I was still able to see very little for tears welled out of them, blinding me.

Stooping, with my hand across my smarting eyes, I clumsily picked my way through a tangle of squatting figures until I found a vacant space at the far end of the hut where I could sit down. As soon as I did so, to my relief and surprise, my eyes stopped watering for the smoke was hanging only in the rafters and beneath the air was clear. I looked around.

The smoke came from a wood fire which smouldered in the centre of the earth floor, its flames providing the only light in the hut. By its side, his back against one of the soot-blackened centre poles, sat an old bearded man. Apart from ourselves, he was the only man in the hut; the people among whom I had stumbled as I entered were all young and buxom girls. They sat in two long lines facing inwards and were watching me curiously, giggling among themselves.

None of the girls flaunted a magnificent headdress like Garai's which we had seen on our first day, for the low roof of the hut would have made it impractical to wear them. Instead they wore small skull caps, crocheted from the wool of tree kangaroos or opossums and bound on to their heads with circlets of glittering green beetles enclosed in a framework of split cane. Their faces were painted with dots and stripes of many colours, each girl having her own design which had been dictated not by any ritual compulsion but by her own personal fancy. Most wore necklaces of beads or crescents of pearl shell either round their necks or through their noses, and all had the wide waistband of woven orchid fibre that denotes an unmarried girl. Their bodies had been smeared with pig fat and soot, and glistened in the dim, flickering firelight.

No sooner had we found a place to sit than a line of men, headed by a grinning Garai, crawled in. They sat themselves in between the girls, but facing the walls of the hut. They, like the girls, were splendidly decorated and painted but, in addition, most had stuck leaves and pieces of fern in their skull caps. They were not, however, all young. Some had bushy beards; some, like Garai, we knew to be already married, but, although the kanana is a love-making ritual, this was not improper, for the Wahgi society is a polygamous one. These men had all been specially and personally invited to the ceremony and many had come from hamlets many miles away.

For a few minutes, while people settled themselves, there was gossip and laughter. Then a single voice began hesitatingly to sing. One by one, other voices joined in until everyone was singing a slow chant. As the song gained momentum, the men and the girls began to sway their bodies from side to side, rolling their heads as they did so. The cadences of the chant were repeated hypnotically, and the swaying bodies came closer together, each man inclining his torso towards the girl sitting facing him on his right. Closer they came, the droning chant mounting to a climax until, with eyes shut, the pairs of faces met nose to nose, forehead to forehead. Ecstatically each couple rolled their heads from cheekbone to cheekbone in a delirium of sensuous delight.

A few dancers broke away from one another quite quickly, and looked abstractedly around the hut, ignoring their partners. Most of them, however, continued swaying, lost in their pleasure, their faces joined.

The song died and at last everyone separated and began to chatter. One of the girls lit a long cigarette made from newspaper and drew in lazy lungfuls of smoke. Each man crawled around the girl with whom he had danced and sat down by the side of the next girl in line so that everyone, as in a Paul Jones dance, had changed partners. Once again the chant started, the dancers began to sway, and once again as the climax of the song was reached, faces met together and rocked from cheek to cheek.

We sat watching for hours. It became so hot that I took off my shirt. The fire smouldered lower until all I could see of the dancers was a glint of an oiled body or the moving shape of a white owl's wing which one of the men wore in his skull cap.

One of the dim figures close to me let out a deep chuckle. It was Garai.

'Eh lookim,' he whispered, and pointed to a couple who had broken away from the main dance and were sitting in the shadows with their arms around one another, the girl's legs resting over one of the man's thighs.

'Im e carry-leg,' said Garai.

During the kanana ceremony itself, the dancers are forbidden to touch one another except with their faces. The old man sitting in the centre was there to enforce the rule. But a girl can indicate by the enthusiasm with which she rubs noses whether she likes her partner or not. If a pair are mutually attracted then they may leave the line of dancers and 'carry-leg', and such friendships made during the kananas often ripen into marriage. It was indeed like a Saturday night dance in England.

By three o'clock, the ranks of the dancers had thinned considerably. We crawled out of the hut and into the cold night.

The next day, Garai, looking very tired but having lost none of his cheerful ebullience, escorted us on a walk through the nearby hills.

We had not been walking for more than ten minutes when I heard a distant drumming and singing. We crossed one of the kunai patches and saw coming down the path towards us a spectacular procession. At its head strode several men resplendent in enormous feather headdresses and carrying long three-pronged spears. But they were merely the heralds of an even more impressive sight, for behind them came a man carrying aloft on top of a pole a giant standard, three feet across, ablaze with gorgeous colour. It was a banner of woven cane and grass hung with a dozen shining pearl shells, mats sewn with valuable cowrie shells, tiaras of scarlet parrot feathers, and around its rim thirty or forty sets of bird of paradise plumes. Behind the standard-bearer walked more men, women and children each of whom carried pieces of smoked pig flesh – a flank, a spine, a leg, a head or entrails wrapped up in leaves. One man held a drum which he thumped to accompany his yells as the whole party advanced towards us down the path through the kunai.

We stood to one side to let them pass and Garai told me

what was happening. The men had come from the hills on the other side of the Wahgi valley and were on their way to collect a bride. The arrangements for the marriage had been made long before, when representatives from both families had met and agreed between them the exact price in feathers, shells and pigs that the groom must pay for his bride. The price was high and to have amassed it all would have taken years, so the bride's parents had agreed that the marriage could come into effect on payment of a substantial part of the price, provided that regular instalments were made afterwards until the full sum had been paid off. The bridegroom had then made long and arduous trips into the forest hunting birds of paradise for their plumes. Some of the pearl shells he had borrowed from relations, some he had earned by working for one of the older and wealthier men in the village. At last he had enough to serve as a deposit and two days ago he and other members of his family had set out on the long march to the bride's hamlet. With them they took the bride-price – the pearl shells, the pig meat and the paradise plumes, which were carefully wrapped in protective folders of dried leaves stiffened with split cane lest during the journey their filigree beauty should be marred. Last night the party had slept in the forest. When they arose at dawn, they had constructed the huge banner and decked it with the shells and the feathers so that the munificence and fine quality of the bride-price should be seen by all. Now they were nearing the bride's home which lay only another hour's walk away. Garai spoke to one of the warriors who followed in the banner's wake and asked for permission for us to follow them.

We walked behind the wedding party for mile after mile. Eventually we emerged from the bush and began toiling up the long grassy spur that led to the bride's house. A hundred yards from it, we had to climb over a savagely spiked fence that formed a defensive palisade, a relic of the warlike period that had ended only a few years ago. On the other side of it, the standard-bearer was waiting to allow stragglers to catch up with him. Then, when all had assembled and smartened themselves up, the procession slowly and in a dignified manner advanced into the village.

The wedding party

The bride and her family were sitting in the small clearing in front of their hut awaiting the banner's arrival. I was unsure as to which was the bride until Garai pointed her out to me. She was the most unlikely looking member of the group for such a role, for not only was she comparatively old, but she was also holding a young baby. She was, Garai explained, a widow.

The standard was planted firmly in the ground in the middle of the clearing, and the bride and her family got to their feet to welcome the visitors formally. They embraced, putting their arms around one another's shoulders and waists with an air of slightly forced affability not unlike the handshakes between comparative strangers who find themselves newly related by law at a European wedding reception.

Everyone sat down and one of the senior members of the groom's party, a big powerful man with a luxuriant beard and a headdress consisting of a shock of brown cassowary feathers, delivered a speech, striding up and down in front of his audience and declaiming in a stylized and highly theatrical manner. The bride listened open-mouthed.

The pig meat had been laid out in a neat rectangle on one side under a casuarina tree, the four brown, smoked heads being laid in a row. When the speech was over, another of the visiting men picked up a flank of flesh. The bride's menfolk sat in a line to receive it. As the meat was offered to them by the groom's relative, each man bit off several gobbets of fatty, greasy flesh which he let fall from his mouth into his hand and then laid on a piece of banana leaf. Several wretched dogs observed this distribution of food with pathetic anxiety but none received even the tiniest fragment, for when each man had bitten off his share he took it away to his womenfolk.

The banner was now dismantled, and the feathers and shells laid out in rows on a mat. All the bride's male relations squatted around, and as each item was handed down from the banner there was a long and sometimes heated discussion as to who should ultimately possess it.

When all was finished the visitors took some of the pig flesh, opened banana-leaf packages of cooked vegetables and began to feast. The bride left her family group and sat by her husband's side and for the first time there was an atmosphere of relaxed festivity. One of the men was obligingly seasoning everyone's meal by chewing ginger and spices and spitting on to each piece of meat in turn. It was now evening and as I saw everyone eating with such relish I remembered that I had not had any food myself since early morning. One of the men, seeing me staring, offered me a greasy hunk of pork liberally spattered with chewed ginger. It was a kind and hospitable gesture. Hoping that I might not be considered impolite, I shook my head and pointed to a pile of bananas. Laughingly, the man handed me one and we joined in the wedding breakfast.

———

Sir Edward Hallstrom, the owner of the station at Nondugl, had had a lifelong interest in tropical birds and agriculture. Here he had built huge aviaries in which to assemble a collection of Paradisea which would provide birds for zoos all over the world. But this part of his plan could not be fully implemented, for Australian immigration laws prohibited the entry of any livestock of any kind into Australia for fear of the accidental introduction of disease. This law applied to Paradisea as to everything else, in spite of the fact that each year thousands of birds of many different kinds fly on their migrations from New Guinea to Australia and back again, oblivious of bureaucratic restrictions. The main commercial airlines to eastern New Guinea all ran through Australia, so unless a special permit was given – and such exceptions were hardly ever made – any birds from Nondugl had to be taken to the outside world by a lengthy sea voyage without calling at any Australian port. This was very hard to arrange, and we ourselves would have to face this problem if we were to take back a collection of Paradisea to the London Zoo.

Nonetheless there was at Nondugl a collection of birds of paradise unparalleled anywhere else in the world, and ornithologists of many nationalities went there to study them.

The man in charge of these birds was Fred Shaw Mayer. He was a thin, greying, gentle person with a slight stoop. If you met him in a city street you might suppose that he was of such a timid disposition that he had never dared to leave his office desk or venture farther abroad than the suburbs of his own town. Yet Fred was one of the greatest of all animal collectors. Born in Australia, he had travelled in some of the wildest and most dangerous parts of the world in search of birds and mammals, insects and reptiles. He had wandered over both the Dutch and the Australian territories of New Guinea; he had made special journeys to remote islands just to find one particular species of bird. He had caught animals in the Moluccas, in Java and Sumatra and in Borneo, and his collections of specimens are now the treasured possessions of many scientific institutions including the Natural History Museum in London. Many of the creatures he found on his expeditions turned out to be previously unknown to science. Three species of birds of paradise were first discovered by him and several creatures bear as part of their scientific name the word 'Shaw-mayeri', a tribute to his skill from the zoologists who named them.

None of this, however, would you suspect when you first met him. Indeed he was so reticent that it was often difficult to find him at all, for his days were devoted to the birds in his aviaries. He rose well before dawn in order to prepare food for the birds so that they could feed just after the sun rose, as they would do in the wild state. He admitted that his local helpers were probably quite capable of mixing the bird food by themselves, but he said mildly that he preferred to do the job himself. At that early hour in the morning it was very cold and Fred habitually wore a number of long woolly cardigans, heavy army boots and an odd deer-stalker hat with flaps which came down over his ears; and in this garb, by the light of a paraffin lamp, he mixed big bowls of special meal with diced pawpaw, pandanus fruit, plantains and boiled eggs. Each group of birds had its own requirements. Some liked meat in their diet, so tadpoles and spiders had to be found for them; others had a taste for wasp grubs or the yellow of hard-boiled eggs. Sometimes, if other meat was not available, Fred went to his refrigerator and cut up the fresh mutton which should have provided his own evening meal. The rest of his day was spent walking round the aviaries, tending and cleaning his charges. It is little wonder that he was known by all the local people as Masta Pidgin.

There were many different kinds of birds in Fred's care: parrots of all sizes and colours; flocks of huge blue-grey pigeons each crested with a fan of gauzy feathers spotted with silver; and on an ornamental pond several of one of the rarest species of duck in the world, Salvadori's Duck, which came from a high tarn in the mountains behind Nondugl.

Crested pigeons

But it was the birds of paradise which captured our attention. Here Charles and I saw some of the species which hitherto we had known only from illustrations in books. Day after day we walked round the aviaries watching the birds and trying to familiarize ourselves with their harsh strident calls so that later, when we went into the forest, we should be able to identify distant bird-call and so know what species were in the neighbourhood.

Some of the birds in the aviaries were drab thrush-like creatures. These were either hen birds or else young cocks, for the male bird does not grow his magnificent plumes until he is four or five years old. When he does, he is so completely transformed that the linking of hens and immature cocks with the fully plumed and quite dissimilar adult males can be exceedingly difficult. Most of Fred's male birds had come to him as youngsters, for if a Wahgi hunter caught an adult the temptation to keep and kill it for the sake of its plumes was very often proof against the rewards, high as they were, that Fred could offer for it. Many such birds had now been in the aviaries so long that they had grown their plumes and we were enthralled by their beauty – the gorgeous Prince Rudolph's Bird with its haze of sapphire-blue plumes rimmed with red; the magnificent, arrogant-looking Princess Stephanie's Bird, glossy black with a throat patch of rippling green iridescence; the bizarre Superb Bird with two curling wires projecting from its stumpy tail, a green chest, a scarlet back and a shining yellow cape round its shoulders, a creature which failed to match the grace of other species of Paradisea and looked almost as though it were some amateur's first inexpert attempt at designing the most extravagantly decorated bird he could assemble.

I was fascinated by two species in particular. The first was the size of a starling, the King of Saxony's Bird of Paradise. It is the possessor of one of the most remarkable of all feather adornments, a pair of long streamers, twice the length of its body, which spring from the back of its head and are decorated with a line of enamel-blue plates, glistening like mother-of-pearl. The second was Count Raggi's Bird of Paradise, for this one, which lives in the forests surrounding Nondugl, is the local representative of the classic and most famous species which Pigafetti described and which Linnaeus named *Paradisea apoda*. Like Pigafetti's bird it has a green gorget, a yellow head and long filigree plumes sprouting from beneath its wings. It differs in that the original bird had golden plumes whereas Count Raggi's has deep red ones. I watched the Nondugl specimens with the greatest care. They were unfortunately not in full plumage, but they were the kind which Charles and I were hoping to find in the wild so that we might film their courtship dances. They were the creatures which had brought us to New Guinea.

The local people valued the birds highly for their plumes, which they used not only for personal adornment but also, in many transactions, as an essential currency. We had massive proof of the scale on which the birds were hunted only a few days later. Frank heard that a big sing-sing was to be held at Minj, a place a few miles away across the Wahgi River on the other side of the valley. The sing-sing ground was a wide expanse of clipped kunai grass rather like a football pitch, which had been specially cleared for the occasion. Just beyond the ground ran a deep bush-filled ravine and behind rose the southern wall of the valley, the Kubor Mountains, steep and yellow-green, clear in the cloudless sky. Dancers were due to come down from the mountains to visit a part of their clan which had settled down in the valley. On their way they would stop at each settlement to join with the local people in a dance, so that the whole journey, normally a few hours' march, would take several days. No one could tell us exactly why they were making the visit. It might be that they were going to transact some business or to make a ritual exchange of food and gifts, thereby reaffirming their tribal bond, or that they were indebted to their clansmen and were going to discharge their obligations by giving a big feast.

Towards mid morning a few women from Minj, heavily painted and dressed in full ceremonial costume, appeared on the kunai ground. They had come to see the performance.

After another hour, we heard faint chantings and through binoculars I saw, high up on one of the mountain spurs, a line of tiny figures emerge from a cluster of huts. As I watched, Charles spotted another similar group descending one of the ridges away to the right. Every few minutes, the line stopped moving forward and contracted into a blob. As it did so the sound of chanting swelled and was joined by the faint thud of drums. Then the blob elongated into a line again and continued slowly downwards. At last they reached the ravine and disappeared into the bush. The singing grew louder and louder as they climbed unseen towards us until suddenly and dramatically, a dancer crested the near side of the ravine. Clutching his drum, his vast headdress waving, he moved slowly towards us, chanting as he came. Warrior after warrior followed him in a seemingly never-ending line until by midday, when the sun directly overhead was beating down with almost intolerable brilliance, the sing-sing ground was packed with hundreds of wildly chanting dancers.

They formed themselves in platoons, five in a rank, ten ranks deep, and, pounding their drums and yelling hoarsely, they stamped fiercely across the ground. Their dance, though simple, absorbed them totally and as the dust thrown up from their naked feet rose around them, caking the rivulets of sweat which ran down their chests and backs, they seemed almost in a state of trance.

Sometimes they halted, but even then they continued to sway in unison to the rhythm of their drums, rising on their toes and bending their knees, the shimmering canopy of their headdresses undulating like a sea swept by a heavy swell. Many of the men had smeared their muscular bodies with red clay; nearly all of them had thrust leaves of a red shrub in their arm bands and wore bracelets of possum fur. Several were armed with spears or bows and arrows, and one or two carried giant stone axes, the blades fixed in a long, curving piece of wood covered in a decorative basket-work which seemed to serve as a counterbalance to the heavy blade.

I was overwhelmed by the glory of their headdresses. Many kinds of paradise birds had been killed to provide these feathers. Nearly every man had two King of Saxony plumes stuck through his nose and fastened in the centre of his forehead so that the feathers formed a superb beaded hoop around the upper part of his face. Some men had so many Saxony plumes that they had included them in their headdresses as well. One warrior had sixteen of them in addition to the feathers of twenty or thirty

Lesser, Count Raggi, Magnificent, Princess Stephanie and Prince Rudolph Birds of Paradise.

It was one of the most spectacular sights I have ever seen. I made a rough calculation. There were over five hundred beplumed dancers. Between them, they must have killed at least ten thousand birds of paradise to adorn themselves for this ceremony.

Charles filming during the preparations for a feast

2

Into the Jimi Valley

I had hoped that we should be able to film the display dances of the paradise birds in the forest close to Nondugl, even though it would doubtless require a great deal of time and patience, but from what we had seen, it was clear that we had a much better chance of doing so if we left the Wahgi altogether and went into a wilder and less settled area.

I had also developed another ambition, for my imagination had been caught by the spectacular stone axes which I had seen being carried by some of the Minj dancers. Fred told me that when the Wahgi was first explored twenty-five years earlier, these axes were used throughout the valley but that nowadays the newly introduced metal ones had almost entirely displaced them. Such stone axes as remained were only brought out on ceremonial occasions. No one in the Wahgi still made them but they were traded from tribes living in the Jimi valley over the mountains to the north.

'And what chance is there of finding birds of paradise in the Jimi valley?' I asked.

'Excellent,' Fred replied, 'because there is only a small native population. And not only might you find birds of paradise and an axe factory, but you might also meet some of the pygmies who are supposed to live around there.'

Arranging a trip into the Jimi valley, however, was not easy. In the first place, it was an uncontrolled area and only people with special permits were allowed to enter it. The man responsible for granting permission was the District Commissioner at Mount Hagen Station near the head of the Wahgi valley.

We sent a message to him on the Nondugl radio transmitter asking if we might come to see him, and when the next supply plane landed at Nondugl we climbed on board and flew up to Hagen.

We were shown into the DC's office by one of his ADOs. The Commissioner himself, a bluff Australian in immaculate, neatly pressed khaki, sat behind his desk and looked at us searchingly from beneath heavy eyebrows.

Rather nervously, I explained as best I could what I was proposing: that Charles and I should go into the Jimi valley and spend a month trying to make a film about birds of paradise and the manufacture of stone axes. I added that, if possible, we would like to walk out of the valley along some route other than that we might take on our way in, so that we should see as much as possible of the country.

The DC listened silently until I had finished and then took a map out of a drawer and spread it on his desk.

'Look here,' he said brusquely. 'The Jimi is pretty wild country. So far, we've only sent a few exploratory patrols through it,' and he traced with his finger the dotted lines which crossed a large white blank on his map.

'A couple of years ago pilots who were flying from the Wahgi to Madang on the northern coast reported seeing villages in flames and some of the people came over the hills with stories of women and children being slaughtered wholesale. I sent a patrol in to investigate and they walked into the middle of a tribal war; they were ambushed, several of the policemen were wounded and they had to come out in a hurry. So I went in myself with another patrol officer, Barry Griffin, and a dozen or so armed native policemen. We found a site for a station at a place called Tabibuga and I left Griffin there to build it and to try to restore some sort of order. He's only been out once or twice since and then only for a day or so's rest here at Hagen. Although things seem to be going all right, he's obviously got his hands full. I'm not going to let you go in unless he is quite happy to have you. For one thing,

28

if you start traipsing around the Jimi looking for birds and stone axes you will have to have an escort. He is the only bloke who can provide it and maybe he will reckon he's got other things to do with his policemen than to let them spend their time looking for dicky birds. Apart from that, he may not want to have you anyway. He's one of those chaps who really like solitude and who ask no more than to be left alone so that they can get on with their jobs. No one has visited him there since he first built the place and he may not like the idea of two strange blokes with no experience of the country arriving out of the blue and dumping themselves on his doorstep. And if he feels that way, I'm certainly not going to order him to have you.'

The DC paused and looked at us hard.

'If he did agree, I would suggest that you go in to Tabibuga by the trail over the mountains along which his supplies are usually carried. It's a two-day march; there's quite a good track now and the people in the villages on the way are, by and large, willing to act as porters. Once you get to Tabibuga, you can sort out with Griffin just how to spend your time. I know he is planning to do a patrol westwards from his station and he might let you go with him. If you want to go out of the valley along a different route, then you'd better cross the Jimi River, go up the other side into the Bismarck Mountains and come out at a place called Aiome in the Ramu valley. There's an airstrip there and no doubt you could charter a plane to come and pick you up. Would that suit you?'

'Yes, sir,' I said.

'Very well,' he replied, getting to his feet, 'the next time Griffin comes up on the radio, I'll put the proposition to him. But understand, if he says no, the whole trip is cancelled.'

Suddenly he grinned.

'I hope you blokes like walking,' he added, 'because if you do go in, you will have to do a hell of a lot of it.'

Four days later, we received a radio message at Nondugl from the DC: Griffin had agreed to have us, and two of his native policemen would be waiting to escort us in at the Wahgi end of the Tabibuga trail in one week's time.

Immediately we were overwhelmed with the preparations necessary for the journey. We flew back to Lae to get food for ourselves, sacks of rice for the porters, paraffin lamps, saucepans, and tarpaulins to serve as tents. We visited the airline office and arranged that a small, single-engined plane should fly to Aiome on a day just over four weeks ahead to collect us after our journey and fly us back to Nondugl. We purchased bags of salt and beads, knives, combs, mouth organs, mirrors and pearl shells with which to pay porters and reward anyone who brought us animals. We also bought plenty of matches and piles of old newspapers, both of which we knew to be highly valued in the remoter parts of the highlands.

We returned to Nondugl and tried to sort out all our gear into 40-lb loads. This was not easy, for the only scales at Nondugl had just broken and I had to proceed by guesswork. Time after time I filled a patrol box, lifted it and decided that it was so appallingly heavy that it must exceed the stipulated weight as no one could possibly carry it for more than a few minutes. Then I would have to take out some of its contents and replace them with lighter things such as clothes.

We should be walking for a month and during that time we could not rely on finding either food or shelter. The pile of gear needed seemed enormous and no matter how carefully I checked my calculations and cut down on personal belongings, I could not avoid the conclusion that we should need a huge number of porters.

One evening I confessed to Fred.

'Maybe we are travelling soft and taking too many luxuries among our food and clothes,' I said, 'but it looks as though we might need perhaps forty porters.'

'Oh! That *is* good,' replied Fred mildly. 'I never seem to be able to manage with less than seventy and you know it can be *so* tiresome trying to recruit as many as that when the locals are not feeling cooperative.'

Nevertheless, I was still quite worried when, on the day before the date of our rendezvous, we found we had so much luggage that we could not possibly pack it all into one jeep. Instead, we had to load the bulk of it on to a farm trailer, hitch it to a tractor and send it ahead driven by one of Frank's senior farm hands. We followed with Frank and the remainder of our gear in the jeep during the afternoon.

Kwiana, the little settlement at the foot of the Tabibuga trail, consisted only of three small huts and a *house-kiap*, a government rest-house, thatched and built of plaited cane round a timber framework. Two huge, muscular native policemen were already there to meet us. Barefooted and barechested, they wore only a neat khaki wrap around their waists and a polished leather belt from which hung a bayonet in its sheath. In appearance they were quite different from the bearded, hook-nosed Wahgi people, for they, like most New Guinea policemen, had been recruited on the coast.

The senior one saluted me smartly.

'Arpi-noon, masta,' he said and handed me a letter. It was from Barry Griffin. He had written that the bearer of the note, Wawawi, was a trustworthy policeman from his staff who knew the trail well and would escort us to Tabibuga. He listed the names of the villages on the route, suggested that we should sleep at one called Karap and ended by saying that he looked forward to meeting us.

Wawawi had assembled a large crowd of villagers in the open space in front of the house-kiap. They were typical Hagen men, bearded and naked but for their woven waistbands and leafy bustles. Most carried in their belts knives or axes which hung over their bare thighs, blade to flesh, in what seemed to me to be a most hazardous position. They appeared to have only recently woken up, for many were bleary-eyed, their bustles crumpled and soiled. A few had the smudged remains of painted designs on their faces. It was still cold for the sun had not yet risen and the men wrapped their arms around their bare chests to keep warm.

Under Wawawi's direction, our baggage was brought out and laid in a long line. The porters-to-be stared dejectedly at the loads, occasionally lifting one to confirm their worst fears as to its weight and surreptitiously moving away from it towards some other which appeared to be lighter. Wawawi, however, moved briskly along the baggage, allocating a pair of men to each item.

When this was complete, Wawawi reclaimed his rifle from the small urchin who, bursting with importance, had been holding it for him, looked towards me to see if I was ready and called an order to the porters. They picked up their loads and followed Wawawi as he strode up the wide red earth track which led into the mountains.

For the first mile or so the path ran along the side of a narrow, steep-walled valley. Beneath us a small river frothed and sparkled as it tumbled over jams of boulders on its way to join the Wahgi River. The sun had at last risen, warming our bodies and dissolving the remnants of mist that hung around us. One of the carriers yodelled at the top of his voice 'Hooo-aaah' and prolonged the last lower note as long as his lungs allowed him. As soon as he started everyone else joined in, so that the resultant clamour sounded like a continuous long-drawn-out 'aaaah' with a higher obbligato of staccato 'hoo's'. It was a music which was to continue throughout that day and become our constant marching companion during the next few weeks.

Soon the track steepened and began to zigzag up the spine of a long grassy ridge. The barefooted porters plodded gamely upwards, digging their toes into the steep mud upon which my nailed boots skidded and slipped. Every hour or so, Wawawi called a halt, and while the men rested he re-allocated the loads so that each porter took a turn in carrying one of the heavier boxes.

Towards midday we passed the last of the pleasant casuarina trees and verdant bush that had clothed the slopes so far and entered a thin forest of gaunt trees, their branches trailing withered moss and gnarled creepers. At one point, the track snaked up a series of dripping rock faces which caused the men a lot of trouble. I lingered here to assist where I could, until all the loads had been hauled up it. Just above, the gradient lessened and it seemed that we were approaching the top of the pass. Thin mist was swirling through the bleak forest. I walked slowly, my eyes on the ground, picking my way through boulders and panting slightly, for we were now at an altitude of over 8,000 feet. Ahead, I noticed that the porters had stopped once again. I reflected that it was hardly the best place for a rest and decided to pass them and go over the crest of the col to find somewhere more sheltered. But as I neared them I saw that instead of sitting down the men were clustered round Wawawi and arguing heatedly.

'Dis-fella men, im 'e talk 'e no like go more,' said Wawawi as I neared him.

Certainly they looked cold and tired, but I could see no real reason why they should suddenly go on strike, just when it seemed that the worst part of the climb was over. I did not care to think how we should manage if they did abandon their loads in this remote and lonely spot. In my most persuasive tones I explained that now we were at the top, things would be easier, and from here, I said optimistically, the track will go downhill. Have a good rest, I said, and we will pay well when we arrive at the next village; but we must go on. I doubt if they understood what I was trying to say, and it was Wawawi who answered me. The reason they would go no farther, he said, was that the crest of the pass marked their tribal frontier. Beyond lay the territory of another tribe, who were 'bad-fella too much. Im 'e kai-kai man.'

'Oh,' said Charles mildly, 'he means they are cannibals.'

We both laughed, for the situation seemed so like a far-fetched adventure story as to be farcical. At that moment, I noticed the tip of a feather headdress projecting from behind a pile of boulders, two hundred yards away in the mist. I blinked in astonishment and then noticed another close by it. My smile faded rapidly.

'Well, cannibals or not,' I replied with slightly forced gaiety, 'I think they are over there waiting for us.'

Suddenly, with ear-splitting yells, a horde of men leaped from behind the rocks and rushed towards us brandishing knives and axes. My only conscious thought was that I must urgently convince them that we were friendly. With my heart banging against my ribs, I walked towards them and extended my right hand. My meagre vocabulary of pidgin deserted me and, rather to my surprise, I heard myself saying loudly, in what sounded like absurdly cultured tones, 'Good afternoon'. This had no effect whatsoever, for they could never have heard it above their own ferocious yells. Within seconds they were upon me. To my total astonishment, several of them seized my right hand and pumped it up and down. Others grabbed my left hand and those that could grasp neither contented themselves with smacking me violently on the shoulder. 'Arpi-noon, masta, arpi-noon,' they chorused.

Why they should have concealed themselves and then charged us in such a frightening manner when their intentions were in fact friendly puzzled me for a few minutes. Then it dawned on me that this aggressive display on the frontier was probably merely a routine ploy in their cold war with the Wahgi tribes, designed to emphasize their strength and warlike character, lest their neighbours should decide that they were weak and therefore an easy target for plunder. The Wahgi men, however, seemed unlikely ever to attack anybody as they sat miserably on their heels, shivering in the drizzle which was now falling. Wawawi lined them up and counted them.

'Four fella ten tree, masta,' he said. I unlocked my box, hauled out a bag of coins and handed Wawawi forty-three shillings for distribution. This was regulation government pay for a day's porterage and it was the last time we were able to use money before we got back to Nondugl. As soon as each porter received his pay, he turned and walked away down the trail into the mist.

Our new carriers were a more cheerful bunch. They seized the loads with enthusiasm and, raising a triumphant yell, moved away at a gallop. The ground began to fall and I hurried on ahead, anxious to get below the clouds and look for the first time at the Jimi valley. I imagined that it would be similar to the Wahgi, a single, wide, grass-filled valley with a silver river meandering along the bottom, but when at last I got a clear view I saw something very different. Below me stretched a vast tract of wild country, a complex maze of interlocking ridges and mountains, entirely covered with forest. I could see no rivers, no stretches of kunai grass, and no villages; nothing but an endless rucked carpet of trees.

The ridge we were descending seemed to run towards a small valley, close at hand on our left. One of the tribesmen came and stood by my side. I pointed to the valley. 'Jimi?' I asked. The man burst into a roar of laughter, shook his head and pointed into the far distance, screwing up his eyes. Then with the patient air of a teacher explaining some rudimentary fact to a particularly stupid child, he held his left hand in front of my face and, one by one, touched four of his outstretched fingers.

'Good heavens,' I said to Charles, 'we've got to cross another four valleys before we get to the Jimi.'

'More likely he means we've got another four days' walking,' Charles replied dourly.

I tried to find out exactly what my companion was attempting to indicate with his four fingers, but without success. Indeed, I never did discover. It was merely one of the occasions on which our lack of a common language seemed an insuperable barrier. I was overwhelmed with a surge of loneliness which was not dispelled even when the chanting porters caught up with us. We were entering a new primeval land in which we had no real place. It was true that ahead of us, in a fold of one of the mountains, among the infinity of trees, one Australian had made a clearing in the forest and built himself a house, but he had created no more than a minute pockmark on the landscape. The track at my feet was his creation also, but it was only a slender thread linking us to him. If I left it and walked for five minutes in some other direction, I should be on ground which no European had ever seen before.

We followed the path trustingly as it wound along the crests of ridges, zigzagged down steep muddy slopes and dived into the forest. Every mile or so, we met groups of tribesmen who were standing on the path waiting, no doubt, to see what the shouting was about. As we passed, they enthusiastically attached themselves to our caravan and added their voices to the clamour.

Towards three o'clock, we reached the first sign of habitation which we had seen since we had left the Wahgi, a low palisade of sharp stakes broken only by a narrow gap, flanked by posts painted with tribal markings. Half an hour later we stepped from the forest into a village – two lines of thatched huts strung along the crest of the ridge, enclosing a bare expanse of red earth and girdled by a ring of casuarina trees. The entire population had assembled to meet us, the women sitting in one group, the men in another. The luluai and his lieutenants stood at the far end in front of the largest hut, which I guessed to be the house-kiap built for use by a patrol officer. As we threaded our way towards him, through the squatting villagers, they raised a deafening yell of welcome. The luluai escorted us into the house-kiap and our first day's march was over.

Wawawi once again supervised the stacking of the baggage and paid off the porters, this time in tablespoonfuls of salt. Each man received it in a piece of leaf, wrapped it up carefully, tucked it in his belt and wandered out of the village back to the forest. While our beds were being erected I sat outside on the edge of the ridge, resting my back against a casuarina, and scanning the trees in the valley below me. To my delight, I heard the call of a Lesser Bird of Paradise, but though I searched with my glasses for a long time, I could not see the bird itself. As evening fell, clouds rolled up from the valleys below until the village alone remained clear. Charles and I made our supper and went stiffly to bed.

Paying the porters with salt

We were woken, just after dawn, by a vociferous yodelling. The luluai was standing among the casuarinas, his hands cupped round his mouth, his voice echoing over the cloud-filled valleys. In response to his calls, forty or fifty porters assembled in front of the house-kiap; many of them I recognized as the men we had met on the road during the previous afternoon. Just before we moved off, it began to rain. It was cold and uncomfortable, but our boxes were watertight and the carriers merely pinned a few broad leaves in their skull caps to keep their heads dry. By midday, we had passed through the cloud layer and the rain stopped.

Our progress now became a triumph, for as we went we collected, like a snowball, more and more tribesmen who trotted along with us. The spasmodic hooo-aaah's of the previous day now became continuous. I yearned for a little peace and quickened my pace to outdistance the carriers, but the main supporting party of chanting men ran after me and it was impossible to escape.

At one o'clock we had a sudden distant view through a small gap in the bush and I saw below us a tiny red spot in the dark green forest. Through my binoculars I could distinguish a few rectangular buildings and, in the middle, a flag flying from the top of a mast. It was Tabibuga.

An hour later we reached it. Our entry was dramatic in the extreme. Our escort now numbered several hundred. The vanguard consisted of thirty or forty warriors with painted faces and feather headdresses who advanced in short spurts. At the end of each run, they redoubled their shouts, stamped furiously with their right feet and waved their knives and spears. Wawawi had reclaimed his rifle, which for most of the day had been

Our baggage arrives at Tabibuga

carried by one of the local men, and was marching just behind us with it on his shoulder in the correct military manner. Our porters, shouting with excitement, were doing their best in spite of their loads to run and caper like the unencumbered warriors ahead. As we flooded on to the huge parade ground of Tabibuga, I saw that we were awaited by at least a thousand people. They added their screams to the general bedlam and cleared out of the way as our advance guard cantered forward towards the large building which dominated the station. On the veranda I could see a man in white sitting reading, totally unperturbed by the riotous demonstration all around him. He did not even look up. When we were no more than twenty yards away from him, he raised his head, got to his feet and slowly walked towards me.

'Griffin,' he said, as he shook my hand. 'Sorry about all the noise. My chaps are bit excited because you are the first Europeans who've come in since I've been here. Guess they thought I was the only one in existence and they're probably pretty shattered to find that there are a couple more.'

———

Tabibuga was Barry Griffin's own creation. His first task on arriving in the valley had been to pacify the warring tribes and he decided therefore to establish his patrol post in the middle of the most troubled area, which lay not in the flat lands of the lower Jimi but high among the mountains and gullies near the head of the valley, many miles from the river itself. To create a suitably level site in this rugged country, he had cut a wide platform a hundred yards across in the side of a ridge. This formed the parade ground. Along one side of it were ranged Barry's office, the courtroom from which he administered justice, and a trade-store stocked with knives and axes, cloth, beads, paint and shells. Below it lay the quarters of his native staff, vegetable gardens, pens for pigs and goats, and a *house-sick* – a tiny hospital administered by two native medical orderlies. On the crest of the ridge, beneath a tall pine and overlooking the station, stood his own house, built so close to the ridge's edge that the washroom overhung it and was supported by stilts, a convenient arrangement for the water from the canvas bucket which served as a shower could fall straight through the loosely woven cane floor and drain away down the hillside.

Apart from the bathroom, his house consisted only of one large room with glassless windows closed by shutters, and a cook-house connected to the main building by a short, covered passage. Everything inside was immaculately arranged. Magazines were stacked in neat piles according to their date, their type and whether they were read or unread. The boots by the door stood in orderly line. The blankets on the camp bed in the corner were carefully folded and covered with an embroidered counterpane. The table was bare except for a bowl of forest flowers. Nowhere was there the litter of domestic trivia which most people accumulate. It was the home of a man with a passion for tidiness.

Barry himself was tall and slim with closely cropped black hair. As we sat talking politely in his house, I could detect no expression on his face which would help me decide whether he was glad or irritated by our arrival. He spoke softly with the minimum movement of his lips. With a curt order he called his houseboy, who entered carrying three bottles of beer on a tray. They had been brewed in Australia and here in the Jimi they were as valuable as bottles of the best champagne in London. As we drank he seemed to relax.

'Well,' he said, 'I'm both surprised and relieved to meet you. All I knew from Hagen radio was that you were film-makers and ornithologists, which seemed to me an odd mixture, and I didn't know whether to expect Hollywood types in loud clothes and horn-rimmed spectacles or elderly bearded blokes with butterfly nets. It's good to discover that you are neither. Anyway, come and eat.'

Apart from the bread and potatoes the meal had been produced entirely from tins – lambs' tongues, asparagus tips and fruit salad – and although Barry made deprecating remarks about it, clearly he had broached a carefully hoarded store of luxuries to provide it. I was anxious not to presume too much on his hospitality and suggested that we should pitch camp farther along the ridge. Barry quietly replied that he had arranged for us to sleep in the house, should we wish to do so, and as night fell the houseboy came in again and set up two more camp beds complete with blankets.

Over breakfast the next day, we asked Barry about birds of paradise. He was not optimistic.

'I doubt if the locals will bring you any birds of paradise or tell you much about their dancing trees. They are pretty possessive and secretive about their birds. If a man has a dancing tree on his land, all the birds that come to it are reckoned to be his property even though they fly over other people's ground. He may watch a young bird for several years waiting for it to grow its plumes, so he gets rather upset if, just when its feathers are at their best, someone else manages to shoot it before he does. Of all the cases which I have to try in the native court, the ones which cause the most trouble and bloodshed are quarrels over land, women and birds of paradise – and not necessarily in that order. So you can understand that they don't like strangers knowing where the trees are. However, I've asked the station luluai to come up this morning and I'll see if I can get him to tell you anything.'

When the luluai arrived, he stood at the door, nodding respectfully as Barry spoke to him in rapid pidgin.

'If you go along with him,' Barry said to me, 'he will show you a dancing tree.'

I followed the luluai down from the house, across the parade ground, through the little village that lay beyond, and along the steeply descending muddy track. Soon we had left the station buildings far behind and were walking through dense forest, a moist tangle of trees and creepers interspersed with elegant tree ferns. At last we came to a giant fig tree which soared high above the bush surrounding it. A ladder of notches had been cut in its massive runnelled trunk. They must have been made a long time previously, for their edges were softened and concealed by overgrowing bark. Looking up into the branches, I could see, forty feet above the ground, a crude wooden cabin. The luluai explained by a mixture of dumb show and pidgin that the birds came to dance on a bough a few yards away from the cabin. When the time was ripe he would climb into the hide during the night and wait until dawn with his bow and arrows ready. As the sun came up, a male bird of paradise would come to the branch and begin his performance. Then, a single twang of the bow string would turn a strutting, vibrant fountain of plumes into a limp, bloody corpse.

With difficulty, I climbed up the trunk, using dangling sinewy creepers as handholds, until I could see the bough on which the birds danced. It had been used recently for its bark bore fresh scratches and was shorn of twigs. Remembering the age of the notches below, it was clear that the hide had been in use for many years. Generations of birds must have been slaughtered here.

The foliage of the fig tree was so luxuriant that it was not possible to get a clear view of the place where the bird danced either from the ground or, as I now discovered, from the hide itself. I could see only enough to give me a sight for a shot with a gun – but not with a camera. We should not be able to film here, even if any birds still survived to dance.

When I descended I asked the luluai if plumed birds still came to the tree. He shook his head. As we walked back to the station we passed his own hut. He left me for a moment, crawled into the hut and emerged holding a dried bird of paradise skin, with a splinter of bamboo thrust through its beak so that it could be fixed in a headdress, head-down with its gorgeous plumes upper-most. He had shot it a week earlier in the fig tree.

The next day, the parade ground was invaded by a thousand Milma tribesmen. They came not from the country close to Tabibuga but from an area almost a day's march away on the other side of one of the bigger tributaries of the Jimi River. Two years ago they had been fighting with the Marakas, the local Tabibuga people, and it was this war that had made the establishment of the patrol post an urgent necessity. When Barry arrived he found that the Milmas had been driven from their farms and villages by the Marakas and one of his first actions had been to order the Marakas to relinquish their newly acquired territory and to reinstate the Milmas on their original tribal lands. Now they came to the patrol post once a week bringing loads of cassava, pawpaws, yams and sugar cane which Barry required to feed his station staff, and which he exchanged for knives, shells and cloth from his store. Barry had been compelled to allot a special day of the week for these visits, so that he could ensure that there were no large parties of Marakas on the station in case the meeting of the two enemies might cause old quarrels to flare up again.

The Milmas at first sight resembled the Wahgi people for they were bearded, their faces were painted, they had pierced their noses to carry pearl-shell crescents, and they were dressed in broad waistbands with crocheted laps in front and bustles of leaves at the back. Yet they had about them a wilder, more savage air. Nearly all wore the brown, furry tailskin of a tree kangaroo slung from their necks and hanging down their chests. Their headdresses were not made up exclusively of paradise plumes but contained feathers from owls, eagles and cockatoos, and these, though they were faded and bedraggled, invested the men with an air of barbaric virility which contrasted markedly with the gaudy but faintly effete opulence of the Wahgi men. And nearly all of the Milmas were armed with knives, bows and arrows, huge three-pronged spears and war-lances ten feet long.

Several days before our arrival Barry had sent messages to these people asking them to bring in animals and birds, and after he had introduced us in a short speech which was relayed to them by the station interpreter, or *turnim-talk*, they came up to us, one by one, and presented us with enigmatic bundles.

As we unpacked each one and examined its contents, I assessed its value in terms of rarity and condition, and Barry priced it accordingly in terms of trade goods. The first was an oval parcel wrapped in leaves and carried in a neatly tied harness of creepers. I opened it and found the gigantic green egg of a cassowary. Although we did not want it, we paid the man a handful of blue beads for it. The second man, with an air of unconcealed pride, held out a splinter of bamboo on which were spitted the corpses of several dozen identical beetles. In spite of the fact that he had slightly misunderstood Barry's request, he had obviously spent a great deal of time collecting the creatures and we paid him two handfuls of beads. The third and fourth offerings were also eggs, those of a bush-turkey, white and, though smaller than the cassowary, still very large. The fifth man handed me a length of bamboo stopped at its open end with a twist of grass. I unplugged it and carefully shook out on to the ground a snake. The turnim-talk leaped backwards with an unintelligible but vehement expostulation. I took a stick, pinned the reptile's head to the ground and, seizing it with my thumb and forefinger at the back of its neck, picked it up. It was a beautiful emerald green python, decorated with a broken line of white scales along its spine. I knew the London Zoo would wish to have such a handsome and interesting snake but, to my sorrow, I saw that it had a bad wound on its mouth from which it would soon die.

Next came three quite different objects. They were all made of stone – a slim polished axe-head with the smooth tactile beauty of a Chinese jade, a mace-head of rough pitted stone shaped like a pierced pineapple and the size of a tennis ball, and a heavy stone bowl. This last object belonged to a type which, although well known, is nevertheless an enigma. The tribesmen in the central highlands frequently come across such bowls when they are digging in their fields. But they themselves have never made them, nor are they sure what their use was. It seems likely that they are the relics of an earlier people who lived in the New Guinea mountains before the present population arrived.

The last offering was even more exciting. A warrior stretched out his brown hand and I saw, cowering in his palm, two tiny fledglings. Their bodies were covered with quills, just poking through the goose-pimpled skin, which gave them the bluish tinge of an unshaven chin. They had disproportionately large beaks of a shape which was unmistakably that of a parrot, but until they were fully fledged I could not be certain as to exactly what they were. I hoped that they might be Dwarf Fig Parrots, a particularly rare and interesting branch of the parrot family which occurs only in New Guinea.

Young Dwarf Fig Parrots

It was imperative to give them some food immediately and I took them back to the house, so beginning a process which over the next few days was to transform Barry's immaculate home into something resembling the annexe of a zoo. He viewed the parrots' arrival with stoical calm. Fortunately, the little creatures were old enough to be able to eat by themselves and readily nibbled bananas. But bananas alone would not, I knew, sustain them for long and it was vital that I should persuade them to eat some seeds as well. I had brought with me a small supply of sunflower seeds but the parrots, never having seen such things before, did not regard these shiny, polished, tasteless objects as food. Accordingly I spent a long time that day – and many days that followed – cracking each seed, extracting the kernels and sticking them into bananas. The chicks in their eagerness to eat their bananas inadvertently took some of the kernels and soon acquired a taste for them. Eventually, before we left New Guinea, the little birds were shelling the seeds for themselves and eating them with enthusiasm. By this time, too, they had fledged completely and developed brilliant green bodies, scarlet foreheads and cheeks and a small patch of blue above their eyes, showing that they were, indeed, Dwarf Fig Parrots. No bigger than sparrows, they were the most captivatingly tame of all the creatures we finally took back to the London Zoo and the first of their kind ever to be seen there.

3

The Axe-Makers

The ridge on which Barry had built his house proved to be an excellent vantage point for watching birds. Every day we saw several Paradisea but always they were so far distant that even with our most powerful telephoto lens we were unable to film them adequately. We also occasionally caught glimpses of them when we walked in the forest but our views of the birds were so fleeting that again photography was impossible. To film them, we had to find some place to which they paid regular visits and then to build a hide close to it so that we could wait, with our cameras ready, for the bird to appear. A dancing tree or a nest would provide just such a situation, but though we searched we were unable to discover either, and the local people, as we expected, professed complete ignorance.

In the course of our explorations, we found several snakes, a stick insect nearly a foot long, a number of brilliantly coloured tree frogs, a swarm of huge caterpillars, and many other small creatures which provided subjects for our cameras, but these animals seemed to us to be very inadequate substitutes for our main quarry – the birds of paradise.

In the chilly evenings, we sat with Barry around the stove heaped with blazing wood that stood by one wall of his living room and planned our route to Aiome. Barry had never made the complete journey in one trek but had travelled along most of the route at one time or another on his patrols, and with the aid of his own sketch maps we were able to draw up a time-table. He told us that stone axes were still made at a village called Menjim which lay two days' march down the Jimi valley, on the same side of the river and about as far from it as Tabibuga. The journey to Menjim would not be an easy one, for the only existing track crossed numerous tributary valleys running down at right-angles to the Jimi River, and to travel from one to the other would involve each time toiling up steep jungle-covered slopes to a high pass and then descending several thousand feet to the next river. Menjim lay on one of these tributary rivers, the Ganz. From there we planned to walk down the Ganz valley in one day to the Jimi itself, where, at a place called Tumbungi, we could cross it by a native-made cane suspension bridge. On the other side lay the Bismarck Mountains, the country of the pygmies. To cross the main range we should have to climb to over six thousand feet, and it would take us five days of hard marching to complete our journey down to Aiome, in the valley of the Ramu, the huge river which drains the northern flanks of the Central Highlands of New Guinea and empties into the Bismarck Sea.

As a result of these calculations, we knew it would take at least eight full days of travel to reach Aiome. The date for our rendezvous there with the charter plane was unchangeable and if we spent too long at Tabibuga, we might be unable to spare any time for filming on the journey ahead. I became anxious to leave. Barry, however, was unexpectedly faced with some local problems on the station which he felt he could not abandon until they had been settled, so we agreed that Charles and I should go on ahead to Menjim, and that Barry should join us there as soon as he could.

We left early one morning, six days after we had arrived at Tabibuga. Once again Wawawi came with us. He led the way, Charles and I followed, and behind us came a long, winding column of porters, three of the more responsible and careful ones carrying the cages containing the two little parrots and some snakes. For the first hour or so the journey was deceptively easy, the track descending gently down kunai ridges and occasionally passing through small patches of forest. Wawawi sent runners ahead to conscript relays of porters and as we reached each new tribal territory, we found men waiting on the frontier to carry our baggage onwards.

At about ten o'clock we reached Kwibun, the first village on the route. Here we stopped for a rest. The local people collected in a group around us chattering with excitement, and while the porters refreshed themselves with snacks of cold cassava, I unlocked the patrol box which contained our trade goods and extracted a large pearl shell. We had come to look for 'stone-akis' and 'all-kind pidgin' which 'no got wound', I explained, waving the shell in the air, and I would exchange 'dis-fella keena' for a good example of either. The villagers listened to me wonderingly. Then one of them left the group, went into his hut and returned with an axe.

Like the ones we had seen at the Minj sing-sing, it was T-shaped, the stone blade having a long, curving, wooden counter-balance, but it was smaller and completely covered with a black, sticky tar. Clearly it had been lying disused for many years above the smoking fire in the rafters of the tribesman's hut, and he had only brought it to me because, of all his implements, it was the one he least valued. It was, however, exactly what I wanted, for its obvious signs of age implied that it had been made, and perhaps used in battle, before the arrival of any metal tools into the Jimi, and I gladly traded it for the pearl shell.

No one produced anything else of interest, so we left and continued westwards. After another two hours' marching, the spring began to disappear from my stride. I had assumed that in this rainy country there would be many streams and consequently I had not brought water bottles. But the sun shone fiercely from a clear sky, scorching my skin, the dust from the kunai grass caked my lips and my throat became painfully parched. We marched on for mile after mile without finding the smallest rivulet which could provide us with a drink. Charles seemed to feel the lack of water even worse than I. He was sweating so profusely that not only was his shirt soaked but his trousers back and front became saturated and frequently he was able to wring a cupful of liquid from the hems at the bottom of his trouser legs. This was very worrying for although the day was hot, the journey was no more strenuous than the one we had made to Tabibuga when Charles had not perspired in this abnormal way, and I feared that he might be suffering from a fever of some sort. With no drink to make good this constant drain of water from his body, he soon began to feel really ill, but in spite of this he gamely trudged on.

Early in the afternoon, we descended into a deep valley and found at the bottom a wide river at which Charles at last was able to slake his thirst. We took a protracted rest, and then began the long climb up steep forest-covered slopes on the other side. Barry had recommended that we should sleep that night at a village called Wum, and at last I thought I could see it in the distance on the crest of a high knoll. It looked impossibly far away and the two hours it took us to reach it seemed interminable. Wawawi strode at my side, laughing at my weariness, and we entered the village together. I sat down outside the small house-kiap, which Barry had ordered to be built on his last visit, and called for water. The village luluai brought it to me in long hollow stems of bamboo. I drank greedily. I sluiced the cool water over my chest. I poured it wastefully over my face and neck and washed away the dust.

'This place Wum, im number one place true,' I said to Wawawi. 'Walkabout finis. Me like die now.'

'Name belong dis place, Tsenga,' said Wawawi cheerfully. 'Wum long-way more.'

'Wawawi,' I said with decision, 'me sleep 'long dis place. Makim bed, quick time.'

When Charles hobbled into the village an hour later, I had a large mug of tea waiting for him and his bed ready. He collapsed exhausted on to it and confessed that he had nearly been sick on the way up.

The next day he felt considerably better, but the journey was if anything harder than the previous day's. Several times we had to descend a thousand feet, slithering and skidding down a muddy forest track, ford a river and then, panting and sweating, trudge up the mountain on the other side of the valley to regain our original height. Each time I hoped that Wawawi would tell me that the river in the valley over the next divide was the Ganz, but it was not until the late afternoon as we sat resting on the crest of a pass that he announced that Menjim lay immediately below us. By this time I had gained my second wind and I took the steeply winding path at a run. The Menjim villagers having heard the chants of our carriers had come part way up the track to meet us, and as I trotted past them, unwilling to break the rhythm of my pace, they cheered and grinned and momentarily clasped my hand so that I felt as though I were an Olympic athlete entering the stadium for the last lap of the marathon.

The Ganz valley was beautiful and, as it was the end of this stage of our journey, it seemed to me to be particularly so. The river frothed and cascaded through a forest of giant pine trees, and on its bank in a spacious clearing we finally found Menjim itself. The house-kiap was large and roomy and as the porters carried in our loads, the villagers brought us gifts of pineapples, pawpaws and breadfruit. Only one of them, a young man with a large leaf and two tufts of cockatoo feathers stuck in his hair, understood any of my pidgin. Proud of his unique ability, he seated himself on the veranda and waited patiently to act as turnim-talk whenever we might require him.

It was he who agreed the next morning to take us to the place where the axes were made. It lay only a few minutes from the village on the hillside lower down the valley. A group of men were sitting around a fire by the side of a small stream, chipping pieces of stone and gossiping and singing as they worked. As we arrived they got to their feet and clustered round us while Turnim-talk explained to them in a patronizing way who we were and what we had come to see. I asked where the stone came from and, in explanation, one of the older axe-makers waded into the stream. After a few minutes' search, he bent, heaved up a large dripping boulder, and staggered back to lay it at our feet. It was roughly oblong in shape and several of the axe-makers squatted beside it and began to talk volubly. One of them scratched lines along its length with a pebble, gestured to a point on it, and explained that if it were struck there it would split lengthways.

'Lookim,' said Turnim-talk admiringly, 'dis good-fella stone too much. Im workim big-fella axe.'

Certainly, an axe blade the length of the boulder would be gigantic, and much larger than any we had seen so far.

The suggested method of cleavage was not, however, accepted by everybody and several more men made alternative recommendations. The old man listened patiently to them all. Then, his mind made up, he picked up a heavy stone, placed it carefully on the point on which he proposed to hit the boulder and lifted it above his head. He stood poised, then hurled the stone down with all his strength.

There was a moment's silence, then a shout of laughter from all the axe-makers. The boulder had split, but across its length, exactly at right-angles to the direction which had been so carefully planned. Everyone seemed to regard this misfortune as a great joke.

Turnim-talk wiped tears of laughter from his eyes.

'Two-fella lik-lik akis, t'a's-all,' he said.

When the old man had recovered from the humour of the situation, he lifted his stone maul again and attacked the bigger of the two halves. This time he had more success, for it cleaved neatly into long smooth flakes. He continued smashing the remnants of the boulder until it was reduced to a pile of chips and over a dozen flakes. He selected the largest of them and surrendered the rest to the other men. Then he sat down, took a pebble and patiently began chipping his chosen fragment into the approximate shape of an axe head. Every few minutes he picked up the axe-blade-to-be and, holding the narrower end lightly between his thumb and forefinger, tapped the lower end with his pebble so that the stone rang. Each time he did so he smiled broadly and I assumed he was able to tell from the tapping sound whether or not the stone was perfect and uncracked.

Chipping an axe blade

'Finis im akis long dis place?' I asked Turnim-talk.

'No got,' he replied. 'Come.'

We followed him down the stream to the main river and there we found an even larger group of men sitting among the jumble of boulders at the river's edge, grinding and polishing their axe blades. They were using whetstones of a coarse sandstone which Turnim-talk informed us also occurred as boulders in the river. There was no uniformly accepted method of working. One man had embedded his whetstone in the soft stem of a banana palm and, with this in front of him, was rhythmically rubbing his axe blade back and forth on it, stopping every few minutes to dip the blade in the river swirling by him and examine its progress. Another worked in the opposite way: he had laid his blade on the ground and was filing it methodically with a rather smaller whetstone. Some, who had finished the main work on the axe head, were carefully bevelling the curved cutting edge. Others were shaping the wooden counterweights, weaving the decorative cane covering and binding on the wooden hafts.

Polishing an axe blade

I asked Turnim-talk how long it took to complete one axe.

'Some-fella time, tree fella moon,' he replied. 'Some-fella time, six-fella moon.'

If this were so, it was only because the men approached their work in such an unhurried spirit for, from what we had

Fitting the haft

seen, I felt sure that if a man were prepared to work hard every day he could finish one axe in two or three weeks. But such ridiculous single-minded application to a task is largely a Western habit; these people worked only when they felt inclined to do so.

It was an astonishing scene, for as we watched these semi-naked craftsmen, their head-plumes bobbing as they worked, their chants almost drowned by the rush of the river, we were watching life in the Stone Age. But one significant alien detail caught my eye. One man, like his companions in every other respect, was putting the finishing touches to the haft of his axe, not with a stone blade, but with a shining metal knife. If we were watching the Stone Age, we were witnessing one of its last stages. Furthermore, the axes these craftsmen were making had no real utilitarian function. The blades were too thin, they flared too widely, their cutting edge was too finely tapered for them

A finished Highland axe

to be really serviceable. If one were used to fell a tree, it would chip and splinter. If it were taken to war, its huge cumbersome counterbalance would prove disastrously unwieldy.

These axes were larger, more flamboyant and more decorative than the stubby, begrimed and workmanlike example with its steel-sharp cutting edge which I had acquired at Kwibun; but to my eyes they were also less beautiful, and without doubt they had no practical value. Splendid though they looked, they had become decorative and non-functional. These men were now only making them to serve ritual purposes – for display at sing-sings or perhaps, since custom sometimes demanded it, for inclusion in a bride-price.

Two things may happen to the stone axes in the future. As the craftsmen realize that their products need no longer be serviceable, they may employ softer and more easily worked stone and tend to make the blades even more ornamental; or else tribal traditions, already weakened by the teaching of mission-aries, will no longer insist on the presence of axes at ritual occasions. When either happens, the Stone Age in this part of New Guinea will be over.

That night, as we sat in the house-kiap, a panting tribesman appeared on the veranda with a message. To my joy, he had brought it in a cleft stick. I had hardly dared to believe that such a custom, so reminiscent of the old-style adventure stories, could still exist, but the New Guinea tribesman has no pockets in his scanty costume, nowhere to keep a letter uncrumpled and unsoiled, and the cleft stick still provides the best solution.

I undid the binding at the top and extracted the letter. It was from Barry. He had finished his work at Tabibuga and would join us the next day.

I called Turnim-talk in from the veranda, and explained that we should be staying in Menjim for one more day when the kiap would arrive. Now that I had seen the 'stone-akis' I was anxious to see 'kumul e go sing-sing long diwai'. (Since we had been travelling without any Europeans our pidgin of necessity had improved and 'diwai', meaning tree, was one of my more recently acquired words.) I emphasized that we would not harm the birds in any way, that we would not shoot them, nor would we attempt to catch them. We wished only to see them and to point our 'box picture' at them. If any man could show us the dancing birds, I would give him a pearl shell of the finest quality – a 'number-one keena'.

Turnim-talk's eyes sparkled.

'Me savvy,' he said. 'Diwai belong kumul, im e close-to.'

Hardly able to believe our luck, I arranged that he should collect us early the next morning and take us to the tree.

'We no lookim kumul,' I warned. 'We no givim keena.'

Turnim-talk took no risks. He called us not merely at dawn but in the middle of the night, or so it seemed to me as I sleepily pulled on my clothes by the light of a torch. We picked up our cameras and stumbled down the path leading out of the village, our boots clinking unnaturally loudly on the stones. We crossed the river by a fallen tree trunk and walked up to a plantation of cassava. Faintly in the grey before-dawn light, I could see beyond it a group of casuarina trees.

'Sun i come up,' whispered Turnim-talk. 'Kumul i come sing-sing long diwai.'

We nodded, and wormed our way into the centre of a group of bushes where we set up the camera. Then we settled down to wait. The leaves around us were heavy with dew and I felt cold even though I was wearing a thick jersey. Slowly, almost imperceptibly, the grey sky brightened. I was impatient for the bird to arrive, but every time I mentioned the possibility, Charles countered by holding up his exposure meter and pointing out that it would in fact be disastrous if the bird came so soon as there was not yet enough light to film it by. At last he grudgingly admitted that if he opened the aperture of his lens to the widest extent (thereby, he did not fail to add, reducing the depth of focus to nothing) there might be just enough light to register a dim image on the film.

As he said this, I heard a bird call which I recognized as being that of a Lesser Bird of Paradise. It came from behind us and I slowly turned round to look for it. There was another call and a flutter drew my eyes to a distant tree in which I could distinguish the vague shape of a bird. It called a third time and flew in a swooping arc above us, its brilliant plumes trailing behind it, and alighted in the casuarinas ahead of us. Maddeningly, it settled in the densest part of the tree's foliage and disappeared from our sight.

It began to call, with a new urgency in its note, while I searched despairingly with my binoculars. For what seemed like an age, the shrieks continued and all we could see was an indeterminate agitation among the leaves. Then there was silence. Abruptly the bird shot from the tree and flew off down the valley.

Lesser Bird of Paradise

'T'a's all,' announced Turnim-talk loudly. 'Masta givim one fella number one keena.'

'E no come back?' I asked.

'E no come back, altogether,' he replied with finality.

'Orright. Me givim,' I said. 'Turnim-talk go back long house-kiap. We stop lik-lik.'

Triumphantly, Turnim-talk left us. Miserably we waited for another half-hour in the faint hope that the bird might return. I scanned the trees with my binoculars and in doing so I turned them idly on to a pawpaw growing close by us. To my surprise I found myself looking at two large eyes peering at me through the leaves.

I handed the binoculars to Charles. He could see them also, but neither of us could imagine what creature it was that owned them. The bird of paradise would not return now, for the sun was already rising in the sky, so we stood up from our conceal-ment and walked over to the pawpaw to investigate.

I looked up into the tree. Nestling in the top crown of leaves I saw a white furry creature the size of a cat. It was a cuscus, one of the most charming of the mammals of New Guinea and a creature I dearly wanted to take back to London. As I watched, he uncurled himself and, blinking myopically, began to clamber down towards me, gripping the trunk with his long curling tail. On his way he encountered a vine twisting round the trunk and stopped to munch a few of the leaves in a contemplative fashion. Then he continued to descend towards me, and for a moment I thought he would walk straight into my hands. So that I should be in a position ready to receive him, I made a slight movement. He whirled round and scampered back up the trunk to the shelter of the leaves.

We had reached an impasse. He would not come down while we stood there, and I could not climb up for the pawpaw was so slender that it would not carry my weight. The only solution

The cuscus

was to chop it down. I took out my bush knife and began to do so. The cuscus reappeared from among the leaves and gravely inspected what I was doing. Soon the tree began to shake with each blow. This the cuscus did not like, so he descended a little way, and with his tail wound round the trunk and bracing himself with his hind legs, he leaned outwards, clasped the nearby branch of a bush and left the pawpaw altogether. This, though at first sight a clever move, was unwise, for the bush was low and one in which I could clamber myself. I put down my knife and took off my jersey for, in a cowardly way, I much prefer to catch such creatures in a cloth of some sort as I believe it minimizes the chances of being bitten. As I reached up towards him the cuscus gargled at me in a threatening way and retreated a few inches. The branch supporting him was thin, however, and began to bend under his weight. He could go back no farther. With a swoop of my jersey, I caught him by the back of his neck, unwound his tail and brought him down growling fiercely.

The cuscus, like all the truly indigenous mammals of New Guinea, is a marsupial and has a pouch like a kangaroo. Its range is widespread for it is found not only in New Guinea, but also in northern Australia and in many of the islands of eastern Indonesia. It exists in many different colours. Our capture was unusual in being pure white, the commoner colours being brown or white spotted with orange. He had a moist pink nose, and naked paws, and had coiled his tail like a watch spring. Our joy in having found him temporarily outweighed our disappointment at having failed to see the paradise bird's dance, and we hurried back to the house-kiap to prepare a comfortable cage.

4

Pygmies and Dancing Birds

That evening, in a cloudburst, Barry arrived at Menjim. The monotonous swishing of the rain prevented us from hearing his entrance and we were quite startled when he suddenly appeared and stood, dripping, on the veranda. He brought news which added a further complication to our plans. The night before he had left Tabibuga, he had called Hagen on the radio to report his departure and had been asked by the DC to inspect an airstrip which a gold prospector named Jim MacKinnon had just completed at a place called Kumburuf, on the northern flanks of the Bismarck Mountains. A plane had been chartered to fly over the strip in four days' time and if the pilot saw ground signals indicating that the new strip was serviceable, he would land with a load of stores. The only person qualified to give such a signal was a government officer and, if Barry were to get there in time to do so, we should all have to leave Menjim the next morning.

As Barry told us all this, the rain continued to hurl itself on the roof of the house-kiap and poured from the eaves so that the windows seemed curtained with a continuous sheet of water. I gloomily contemplated the prospect of marching for several days in such conditions and, in an endeavour to be philosophical, reasoned that it was better that the weather should be bad during a day committed to travelling than during one on which we were trying to film. The logic of this, however, gave me little solace when in the morning we found that it was still raining as hard as ever.

Marching through the rainforest

We had waterproof capes with us, but there seemed little point in wearing them for, if we did so, they would not only flap uncomfortably around our legs, but we would become as wet with sweat as we would do if we walked unprotected in the rain. We therefore packed them in the top of our boxes to ensure that, even if the lids leaked, the contents would remain dry. Then we put on jerseys and bravely set out. When we saw the near-naked porters uncomplainingly shouldering the loads in the drenching downpour, however, it was impossible to feel sorry for ourselves, even though I noted, uncharitably, that the carriers' skins were so greasy that the rain fell off them in silver drops as it does off a bird's feathers.

The march down the Ganz was an easy one for we were travelling downhill and we were able to fall into a rhythmic stride with our heavy, mud-clogged boots swinging like pendulum bobs. In the late morning the rain stopped and the forest smelt deliciously clean and fresh; the ground was covered with a deep layer of mouldered leaves and was delightfully springy underfoot. We had never travelled in this kind of bush before. The commonest trees were the giant araucaria pines, the enormous trunks of which, as thick and as tall as factory chimneys, rose vertically, untrammelled by branches or creepers until, nearly two hundred feet above the ground, they burgeoned into a crown of monkey-puzzle-like foliage. Some of these living pillars had been blazed with axes to mark the route, and the wounds exuded copious and sweetly fragrant resin. Among the pines grew other trees, some stilted and buttressed with aerial roots, some draped with lianas from which hung epiphytic ferns like ornate chandeliers. Occasionally we saw in the gardens growing on the branches a cascade of vivid orchid blooms. There were birds, too, high in the forest canopy above us. Usually we only heard them – perhaps a shrill, piercing call or, very commonly, the heavy, noisy beating of wings which is characteristic of a hornbill – but occasionally we saw them also. Lesser Birds of Paradise seemed particularly abundant, their sulphur plumes flashing brilliantly as they took to flight ahead of us.

As our clothes dried on our backs, I felt exhilarated and very happy, and the carriers began to sing.

Our line of porters stretched far behind us, for now that Barry had joined us we needed at least a hundred men to carry all our loads. The track to Tumbungi ran down the right side of the valley and for most of the day we had the Ganz River beside and below us as our constant companion, rushing through gorges and tumbling over waterfalls until, as we neared the Jimi River, it slackened its pace and divided into many channels to braid over a wide, boulder-strewn delta at its confluence. Here we waded across it, climbed a low divide on the other side, and then descended steeply to Tumbungi by the side of the Jimi River.

Wading across the Ganz River

Instead of a village or a hamlet, all we found was a house-kiap and a shelter for porters, standing lonely and deserted in a small clearing. At the riverside grew a giant tree from which a dilapidated suspension bridge of vines sagged across the river to another tree on a rocky bluff fifty yards away on the opposite bank. There was silence but for the buzz of insects, the rippling of the river water, and the faint creak of the bridge as it swayed gently in the wind.

This was the settlement from which Barry had planned to recruit new porters. If we could find no new carriers we should be in trouble, for the Menjim men would almost certainly refuse to carry our baggage any farther. The country across the river belonged to a totally different tribe, the pygmies, and though the Menjim carriers might be persuaded to go into it under the protection of a kiap and his armed policemen, they certainly would not do so if they were to be abandoned in strange and possibly hostile country and had to make their way back home unprotected.

Furthermore, if we induced them to go beyond their own territory, they would not be able to gather breadfruit, pawpaws or cassava from the forest as they could do if they were in their own tribal area. They would therefore rely entirely on us for food and we had not enough rice to provide for them. We had no alternative but to pay them off.

Barry sat himself on a stool outside the house-kiap and watched impassively as the loads arrived and were checked by the policemen. Wawawi, who was standing by him, suddenly pointed across the river. A small group of people had come out of the forest and were standing by the water's edge looking at us. They were pygmies. Wawawi climbed up to the bridge and crossed to invite them over.

Crossing the suspension bridge

He led them back over the bridge and in comparison with Wawawi, who was six feet tall, they seemed so tiny that it was difficult to believe that they were fully grown. Their leader was a barrel-chested little man, with splinters of bamboo stuck through his nostrils, three on each side, whitening bird skulls hanging from his ears and a hornbill beak slung at the back of his neck. His brown, beardless face was covered with herring-bone stripes of blue-black scars and on his head he had an extraordinary bulbous hat which gave him the appearance of an animated mushroom. Later, when we got to know one another better, I was able to examine this hat in more detail. Its top layer was a cloth made from beaten bark fibre and when, at my request, he removed it, I discovered that the substance of the hat was made up of his own hair clippings which had been mixed with red mud and kneaded into his growing hair so that it formed a stiff solid mass. In fact, it was not so much a hat as an irremovable wig, the lower layers of which were still attached organically to his scalp.

The leader of the pygmies

He stood rather nervously in front of Barry, shifting uneasily from foot to foot, screwing up his face in a worried effort of comprehension as one of the Menjim men did his best to interpret what Barry was saying.

Barry asked for two things: he wanted to buy food, and he wanted porters to carry our loads onwards. For both he promised to pay well in beads, paint or salt. He added, on our behalf, that if any of the pygmies had tame animals, we would pay well for these also. The pygmy grunted as he listened, and with every nod his wig wobbled on his head and slipped over his eyes, so that he had to push it back into place. We understood from his muttered reply that he would go back across the river and send messages to the rest of his tribe telling them of our requests. More than this he could not do. Barry thanked him, and he and his companions, stoutly independent, returned over the bridge.

The next morning, pygmies carrying food began to cross the river and continued to flood into our camp until well into the afternoon. They brought stems of bananas, breadfruit spitted in dozens on long poles and carried by bandoliers of vines, bundles of sugar cane, taro, yams and cassava. Of all the people who came, none was over five feet high and most were some six inches shorter. All, men as well as women, wore wigs, some of which were decorated with feathers, leaves, panels of green beetle-shards threaded on bamboo splinters or strips of bark scored with simple geometrical designs. Some of the people had tied round their necks ropes of beads or heavy necklaces of cowrie shells which proved that even in this remote valley, so far from the sea, there was still a chain of trade routes along which the shells could come from the coast. One man wore a repulsive necklace of mummified human fingers.

As the food arrived, the Menjim men built huge fires and began to cook some of the vegetables. We ourselves took some of the breadfruit, large oval green objects, the size of footballs, with a prickly green rind. We roasted them on a fire for a few

A pygmy wearing hair ornaments of beetles and shells

minutes and then split them and extracted the numerous white kernels which tasted like chestnuts. They were delicious.

In the afternoon, our first acquaintance reappeared and came to me, carrying over his shoulder a stick on which, struggling to maintain its balance, perched a white yellow-crested cockatoo. I was captivated. It was a hen bird, for her eyes were brown and in a cock they are black. Her eyes also were ringed with a narrow circle of featherless, bright blue skin, a feature which is possessed only by the New Guinea race of cockatoos and does not occur in the almost identical birds which live in Australia. The pygmy set her down and she waddled off to one of the groups of porters seated round a fire and proceeded, with perfect self-confidence and a great deal of success, to beg breadfruit nuts.

We traded her for a pearl shell and Cocky became the least rare, but the most consistently entertaining, member of the menagerie which we took back to London. I assumed that the Zoo would have so many cockatoos that they would not want her and from the first I regarded her as a future pet for my London home. When she did arrive in England, however, I discovered that the Zoo had never possessed a New Guinea Blue-eyed Cockatoo and wanted to have her. But by that time she had wormed her way so deeply into my affections that I could not bring myself to surrender her.

Cocky with her pygmy owner

With the addition of Cocky, we had now quite a large collection – the cuscus, the pythons, fig parrots, a young hornbill which some tribesmen had brought to us earlier – and as I cleaned out the cages, the pygmies clustered round to watch. Each time I relined a cage with clean newspaper and threw away the old sheets, soiled and sodden with droppings, the pygmies pounced on them and carried them away to the riverside, where they gently and carefully washed them clean. Then they dried them over the fires, and that evening I saw them roll some of their native tobacco in the precious paper and sit back, their faces wreathed in smiles of satisfaction, to smoke.

By the next morning nearly a hundred pygmies had congregated on the other side of the river. We could move on. One by one our loads were carried over the swaying bridge, which was so rickety that we dared not risk allowing more than two men and a load on it at one time. Then began the hardest day's march we had so far tackled, up into the Bismarck Mountains.

As evening drew on, we were still trudging wearily up neverending grass ridges with no sign of human habitation in sight. 'What lies there?' I asked Barry, pointing westward to a cloud-filled valley. 'No one knows,' he replied. 'No one has been there.' The sky looked threatening as the sun sank behind heavy grey clouds which had accumulated over the mountains in the west, so we decided to go no farther and pitched camp on the ridge. Within half an hour Barry's police had cut poles in the bush and built a framework over which they spread the tarpaulins so that they formed a long ridge tent. Then they erected a tall bamboo mast up which Wawawi hoisted the Australian flag. At sundown, the police put on their best laps and paraded with fixed bayonets so that the colours could be lowered with due ceremony before the wondering gaze of the pygmies.

The next day's march seemed even harder. It was imperative that we reached Kumburuf, the prospector's camp, by nightfall if Barry was to inspect the airstrip before the plane arrived, so we moved as fast as we could with the minimum number of halts. As we crossed the top of the range we entered moss forest. I heard many Paradisea calls, but we could not spare time to search for them and, indeed, I was glad to keep moving for the permanently sodden forest floor was alive with leeches and, if we stopped, they came looping across the ground towards us. Even while we were marching we were not free from them, for if we brushed through low undergrowth a few always fell on our legs and had to be flicked off with the tip of our knives. The porters were as worried by them as we were, but being barefoot they could easily see the loathsome parasites, whereas if we did not notice them within a few minutes of their arrival, they burrowed through our stockings and disappeared inside our boots to fix their jaws painlessly in our skin and suck blood undetected.

The forest, which we had found at first to be fascinating, began to lose some of its charm. We were marching against time. We could not stop to investigate anything. We could do nothing but wearily keep on putting one foot in front of another and to do so, without stumbling over a root or slipping over a boulder and thereby exhausting more of our energy, we had to keep our eyes fixed to the ground.

At our midday halt, Wawawi arrived carrying a large box himself. Some of the pygmies, unhappy at going so far from their own territory, had dropped their loads and disappeared into the bush. Our carrier line was so reduced as a result that many of the remaining men were carrying even heavier burdens than those with which they had started. If there were any more defections, we might well have to abandon some of our gear.

At last we began to descend through the dripping moss forest and down on to the kunai slopes below at the foot of which lay Kumburuf.

Jim MacKinnon came out to meet us. A stout, jovial man with luxuriant curling grey hair, he looked as though he was almost fifty years old, although in fact he told us he was only in his middle thirties. He welcomed us effusively, shaking our hands, clapping us on the back and laughing excitedly. We were the first Europeans he had seen for many months and he was so overjoyed to be speaking English again that he could not stop talking. Words poured from his lips, tumbling over one another. In his excitement, he stammered badly; he never finished a sentence and every other word was either pidgin English or an Australian expletive.

'Come on in, come on in, my dear old . . . By golly, I'm bloody glad to see you and to . . . It's a terrible bloody mess in here, but I'm only . . . Aw hell, have some bloody whisky.'

The barn-like shack he took us into was indeed in something of a mess. The table in the centre was sticky with smears from past meals, littered with half-used cans of butter, jam and condensed milk, and covered with crumbs. On the pile of trek boxes lay a jumble of red trade cloth, old newspapers and knives. Above them on the wooden wall hung a yellowing calendar decorated with a drawing of an improbably developed chorus girl. An unmade camp bed stood in one corner; there was nothing on which to sit except a torn canvas chair and some upended wooden boxes; and the whole place, as we were to discover later, was infested with rats.

Jim's welcome, however, made up for anything that his house lacked. He was plainly a most generous and kind-hearted man, and pressed on us everything he had that we might want – food, blankets, magazines, drink; we had only to ask and it was ours. He apologized again and again for the lack of luxury in his shack and explained that he himself was only really camping in it, for during the past three months he had been living up at his *place-balus*, his airstrip.

'I'm bloody sorry, but she's . . .' he stuttered. 'The bloody balus from the coast was supposed to bloody drop the . . . After all a bloody roller isn't too bloody heavy, is it, Barry? Can't understand it. Pilot's a bloody nice bloke; nicest bloody bloke as you'll find in the bloody territory. Not his bloody fault. But I didn't get me bloody roller. So, you see, Barry, she's not bloody good enough. Not really. Not by a long bloody chalk.'

He shook his head sadly.

It appeared that after months of work, clearing bush, planing off bumps and ridges, and filling in hollows, the airstrip was almost complete. But to make it safe and serviceable it needed compacting with a heavy roller. Jim had arranged for a charter plane to fly over the strip and drop such a roller, but it had not arrived on the scheduled day and by radio he had learned that the roller exceeded in either weight or size some dimension specified by an air-safety regulation. By the time this happened, however, his request for a Patrol Officer to inspect the strip had been passed to the DC at Hagen and on to Barry. It seemed as though our visit was unnecessary, for Jim himself realized that the plane could not land safely on the strip. Nonetheless Barry pointed out that the plane would be coming over looking for a signal and that he must go to the strip to make it.

Most of the Tumbungi porters left us the next morning, in spite of our attempts to persuade them to stay. There seemed very few people around Kumburuf from whom we could recruit replacements, but Jim said that there would be plenty about in a day or so.

'They're all off on one of their bloody sing-sings,' he said. 'They're up at the place-balus havin' a hell of a party piercin' the young kids' noses with bats' teeth.'

Because of this news, Charles and I decided to accompany Barry and Jim to the airstrip in case we could film the sing-sing. On the way, Jim told me more about his claim. He had been prospecting for gold for nearly twenty years, at first in the northern territories of Australia and then in New Guinea. Until two years ago, he had never made a strike which produced gold in any quantity, but the fever of prospecting gripped him and he was haunted by the stories of Edie Creek, the enormously rich strike that in the 1920s had turned a few lucky prospectors into millionaires. After each of his unsuccessful trips he had returned to some other job to earn enough money to enable him to go once again into the wilds, searching for the gold mine which would make his fortune. At Kumburuf, he believed he had found it.

He had washed gold in small quantities from two parallel creeks running on either side of his shack and he believed that the precious metal was being shed from the ridge which ran between them. He and his partner, who had recently returned

Charles Lagus filming in the Bismarck Mountains

to Australia for a few months, had built a long water conduit down the mountain slopes to provide a race for a monitor, a small gold-washing machine, with which he was now extracting an ounce of gold a day. He had now decided that in order to work profitably he needed several more large monitors.

'When we get those in, Dave,' he said to me, leaning on his stick for a rest and wiping his brow. 'When we get those, she'll come bloody good.'

In order to get them, he had stopped work on the claim itself and had spent the past three months building his place-balus so that the new machinery could be flown in. The decision not to drop the roller had been a bitter, almost crushing, disappointment to him.

We reached the airstrip late in the evening, in pouring rain. A few pygmies were standing disconsolately in one of the shelters Jim had built by its side. They were hollow-eyed and

Pygmies after the dance at the airstrip

exhausted, their cockatoo headdresses bedraggled and awry, for they had been dancing for three days and three nights. Among them were a few boys, their noses newly pierced and their cheeks and upper lips caked with dried trickles of blood. The sing-sing and ceremony were already over, and for Charles and me the excursion to the airstrip had been pointless. It was no more fruitful for Barry, because not only was the strip too soft to be serviceable but, perhaps because of the bad weather, the plane itself never appeared and the sign, which Barry laid out so carefully in white cloth the next day, remained unread.

Gloomily we walked back to Kumburuf in a steady drizzle to find, when we arrived, that all of our Jimi pygmies had now disappeared. We tried that night to muster some porters but, although the sing-sing was over, few people had yet returned to their homes. In the morning we could assemble no more than thirty, and we had no alternative but to abandon some of our loads. Barry anticipated that he would be returning to the Kumburuf area in a few weeks to carry out a new patrol, so he sorted out the kit that he did not need immediately and stacked it in the prospector's hut.

Jim saw us leave with reluctance. He seemed peculiarly ill-suited to the life he had chosen for he was a man who loved company and conviviality, and we knew, as we walked away, that he was wishing dearly that he could be coming with us.

As we descended the ridge, he yelled after us, 'Sink a dozen bottles of bloody beer for me in Lae,' and when, an hour later, I looked back to his hut, toy-like on the skyline, I could just distinguish a small white figure still standing by it, watching us go.

———

That night we pitched camp in the forest close to three small huts which stood huddled together by the side of a stream. Our head porter called the place Kukim Sol. Inside the huts, we found a few pygmies sitting around fires which were burning beneath crudely built cauldrons. They were 'cooking salt'. The cauldrons were made of wet, soft mud, lined with banana leaves and built on top of a rough construction of stones encircling and enclosing the fire. The steaming water in the bowls came from a nearby spring and contained minute traces of dissolved minerals which the pygmies were extracting by slow evaporation. One man showed me a small packet of grey wet salt wrapped in a leaf. It had taken him over a week to produce and I wondered no longer that many of our porters had been glad to carry heavy loads for many hours to earn a tablespoonful of our own trade salt.

Our porters straggled in, many of them carrying double loads, for once again Wawawi, bringing up the rear, had found abandoned bundles on the trail. As we sat in our tent that evening we realized that more of our carriers might desert during the night and that then we would be faced with the choice of abandoning nearly all our cargo – cameras, recording gear, film, the birds – or of spending many days in assembling more porters and missing our plane. Should we do that, it might be a matter of weeks before it would be possible for another plane to come and collect us. Help lay at Aiome, for there the Patrol Officer, with a station far larger than Tabibuga, could undoubtedly produce several hundred carriers if we required them. We decided, therefore, that in the morning Charles and I, with what few carriers remained, should hurry on as fast as we could to Aiome and then send back as many porters as possible to collect Barry and the rest of the cargo. It was a solution we reached with reluctance, for there was a risk that Barry might be stranded for several days before porters reached him. If that happened he would certainly miss the plane on which he was hoping to travel back with us for a few days' holiday in the Wahgi. However, we calculated that, with luck, we might reach Aiome in a day and, if we were able to send back porters immediately, Barry might just arrive at the airstrip a few hours before the plane. This decided, we spent the rest of the evening reducing our kit to its absolute minimum.

The march now became a race. We left Barry just after dawn, promising to travel as fast as we could. Within two hours we had crossed the top of the pass above Kukim Sol. The porters told us that only one river, the Asai, and one high ridge lay between us and Aiome. It seemed that we should reach the station long before nightfall. Jubilantly, we ran down the kunai slopes, descending several thousand feet to the Asai River. We arrived on its banks at midday. To our dismay, we found that the improvised bridge of branches and lianas which spanned it was derelict or partially washed away. Wawawi cautiously crept along it but suddenly there was a crack. Wawawi jumped hastily back to the bank as the centre portion slowly hinged over and crashed into the river.

Meanwhile I had been selecting the shallowest part and gingerly I began to wade across. The water was flowing so swiftly that when I was only knee-deep I began to feel very insecure. By the time the water was waist-high, the swollen river was snatching and tugging at me so powerfully that I could hardly force one foot in front of the other. In taking one step my foot slipped on a submerged boulder and, if it had not been for my staff, I would have been swept away. At last I reached the opposite bank, but my crossing was of no value except to convince me that the pygmies carrying our cameras and film would stand no chance in midstream. We had no alternative but to repair the bridge.

The porters, under Wawawi's direction, began felling casuarina trees and gathering lianas to bind the tree trunks in position. They worked hard, but as the minutes passed I realized that we could not reach Aiome that day.

It took nearly three hours to make the bridge strong enough to support the carriers, and it was not until the middle of the afternoon that we had all crossed to the other side. At six o'clock we made camp halfway up the divide which lay between us and the Ramu valley. Our tent was pitched beneath a breadfruit tree and not far away grew pawpaws and bananas. We gathered the fruit gratefully, for the only food we had packed in our drastically reduced baggage was one tin of corned beef and one of baked beans. Darkness fell quickly and abruptly. We had not brought a lamp with us, so we sat down for our meal by the side of a blazing wood-fire and ate the meat and beans straight from the cans with our knives, for we had neither plates, mugs nor cutlery.

We marched into Aiome the next day at noon. It was civilization: an enormous airstrip, as smooth and as verdant as a bowling green, flanked on either side by a row of spacious villas. As our wild mountain tribesmen strode along the neat gravel paths bordered with low hedges of clipped shrubs, the little Papuan schoolboys in their bright uniform of red loincloths ran in panic across the airstrip to find their mothers. The only two Europeans on the station, a cadet Patrol Officer and a Medical Assistant, welcomed us with hot showers, clean clothes and an enormous meal of steak, and while we relaxed, fifty porters were mustered and sent off to Kukim Sol in charge of one of the station policemen.

To sit once again in a comfortable chair, to drink refrigerator-cold beer, to stroll aimlessly instead of marching against time, all this seemed an incredible luxury. But two thoughts continually thrust themselves into my mind and marred my pleasure: we had deserted Barry and probably robbed him of his chance of a holiday in the Wahgi; and we had not, after all, seen the dance of the paradise birds.

Throughout the next day and late into the evening, Charles and I tried again and again to twist our estimates of marching time to convince ourselves of the possibility of Barry rejoining us before eleven o'clock the next day, when the charter plane was due to arrive. As we reached the conclusion once again that it was simply impossible, Charles lifted up his hand.

'Listen,' he said, 'I thought I heard singing.'

We rushed out into the darkness. Far away on the black silhouette of the mountains we saw two specks of light. We could hardly believe that they could be carried by Barry or his men, and for two hours we watched them as they flickered and slowly came lower. Then they disappeared altogether – whoever it was had entered the patch of forest at the foot of the mountains. At last we could hear clearly a continuous chant and the lights suddenly appeared bright and large at the far end of the airstrip. We ran towards them.

At the head of the column strode Barry. By his side, carrying his loads, were not pygmies, not Aiome men, but tall, grinning Marakas.

'This crowd', said Barry, 'have caught some snakes for you. They brought them down to Tabibuga and were so fed up when they found that we had left the place days before that they chased after us. They are still so cocky that they reckon they can take on anyone in New Guinea if it comes to a fight and they didn't care tuppence that they were walking through hostile country. When they caught up with me at Kukim Sol the day after you left, I just told 'em to pick up the loads and keep on marching.'

He laughed wearily.

'Just when I had a couple of really good foolproof murder charges to hang on them, the old bastards turn up trumps like this.'

The next morning we heard the faint drone of an engine and a tiny speck appeared above the Bismarck Mountains. The plane circled the airstrip and landed. My relief at seeing it turned to worry, for it was a very small single-engined machine and seemed far too tiny to carry Barry, Charles and me, all our baggage and equipment, and the collection of animals. The pilot, however, had no such qualms. He glanced cursorily at the loads lined up on the margin of the airstrip and, calling for them one at a time, began to pack them systematically into the plane's hold. The snake cage was almost the first he selected and, when he heard what was inside, he asked me to put an extra fastening on the lid, remarking mildly that if, during the flight, a python climbed up his back, his mind might be distracted from aviating.

In spite of his confidence about his plane's capacity, however, as the last loads went in we could see that it would be a very tight squeeze. The hornbill had to be taken from his large cage and rehoused in a much smaller one to fit in the only remaining space immediately behind my seat, and there was no room whatever for Cocky, so I took her out of her box and let her perch on my lap.

The journey was a memorable one. It was the first time that Cocky displayed to the full her staggering vocal powers, for as the plane's engine roared to full throttle, she erected her yellow crest and emitted a shriek which cut through the thunder of the engine like a knife. She seemed so perturbed that I feared she might take flight on her own account, but she contented herself with fastening her hooked beak into the ball of my thumb until the most frightening moments of the take-off were over. Soon after she had relaxed, the hornbill behind me discovered that the bamboo mesh of his temporary cage was easily parted, and made me aware of the fact by delivering a sharp and powerful blow on the back of my neck with his enormous beak. I was so tightly jammed next to Charles that it was impossible to move out of the bird's range. In desperation I tried to protect myself by hanging a handkerchief over his cage, but this had no effect whatsoever and he continued to remind me very forcefully of his presence throughout the entire journey.

In scarcely more than an hour, we had crossed the Bismarck Mountains, the Jimi valley and could see the Wahgi River ahead of us. The plane dropped gently downwards and landed at Hagen airstrip. There we left Barry to enjoy a few days' holiday at the station, before he marched back to Tabibuga and resumed his lonely and arduous life.

From Hagen, the flight to Nondugl took only a few minutes. Frank Pemble-Smith and Fred Shaw Mayer were there to greet us, as they had been when we first arrived weeks before, and the warmth of their welcome made us feel almost as though we were returning home. That evening we told Fred of what we had seen and done in the Jimi. In many ways it was a story of success. We had found and filmed the axe-makers, we had seen the pygmies and we had assembled a large collection of animals which, even if it did not contain some of the birds we had hoped to find, was as large as we had intended it to be. Indeed, if it had been any bigger, we should have been unable to get it into the plane at Aiome. But, in spite of all our efforts, we had failed to see the dance of the paradise birds.

Fred smiled gently when we told him this.

'In that case,' he said, 'I think you'll be glad to hear what old Garai has got to tell you. He's coming round tonight.'

Garai appeared after supper, flashing his huge white smile and pulling excitedly at his beard.

'Aaah, na you i come,' he said, shaking my hand vigorously. He was obviously bursting with some tremendous secret. He leaned towards me, his eyes dancing, and whispered hoarsely, 'Me findim, me findim.'

'Wonem Garai find?' I asked.

'Na me findim one fella diwai, kumul i come play long hand belong diwai,' Garai replied triumphantly.

For a moment his pidgin baffled me and when I did sort it out I could hardly believe that I had done so correctly. Could he really be saying that he knew of a 'hand' of a tree on which a paradise bird came to dance, here in Nondugl where every plumed bird was shot as soon as it appeared.

Fred explained.

'When you left for the Jimi,' he said, 'Garai was rather upset that you had not found what you wanted in Nondugl. Quite soon afterwards, he discovered that a Count Raggi's Bird was coming to dance in a casuarina just by the house of one of his wives. So he issued strict orders to the wife concerned and told her it was *tambu* for anyone to touch the bird until the 'masta belong box picture' came back. Ever since then, he's been worried stiff that a poacher will get the poor thing before you photograph it.'

Garai, not understanding a word, continued nodding enthusiastically, his eyes darting from Fred to us and back again.

'Mind you,' said Fred, looking at Garai reproachfully, 'I am not sure how long the old rascal's own self-control is going to last. He's a bit hard up at the moment because he's just bought a new wife and she cost him all the feathers you saw him wearing when you first arrived, as well as a fair number of his pigs and pearl shells. There's bound to be some sing-sing or other due soon, and as he hasn't got anything at all for a head-dress, I expect he'll shoot the bird himself as soon as you've filmed it.'

We met Garai outside Fred's house at half past five the next morning and together, as dawn was breaking, we walked through the dew down the airstrip. In the grey light I saw, crossing the strip ahead of us, a tribesman carrying a bow and arrows. My heart missed a beat, for in his other hand he held the body of a bird. Garai broke into a run, yelling. The tribesman turned round and came towards us. I held out my hand and he gave me the corpse he was carrying. It was a dead Count Raggi's Bird. Its brilliant yellow head flopped tragically sideways as I took it and I saw that its magnificent emerald breast feathers were stained and clotted with blood. The body was still warm; we must have missed seeing the bird dancing by only a few minutes. As I sadly examined it, my mind numb with disappointment, Garai questioned the man vociferously. There was a heated argument at the end of which Garai turned to us, all smiles again.

'Orright,' he said.

The hunter with his newly killed Count Raggi's Bird

I could only hope that this meant that the bird was not Garai's but had been dancing in some other tree. Before I could discover more from Garai, he was walking on down the path.

At the end of the airstrip the track continued, through fields of cassava growing in neat square plots, to Garai's hut, beyond which the ground fell in a heavily wooded slope towards the Wahgi River. As we approached his house, Garai pointed to a casuarina tree growing a few yards from it.

'Diwai belong kumul,' he said.

We looked hard but could see nothing.

'I'll bet that this is where that poor bird was shot,' I muttered to Charles in an undertone. As I spoke a loud call rang from the tree and a fully plumed bird catapulted from the thick foliage near the top.

'Im! Im!' cried Garai, excitedly.

We watched it fly rapidly down into the valley.

'T'a's all,' said Garai with satisfaction. 'Sing-sing im finis.'

Although we were too late on this occasion at least we knew exactly in which tree the bird danced and how early his display finished. I turned to Garai.

'Orright. Tomorrow-time you-me i come plenty plenty early-time long this-fella diwai. Na we lookim dis fella pidgin makim play, me givim Garai one fella number-one keena.'

That day seemed interminable. My mind kept returning again and again to the tree at the bottom of the airstrip, for I knew that now we were nearer to seeing the display I had dreamed of for so many years, than at any other time since we had been in New Guinea. We overhauled the recorder and the cameras and loaded them in readiness for the morning and went to bed early. I had set our alarm clock for 3.45 a.m., but I awoke long before it rang. In the pitch dark we fumbled our way out of the house to a small hut nearby, where Garai had spent the night. At our third call, Garai emerged, clasping his shoulders in the cold.

The night was cloudless. The crescent moon was floating low

in the sky, horns towards the horizon, and above the jagged silhouette of the Kubor Mountains on the opposite side of the valley hung the Southern Cross, glittering like a jewel on velvet. We were nearly at the farther end of the airstrip before the first signs of dawn began to streak the sky away to our left, and as the darkness dwindled a six o'clock beetle began to stridulate loudly in the grass by the side of the path. I looked at the luminous dial of my wristwatch; the little insect was nearly three-quarters of an hour ahead of its schedule. From the hillsides behind us came the faint sound of a man yodelling as he set out on his day's work and, closer to, a cockerel called. The Wahgi valley ahead was cloaked with a smooth, level blanket of cloud. Slowly the stars faded as we walked through the dew-heavy kunai grass towards Garai's wife's house. Steam was rising from its thatched roof and its low entrance was stopped with a pile of banana leaves. Garai called hoarsely through the wooden walls to rouse the occupants. The leaves were pushed aside from the doorway and an old wizened woman crawled out, followed by two young girls, Garai's daughters, naked except for their belts and aprons. As they stretched and rubbed their eyes, Garai questioned them. Their answers seemed to satisfy him.

'Orright,' he said. 'Kumul i come lik-lik time.'

The casuarina tree stood only a few yards away, growing in the middle of a small grove of banana palms. With our equipment in position, we waited anxiously, hardly daring to move or to whisper to one another. Suddenly, we heard a flutter of wings and a fully plumed Count Raggi's Bird flew up from the valley beyond. He came straight to the casuarina and alighted on a slim branch, stripped bare of twigs and leaves, which grew diagonally upwards from the main trunk. Immediately he began to preen himself, combing with his beak the long gauzy plumes that sprouted from beneath his wings and extended past his tail in a glorious red cloud. Charles's camera whirred, sounding startlingly loud, but the bird took no notice and carefully he continued his toilet until, immaculate at last, he straightened up and shook himself. Then, head held high, he called – a single, loud, raucous note which echoed over the valley. He seemed in no hurry to begin his dance, for he continued to call for nearly a quarter of an hour. By now the sun was just rising and shafts of its light, filtering through the foliage, glinted on his splendid feathers. Two other birds flew up from the valley and settled in other parts of the tree. They were drab brown creatures, presumably females, which, attracted by his calls, had come to witness his dance. He disregarded them, and continued his harsh cries, occasionally preening himself. The hens remained silent, flitting from branch to branch. Once one of them approached too near his dancing ground and, with a flurry of beating wings, he drove her off.

With electrifying suddenness, the bird ducked his head and throwing his magnificent plumes over his back, he scuttled down his branch, a tremulous fountain of colour, shrieking passionately. Up and down the branch he danced in a frenzy. After half a minute he seemed to get out of breath, for his shrieks ceased and he danced in silence.

As we watched, enthralled, I remembered that Fred had told us that, according to the local people, the birds sometimes become so overwrought that they fall off their branches exhausted and can be picked up from the ground before they recover. Now, watching the dance, I was well able to believe that this might indeed happen.

Abruptly the tension snapped and the bird stopped dancing. Unconcernedly he resumed his preening; but after a few minutes he began his dance again. Three times he performed this ecstatic display and twice we were able to change our position in the banana grove to get another view of him. Then, as the rays of the rising sun flooded the tree, his passions seemed to subside and his shrieks changed to a growling bubble. This lasted for a few seconds. Then he opened his wings and glided down to the valley from where he had come. The hens flew after him. The dance was over.

Exultantly, we packed up our equipment. It was time to return home.

Just before we left Nondugl, a telegram arrived from Sir Edward Hallstrom. He has decided to present London Zoo with twenty birds of paradise from the station's aviaries and we were to add them to the creatures we had caught ourselves. At least one of the birds, a little King of Saxony male just sprouting his head plumes, belonged to a species that had never before been taken alive out of Australasia. As a whole, the collection would be the most important and comprehensive group of New Guinea species to reach the London Zoo for many years. We could not, of course, take them back by way of Australia. Instead I would have to take them east in a small plane to Rabaul on the island of New Britain. There I could get a passage on a small cargo boat that would take me to Hong Kong – and then London.

5

Return to the Pacific

When, back in London, I came to review all the material we had filmed during our three months in New Guinea, I realized that we had spent more of our time filming people than animals. I had no regrets. Of all the people in the world whose lives were still barely affected by the ways of Western Europe, theirs were the most spectacular. And what is more, had we continued eastwards into the islands of the Pacific we would have encountered still more of them. The thought stuck in my mind.

The following year, Charles and I set off again, this time to film armadillos in Paraguay, a trip that I have described elsewhere. But the thought of returning to the Pacific haunted me. And then, totally unexpectedly, came the chance of doing so. A letter arrived with a Tongan stamp on it.

It came from an anthropologist friend, Jim Spillius. He had written to say that he was currently working on the Polynesian island of Tonga, helping the island's ruler, Queen Salote, to record her kingdom's complex rituals. She was particularly anxious that a film should be made of the most important and sacred of these, the Royal Kava Ceremony. No European so far had been allowed to witness it, but we – and he – might do so if we agreed to film the proceedings.

Queen Salote, as it happened, had already endeared herself to British television viewers. In 1951 she had travelled to London and joined other dignitaries from around the British Commonwealth to attend the Coronation of Queen Elizabeth

II. When the day arrived and the procession to Westminster Abbey began, it began to rain. Most of those travelling in open horse-drawn carriages had their hoods put up and couldn't be seen. But not Queen Salote. She sat smiling in the drizzle happily waving to the cheerful crowds.

So I already had a star for a possible series. I suggested to the BBC I should return to the Pacific to make some more programmes, this time focussing straightforwardly on people. It would start somewhere in the western Pacific, east of New Guinea and then, in the course of six programmes, travel further eastwards to Fiji and end up in the last programme in Tonga with our privileged look at the Royal Kava Ceremony. The BBC accepted the idea and I began a little research.

Which of the many islands in the western Pacific should we select for our start? There are several island groups there and in all, as far as I could see, there were spectacular rituals of one kind or another. Eventually I decided on Vanuatu. It was then known as the New Hebrides and ruled jointly by the British and French in a unique arrangement which they called a condominium. On one of the islands in the group, Pentecost, people still practised what must be one of the most dramatic ceremonies in the whole of the Pacific. Men with vines tied to their ankles dived headfirst from a tower a hundred feet high. I could hardly imagine a more spectacular beginning to the series.

Unfortunately, Charles was unable to come on this trip. Instead, I was joined by Geoffrey Mulligan, a cameraman of my own age and a man with a reputation for having an unquenchable appetite for physical exertion. When I outlined the plans to him, he became as excited as I was by the prospects.

'This jumping ceremony,' he said, 'we must make sure we really do it justice. Would you like me to try the jump myself, filming as I fall?'

At the time, I thought that he had intended this to be a joke. Later on, when we had worked together for some time,

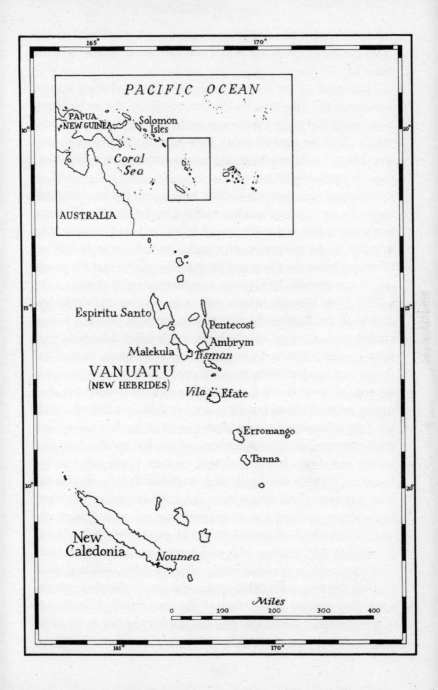

I discovered that if in fact he had been convinced that he would have got first-class pictures that way, he would probably have done it.

The capital of the New Hebrides, Vila, lies sweltering on the west coast of Efate, an island in the middle of the archipelago. The easiest way to get there was to fly, first to New Caledonia, which could be reached either from Australia or from Fiji, and then take a small French-owned twin-engined plane which flew twice a week to Vila.

We stayed only three days in Vila, for passages had been booked for us by an immensely helpful official in the British office on a copra boat that was sailing for Malekula, an island in the north. It called at the plantation of a trader named Oscar Newman. Newman knew the Pentecost people who performed the jump and it was he who had agreed to introduce us to them.

The *Liero*, the ship which was to take us to Malekula, lay dozing in the sun by the jetty in Vila harbour. She was being loaded with a cargo of planks by Melanesian labourers, big heavily muscled men, their skin shiny with sweat, dressed in shorts and singlets with American-style peaked caps jammed on top of their frizzy hair. Garbage and oil floated on the surface of the harbour but there was not sufficient filth to cloud the crystal water, to poison all the coral or to drive away the black sausage-like sea cucumbers which lay on the bottom, twenty feet down, between rusting tin cans. Geoff and I sat in the stern waiting for the loading to finish. It was already an hour past the official sailing time, but none except us had been so recklessly optimistic as to suppose that she would leave on schedule. A shoal of several thousand small silver fish played around her sides moving with such perfect synchronization that they appeared to be one single protean body, twisting and turning, dividing and coalescing. Sometimes they swam upwards until they pocked the surface of the water with a thousand moving dimples; sometimes they dived deep and lost themselves temporarily among the corals.

At last the timber was all loaded and secured. One by one the sweating dockers clambered off her. The French captain appeared on the bridge and shouted some orders, and the *Liero*, grunting and puffing and squirting water from her bilges, moved away from the jetty.

It was difficult to find anywhere to rest. There were only two passenger cabins. One was occupied by a French planter, his pale, plain wife and their young baby; the other by a tiny matchstick-legged shrivelled Australian with red-rimmed eyes and a parboiled complexion, together with his very stout gold-toothed half-Melanesian wife. The ship was blistering in the remorseless sun, which beat on her from a cloudless sky making every part of the upper deck so hot that even the wood was painful to the touch. The only possible place to sit was beneath the awning in the stern. There were no chairs or benches, so Geoff and I lay full length on the deck and dozed.

Towards midday, we sighted the coast of Epi, a bumpy hazy strip on the horizon. The *Liero* crawled towards it, like a snail inching its way over a sheet of blue glass. As we neared the coast, the water shallowed until we could see the coral-studded sea floor. The engines stopped and we lay motionless in unaccustomed quiet. On the coast ahead, I could see a small house half-smothered by the feather-duster-like coconut palms which surrounded it. The French planter with his wife and child appeared for the first time on deck. She was transformed. Lipstick and rouge enlivened her pale face, she wore a newly ironed silk frock and a smart straw hat with a scarlet ribbon dangling down the back. I gathered from the captain that there was no other European within fifty miles of their plantation. There was no one to appreciate her new frock, her hat and her cosmetics except those of us on the ship.

With a great deal of shouting, the native crew lowered one of the ship's boats and took them and their belongings over to the lonely beach. For two hours, the deck hands unloaded planks and ferried them to the shore. Then the ship began to shake again with the rumble of the engines, the water creamed at her stern and once again we steamed off northwards.

Geoff and I moved down from the deck to the cabin vacated by the French family and spent the night sweating on the hard bunks. We woke at dawn the next morning to find that we were lying off the southern tip of Malekula. Tisman, Newman's plantation, was some forty miles away on the east coast, but one of his launches had come down here to meet us. The *Liero* herself would eventually call at Tisman, but not for another thirty-six hours, for she had first to visit several places on the west coast of Malekula to discharge her cargo, so that she might arrive at Newman's plantation with empty holds which could accommodate the several hundred sacks of copra that were waiting for her. We transferred our belongings to the launch and roared away.

Within a few minutes, the *Liero* was out of sight and we were travelling up the east coast of Malekula with the hazy volcanic pyramid of Ambrym away on the horizon to the right. We sat in the hold quivering with the vibration of the engine, our nostrils full of the rancid corroding stench of the copra with which the launch was normally loaded. The noise from the engine was deafening and inescapable, battering our ears so that they ached with very real physical pain. As far as I could see, there was no silencer or muffler of any kind on the roaring, shaking machinery.

Five hours later, we swung into Tisman Bay. Several boats bobbed at anchor close by the shore. Others were drawn up on the dazzlingly white beach. Close-set rows of coconut palms covered the hills behind. Newman, a middle-aged and extremely tough-looking man wearing overalls and a battered trilby hat, stood waiting for us at the head of the beach by a line of corrugated-iron huts. Leaving his men to unload our baggage, he drove us up in a lorry to his house at the top of the hill. It was a single-storeyed timber building with shutters over the long glassless windows and a spacious veranda running along the length of the house on each side.

We sat down on the cane chairs for a drink.

'Enjoy the ride, boys?' Oscar asked, over a glass of iced beer.

'Yes, very much indeed,' I replied untruthfully. 'It's a very nice launch. But she's a little on the noisy side, isn't she? Is the muffler broken?'

'Good Lord, no,' replied Oscar. 'In fact it's lying around in the workshop somewhere almost brand new. The damn thing worked so well that the engine made nothing but a low purring noise. You could hardly hear it. Well that's no damn good in this part of the world. We used to arrive at a landing to collect some copra and then spend the next couple of hours yelling our heads off to let the locals know that we had arrived. So we took the muffler off. Now they can hear us coming while we are still five miles away and they are always on the beach to meet us.'

Oscar was born in the New Hebrides, the son of an Englishman who had planted coconuts on several parts of the coast of Malekula, but who had never made a financial success of his ventures and had died in debt. Oscar told us that he swore to himself that he would pay off all his father's debts himself. That he did and he was now reputedly one of the richest men in the whole of the New Hebrides. Until a year or so previously, his wife and his two sons had lived with him in the big house at Tisman. Now they had gone down to Australia, the boys had got married and Oscar was alone.

At least two or three times a day, he talked by radio to Vila and to other people throughout the group, giving weather reports for the sake of the aircraft company and exchanging news and gossip. The most regular of his calls and one that he enjoyed the most was to a planter on the neighbouring island of Ambrym named Mitchell. They had been acquainted for at least thirty years, but they never called one another by anything except their surnames. Oscar spoke to Mitchell that evening.

'The *Liero* is arriving tomorrow, Mitchell,' he said. 'She's got some cargo on board for you. I've got to go over to Pentecost with two young pommies from London who've come to film the jumping ceremony. We're going to pay a quick visit to find out exactly when they'll jump, but if you like we'll deliver your freight on the way.'

'That's kind of you, Newman,' came the faint voice over the radio. 'It's probably the fancy decorations I ordered for the kids' Christmas party. Glad they've turned up in time. See you then. Over and out.'

Oscar switched off the set. 'He's a bonzer bloke, old Mitchell,' he said, 'but a rum one. He gives a Christmas party every year for the kids of the bushies who work on his plantation and takes no end of trouble, hanging paper chains all over his house. Hell of a scholar, he is. His place is stuffed with books. Can't think what he wants with them. Never throws anything away either. He's got rooms at the back of his place stacked full with empty matchboxes.'

The next day the *Liero* arrived, took on copra and sailed again for Vila. The day after, we ourselves left Tisman in the launch heading for Ambrym and Pentecost. We sailed eastwards across a choppy sea before we reached the lee of the north-west coast of Ambrym. It is a diamond-shaped island, in the centre of which looms a great volcano. In 1912 it erupted with tremendous force, scattering ash and pumice all over the sea and letting off tremendous detonations. A school and a trading store run by Oscar's father-in-law sank into the sea and disappeared. The coastline now is composed of cliffs of muddy grey volcanic ash, runnelled by the tropical rains and sketchily covered by a thin growth of vegetation like the stubble on an unshaven chin.

Darkness fell while we were still several miles from Mitchell's place. Small yellow lights began to appear on the coast and hills ahead. Oscar took out a torch and signalled with flashes. Almost immediately several of the lights winked back at us.

'Damn fools,' Oscar yelled at me over the roar of the engine.

'Every time I try to signal to Mitchell to get my bearings, everyone on the island with a radio decides to be chummy and answer so that I don't know where the hell I am.'

Standing in the stern, his arm over the tiller, leaning outwards to try to see ahead and shouting instructions mixed with abuse to the boat boys, Oscar steered his way through the reefs thundering in the darkness. At last we reached the comparative calm of the inshore waters and dropped anchor.

We went ashore by dinghy. Even in the darkness, I could see that the beach up which we walked was composed of black volcanic sand. Mitchell came down to meet us with a paraffin lamp and took us up to his house. He was a small, gentle white-haired man in his mid seventies. The big high-ceilinged room into which he led us was no doubt clean in the sense that it was occasionally dusted and swept, yet it was enveloped by an aura of mould and decay. A few pictures, hanging high on the wooden walls, were so blackened with mildew that it was quite impossible to see what they had once represented. The shelves of the two large glass-fronted book-cases that stood by the wall were thickly dusted with yellowing naphthalene powder to deter insect pests which might attack the faded books inside. In the centre of the room stood two large deal tables placed side by side. They were heaped with a great mound of miscellaneous odds and ends – stacks of magazines, curling papers, bundles of chickens' feathers, sheaves of pencils, empty jam jars, odd lengths of electrical flex and miscellaneous pieces of engine castings. Mitchell looked at it in a reproachful way. 'Hell and blazes,' he said mildly, 'there are some cigarettes somewhere there. Do either of you young fellers smoke?'

'Now, Mitchell,' said Oscar, 'don't you go and poison these pommies with your rotten cigarettes. They stink so bad that even the bushies won't smoke them.'

'Crumbs,' replied Mitchell, looking at Oscar from beneath his white eyebrows, 'you can talk. There ought to be a law against people *giving away* the rubbish that you sell in your store.' He continued rummaging in the pile on the desk and at last produced an unfamiliar-looking packet of cigarettes.

'Now, fellers,' he said handing them to me, 'see if you don't think those aren't just about the best smoke that you've ever had.'

I took one and lit it. It was so damp that I had considerable difficulty in getting it to light at all. When at last I managed to draw a lungful of smoke, its rank mouldy taste made me choke.

Mitchell looked at me solicitously. 'I was afraid so,' he said. 'It's too good for you. You young fellers have very odd taste these days. Those are the best English cigarettes you can get. Several crates of them were shipped up to me in 1939 by mistake and what with the war and one thing and another I never managed to send them back. To be honest, they've never really caught on with the natives and, of course, the Australians around here don't know a good cigarette from a bad one. I thought,' he added sadly, 'that a couple of chaps out from the old country would be just the people to appreciate really good quality cigarettes like these and I'd have been prepared to cut a little off the price if you had given me a wholesale order.'

Oscar rocked with laughter. 'You'll never flog those rotten things, Mitchell. You'd better throw them into the sea. And anyway, how much longer do we have to wait for a cup of tea?'

Mitchell retreated to the kitchen, saying that his native servants had all gone out for the evening. He soon reappeared with some tinned meat and a tin of peaches. As we ate, the two planters exchanged their news, talked gloomily about copra prices, although they were at the time almost as high as they had ever been, and ribbed one another with enthusiasm.

Oscar carefully wiped his plate clean with a piece of bread and smacked his lips. 'Well, Mitchell,' he said appreciatively, 'if that's the best you can do by way of tucker, I reckon we'll leave right away. I couldn't abide the thought of having to have breakfast with you. I'll call you on the radio when I get back to Tisman.' He clapped his hat on his head and together we went down to the boat.

That night, we sailed across the eight miles of rough water that separates the northern point of Ambrym from the southernmost tip of Pentecost. We anchored in a bay, spread sacks in the hold of the launch, and, doing our best to ignore the stench of copra, went to sleep.

We were woken, just before sunrise, by the sound of a sputtering little launch which came bobbing across the water towards us in the grey light of dawn. At her tiller stood a short fat man with a straw hat on the back of his head and a white woolly beard running around his chin from ear to ear. Skilfully he brought his boat alongside ours and with surprising agility, hopped on board. Although he was certainly very corpulent, he was not flabby, but taut like a balloon inflated to the point of bursting. Oscar greeted him boisterously in pidgin and then introduced him to us.

'This is Wall,' he said. 'He's chief of one of the villages up the coast and he's the chap who will introduce us to the jokers who are going to do the jump. How's it going, Wall?'

'Plenty good, Masta Oscar,' said Wall. 'Six day time, im makim jump.'

This was sooner than we had expected, and as we wanted to spend one or two days filming the preparations for the jump, there seemed little point in Geoff or me returning to Tisman before the ceremony. On the other hand, we had not come prepared for a stay.

'I can't stay with you boys,' said Oscar. 'I've got work to do back at Tisman, but I reckon you'll be OK. There are some tins of tucker somewhere in the hold which you can have and I guess you'll be able to get some yams and coconuts from the bushies, so you won't starve. Can you fix 'em up with some place to sleep, Wall?'

Wall grinned and nodded.

A quarter of an hour later, Wall, Geoff and I were standing on the beach beside a small pile of tinned food and our photographic equipment. Oscar, having promised he would return in time for the ceremony, was sailing out of the bay on his way back to Tisman.

6

The Land Divers of Pentecost

The beach on which we had landed stretched for over a mile in an unbroken graceful curve. Behind it, almost hidden in the thick bush, stood a few huts strung in a discontinuous line along the length of the bay. Wall led us to a particularly small hovel standing by itself beneath a large pandanus tree on the bank of a sluggish stream. It was derelict, its thatch sodden and sagging into holes.

'Im,' said Wall. 'House belong you.'

By now some of the people who lived in the other huts had gathered round and were sitting on their haunches gravely and unabashedly inspecting us. Most of them wore heavily patched shorts, a few were naked except for a *nambas*, the traditional type of loincloth which is abbreviated well beyond the bounds of Western decency. Wall began to organize them into repairing the hut for us. Some he sent to gather leaves for new thatch, some to cut saplings with which to build an extra portico on the front. This he had decided was a necessary addition in order to prevent rain from beating directly into the open door. Within an hour, the hut was beginning to look quite habitable. We constructed a rough table in the portico on which we stacked the tins of food and our enamel plates. Inside the main hut itself, which measured only ten feet by eight feet, we built a platform of split bamboo to serve as a bed. We made it as broad as possible so that we could both sleep on it side by side, for there was no room for the luxury of two separate ones. We hung up our bag of sugar from a string in the corner in an unsuccessful attempt to keep it away from the swarming ants. When all was finished, Wall sent a boy up the palm tree that grew outside to gather some coconuts, and the three of us sat on the hard bed, drinking the fizzy milk from the green coconuts and surveying our new home with considerable satisfaction.

Wall wiped his mouth on the back of his hand, beamed, heaved himself on to his feet and shook us both solemnly by the hand.

'Me go now,' he said. 'Good arpi-noon.' He strode down the beach, back to his boat, and pushed her out through the waves.

Wall, who introduced us to the land divers

That afternoon, we forded the stream by our hut and walked inland along the narrow muddy track that led to the jumping ground. It wound between the strutted pandanus trunks and the smooth boles of palms and then began to climb steeply through dense wet bush. A quarter of a mile up the steep hillside we reached a clearing half the size of a football pitch. At the highest point there stood a single isolated tree, stripped of its branches, around which had been built a scaffold of poles. Already this drunken-looking construction rose some fifty feet into the air and high up in the girders at the top, some twenty men, singing at the tops of their voices, were busy adding further storeys. Others sat on the timbers nearer the ground splitting lianas to serve as lashings, while yet another party were busily grubbing up the stumps of trees from the ground at the foot of the tower.

We spent the rest of that day with the tower builders. They told us that the jumping ceremony would take place in exactly six days' time – which confirmed what Wall had said. I was surprised at this consistency – it is not every unlettered people who place such emphasis on punctuality – but it was clear that the precise timing of the ceremony was of considerable importance to them.

Two days later, Wall's little launch reappeared around the rocky headland that marked the western end of the bay. He waded ashore carrying a large parcel wrapped in newspaper.

Building the tower

'More better kai-kai,' he said, presenting it to us. I unpacked it and found six square loaves of bread and six bottles of anonymous fizzy lemonade. He had bought both bread and bottles from a trade store some twenty miles up the coast to which he had just delivered a load of copra. We were very touched and very grateful, particularly for the lemonade, for the only liquid we had had to drink – apart from coconut milk – came from the muddy stream through which we and every man who went to the jumping ground waded several times a day.

Four days later, the tower was nearing completion. It stood over eighty feet high and looked exceedingly unstable, for the upper storeys lacked the support of the lopped tree trunk which ran like a rigid spine up the centre of the lower section. Attempts had been made to stabilize it by attaching guy ropes of vines to the top and lashing them to the boles of trees at the edge of the clearing, but even so the whole edifice swayed alarmingly as the builders unconcernedly clambered about on it.

Twenty-five men were to make the jump and each of them would dive from a separate platform of his own. These were arranged in tiers up the face of the tower, the lowest only thirty feet above the ground, the highest within a few feet of the very top. Each consisted of two slim boards bound to a simple framework by a rough liana which served the additional purpose of providing a rough surface to the platform on which a diver's feet would not slip. They projected horizontally some eight or nine feet into space, their outer ends supported by several thin struts. It was clear that these supports and the lashings securing their lower ends to the main platform would have to withstand a very great strain when a man jumped and the vines, trailing from his ankles and tied to the tower, suddenly whipped tight over the end of the platform. I asked the builders why they did not use stouter struts and stronger lashings. They explained that the supports were made frail purposely; for the platform was

designed to collapse downwards when the falling diver neared
the ground, thus acting as a shock absorber and lessening the
tremendous jolt on the diver's ankles.

The vines that were to serve as safety ropes were gathered
from the forest exactly two days before the ceremony was due.
Wall told me that this timing was most important, for if they
were more than two days old when they were used, they might
have rotted or dried out and so lost their elasticity and strength.
Should that happen, and the vine break, a man could be killed.
They had to be carefully selected, for only one species of a
particular thickness, length and age was suitable. Even so, the
men did not have to search far, for the vines hung in profusion
from the branches of the forest trees. Men and boys spent the
whole of one day carrying the bundles of them to the tower.
There, other workers tied them to the main cross-stays of the
tower and draped them in pairs over the platforms, so that their
free ends, those that were eventually to be tied around the diver's
ankles, hung down the slightly overhanging face of the tower
like some monstrous shock of crinkled hair.

A man on the ground took hold of each pair in turn, shook
them to make sure that they were not tangled and ran free to
the platform above, and then trimmed them with his bush knife
to the correct length. His job was a vitally important one. If he
miscalculated and made the vines too short, then the diver who
used them would be left hanging in mid-air and would probably
pendulum into the tower with bone-breaking force; and if he
left them overlong, then a man would cannon into the ground
and almost certainly be killed. Nor was this assessment easy, for
allowance had to be made both for the extra length that would
be given to the vines when the platform collapsed during the
dive and for the natural elasticity of the vines themselves. If I
had been due to take part in the ritual, I am sure that I would
have been very careful to check for myself the length of the
vines that I was going to use. Yet although many of the men
who were working on the tower were to dive the next day and

knew the exact platform from which they would be jumping, none of them, as far as I could see, bothered to examine his vines.

When the trimming was over, the cut ends were frayed into tassels, to make it easier to bind them round the divers' ankles, and then bundled and wrapped in leaves to keep them moist and pliable.

Lastly, teams of men dug over the steep slope at the foot of the tower, meticulously sifting the earth through their fingers to make absolutely certain that there were no roots or boulders concealed beneath the surface which could injure a diver as he landed. By the evening of the fifth day after we had first arrived, everything had been completed. The last man had come down from the tower, the last vine had been trimmed and tasselled. The tower stood deserted on the steep hillside, gaunt against the evening sky, like a sinister scaffold.

The author inspecting the diving platforms

When the sun rose from the sea the next morning we saw Oscar's boat rocking at anchor in the bay. He came ashore bringing with him three cold chickens, some tinned fruit and two loaves of bread. After we had eaten the best meal we had tasted for several days, we went up to the jumping ground together. The tower was still deserted. During the next hour men, women and children wandered in one by one and sat themselves at the edge of the clearing. None of them was going to take part in the ceremony. Two of the builders stood at the bottom of the tower keeping watch to prevent anyone walking over the loose soil on which the divers would land. 'No walk 'long dat place,' Wall warned me. 'Im, tambu.'

At ten o'clock, we heard distant chanting in the bush. It grew louder and louder until, with dramatic suddenness, a line of people burst from the bush at the back of the tower and began to dance back and forth, chanting loudly. Some of the women wore long skirts of shredded palm leaves and were bare to the waist; others were clothed in the shapeless cotton smocks introduced by the mission. Many of the men had stuck a young palm leaf into the back of their short trousers so that the frond reached to their shoulder blades. One or two carried sprigs of red croton leaves or a tall spike of scarlet flowers that grew in rush-like thickets in the forest. The dancers stamped up and down across the slope behind the tower in a column six deep. Within a few minutes the ground beneath their feet had been compacted into six parallel terraces of shiny smooth earth.

Unobtrusively, a young boy left the ranks of the dancers and began to climb quickly up the back of the tower. Behind his ear he had tucked a red hibiscus and he had whitened with lime the parting cut in his frizzy hair. Two older men clambered up behind him. They were relatives and were to act as his assistants in the ritual that was about to be enacted. For the first twenty feet they swung themselves upwards on the horizontal spars that formed a giant ladder up the back of the tower. Then they disappeared into the confused tangle of cross bars, diagonals and verticals that made the interior of the tower look almost solid, and emerged on the front by the side of the lowest platform. One of the older men pulled up the two vines that hung from the end. The boy stood impassive, his feet on the base of the platform, gripping the uprights of the tower. His assistant crouched by him tying the vines to his ankles. The platform on which they stood was no more than thirty feet up the tower but the boy would inevitably jump outwards and the ground beneath sloped so steeply that the point where he would first touch the earth, some fifteen feet out, was at least forty feet below him.

The fastening of the vines took no more than a couple of minutes. One of the assistants trimmed the loose ends of the knot with his bush knife and then both of them retreated into the tower, leaving the boy alone.

Holding the red croton leaves in his hand, he released his hold on the tower timbers and walked slowly forward along his narrow platform to stand on the very end, one foot placed on each of the two boards that projected from beneath the liana binding. The dancers below and behind him changed their chant to a rhythmic stabbing yell. They stopped their countermarching and all turned to face the tower, holding out their arms straight in front of them; the women adding to the din by whistling piercingly through their teeth.

The boy, alone on the edge of space, raised his hands. Through my binoculars I could see that his lips were moving, but if he was calling or chanting, I could not hear him above the shrieks of the dancers. With a slow movement, so as not to disturb his balance, he threw the croton leaves into the air. They spun gently downwards to land on the ground forty feet below. The whistles and yells from the dancers grew increasingly insistent. The boy raised his hands once more and clapped three times above his head. Then with his fists clenched, he crossed his arms over his chest and shut his eyes. Slowly, with his body held stiff, he toppled forward. For what seemed an immensity of time he fell spreadeagled through the air. Then, as he plummeted downwards, the vines around his ankles suddenly whipped tight. There was a loud crack like a gunshot as the struts broke and the platform they had supported fell downwards. His head was no more than a few feet from the ground when the vines, stretched to their limit, snatched him backwards and flung him towards the foot of the tower where he landed on his back in the soft earth.

The two men who had guarded the landing ground rushed forward, and while one of them supported the boy in his arms the other cut off the vines. The lad scrambled to his feet, grinning all over his face, and ran back to join the dancers. The two men dug over the soil where the boy had landed and even as they were doing so, another man ran out from among the dancers and climbed into the tower.

At the top of the diving tower

A jumper

One by one during the next three hours, the men jumped, each diving from a higher platform. Forty, fifty, seventy feet they fell. Not all of them were young boys. Geoff and I were filming and photographing from the top of the tower when an old man with hunched shoulders, wrinkled skin and a short white beard came climbing up nimbly towards us. He stood on a platform eighty feet up and put on a spirited display of exuberant gestures before he fell. In the few seconds between his disappearance into space and the moment when the platform crashed downwards and the whole tower shook violently, we heard a high-pitched cackle. He was laughing even as he was tumbling through the air.

But not all the performers enjoyed it as much as he appeared to do. One or two lost their nerve as they stood alone on the end of their platforms face to face with their test of courage. If the urging calls of the dancers failed to make them jump, then the two assistants standing in the tower behind added their own peculiar form of persuasion. They had brought up with them a small branch from a forest tree the leaves of which give an extremely painful sting. But they did not use these on the reluctant diver. Instead they thrashed themselves with the leaves, crying out with the pain and yelling to the diver to jump so that they might stop their self-inflicted punishment.

Only one diver's courage failed him totally. In spite of his assistants' cries and the screams of the dancers he retreated from the end of his platform. The vines were cut from him and he came down the tower, his face stained with tears. Wall told us that he would have to pay a fine of several pigs before he had redeemed himself in the eyes of the community.

It was evening before the last jump of all took place. The diver stood, a tiny figure silhouetted against the sky, a hundred feet above us. For many minutes, standing erect in perfect balance on his platform no more than two feet wide, he waved his arms and clapped his hands and threw down croton leaves. The singers far below him were hoarse, having sung for many hours, but when at last he leaned into the air and fell in a magnificent swooping curve to the earth, they raised a great shout and, still yelling, dashed from their dancing ground behind the tower across the landing ground to pick him up and carry him off shoulder high. It seemed miraculous that his knees and hip joints could have withstood the shattering jerk that must have come when the vines suddenly snatched him short, yet neither he nor anyone who had taken part in the ceremony that afternoon had been injured in any way.

I puzzled for a long time on what could be the meaning of this spectacular ceremony. Wall, who in his youth had been a famous jumper, told me the story of the ritual's origin.

Many years ago, a man from one of the Pentecost villages discovered that his wife was being unfaithful to him. He tried to catch her in order to beat her, but she ran from him and, in an attempt to escape, climbed up a palm tree. He climbed after her, and when he reached the top they began to argue.

'Why did you go to another man?' he asked. 'Am I not man enough for you?'

'No,' she said, 'you are a weakling and a coward. You dare not even jump to the ground from here.'

'That is impossible,' he said.

'I can do it,' said the woman.

'Then if you will do it, so will I. Let us jump together.'

So they jumped. The wife had taken the precaution of tying the end of one of the palm leaves to her ankles so that she came to no harm, but the man was killed. The other men of the village were greatly humiliated that one of their sex should have been tricked by a woman. So they built a tower many times higher than a palm tree and started the jumping ceremony to prove to the women who came to watch them that they are after all the superior sex.

As literal truth, Wall's story was hardly convincing and I was not able to collect enough evidence to speculate responsibly as to its symbolic meaning, if indeed it had one. I asked jumper after jumper why he risked his life in the leap. One man said that he did so because it made him feel better; another amplified this by saying that if ever he had pain in his stomach or a cold in his head, the jump was an unfailing cure. One or two said that they jumped because they positively enjoyed it. Most said simply that they did so because it was 'custom belong dis place'.

I had one clue, however, to a deeper meaning. During the ceremony I had noticed that one of the women standing a few yards from me was nursing in her arms something which I took to be a baby. She watched one youth particularly attentively, and when he fell and swung uninjured, she exultantly threw away the bundle in her arms. It was nothing more than a piece of cloth. Wall told me that the diver was her son and that the bundle was 'all same like baby'. Perhaps the ritual was an ordeal through which adolescents had to pass before they entered the estate of manhood, and as the boy performed it, so his mother cast aside the symbol of his childhood to proclaim to the world that her baby no longer existed and that he had been replaced by the grown man.

If this were indeed the truth, and it seemed to match aspects of the story of the ceremony's origin, then one would expect that only young boys would perform the jump. In corroboration, one woman said that in 'time belong before' a man jumped only once and then it was 'altogedder finis'. But if that had been the case it was no longer so, for I knew that several of the men whom I had seen diving that afternoon had taken part in the ceremony several times before.

One thing only was certain. The people themselves had largely forgotten the original meaning of their ritual, just as we have forgotten the original significance of our 5th November bonfires. Many centuries before Guy Fawkes, our ancestors lit fires at the beginning of November, for in early times the feast of the dead was celebrated at this time. Today's firework parties are almost certainly the direct descendants of those ancient pagan rites. We still retain the custom, not because of its origin, nor because we wish to celebrate the delivery of Parliament from the Gunpowder Plot, but simply because we enjoy it. I suspect the story of the unfaithful wife has little more relevance to the origin of the Pentecost jump than the story of Guy Fawkes has to the origin of November bonfires, and I would guess that the Pentecost people continued their ritual for rather the same reasons as we continue ours – because it was an exciting and enjoyable occasion and because it is 'custom belong dis place'.

7

Cargo Cult

From Pentecost and Malekula, we returned south to Vila. There we managed to get berths on a small vessel owned by the Condominium and optimistically named by them the *Concorde*, which was bound for the island of Tanna, one hundred and forty miles to the south. Tanna might be considered to be the last island in the group to attract anyone hoping to find the old ways of life untouched by outside influences, for it was the first of all the New Hebrides to be visited by missionaries, and since then it has been the scene of energetic and courageous work by the Presbyterian church. On 19 November 1839, the Reverend John Williams, in the mission ship *Camden*, called at Tanna and put ashore three Christian Samoan teachers whose task it was to prepare the way for European missionaries. Williams himself sailed on to the nearby island of Erromango where he landed the next day. Within a few hours of setting foot on shore, he and his companion, James Harris, were murdered by the tribesmen. It was not for a year that another ship from the London Missionary Society called at Tanna. Almost unbelievably, the Samoan teachers had survived, but the relief ship had arrived only just in time, for they were being held captive by the local people and would certainly have been slaughtered and eaten within a very short time had help not come.

Only two years later, the missionaries tried again. The Reverends Turner and Nesbit settled on the island and in spite of great hostility from the local people they succeeded in winning enough converts for Turner to be able to compile and publish in 1845 a Tannese catechism, the first book ever to be printed in a New Hebridean language.

During the next thirty years, there was continuous missionary activity on the island, though progress was slow. On Erromango, thirty miles away to the north, four more missionaries were murdered and although no lives were lost on Tanna, the situation must often have been a desperately dangerous one. But by the turn of the century, the missionaries' persistence and bravery had brought their rewards. Tanna became a showpiece, an example of what Christian endeavour could achieve working with the most difficult and recalcitrant of primitive people. By 1940 there were Tannese men whose fathers, grandfathers and great-grandfathers had all been Christians. The mission ran a flourishing hospital and a well-attended school and most of the Tannese professed to have deserted their pagan gods for Christianity. But in that year a new and strange religion sprang up in the island. The Tannese were in the grip of a cargo cult – a religion as bizarre as any of the ancient pagan rites of the New Hebrides. In spite of all that the mission and the government could do, it still flourished and the greater part of the once-Christian population of the island were its followers.

Cargo cults are not restricted to the New Hebrides. They have arisen independently in many places in the Pacific, on islands as far apart as Tahiti, three thousand miles away to the east, the Solomons to the north-west and the Gilberts in the north. Two years earlier, in the New Guinea highlands, where there have been many cargo movements, I had met a European who had had first-hand experience of one of these cults. He was a Lutheran missionary and he described the origins of these new religions like this.

Before the coming of the European, the peoples of New

Guinea had been living in the Stone Age. The only materials which they knew were stone, wood and vegetable fibres, and many of them had not seen even the pottery which is made by some tribes on the coast. Then suddenly, a strange white people come to their valleys bringing an abundance of astonishing new objects which they call, in pidgin, 'cargo' – petrol lamps, plastic combs, radio sets, china teacups, steel knives – all of them made from entirely new and wonderful materials. The tribesmen are astounded and mystified. But one thing is clear to them: the cargo cannot be of human origin. The very substances of which these objects are made do not occur in nature. And by what magic process are they fashioned? How could you chip or weave or carve such a thing as a shining enamelled refrigerator? Furthermore, the white people do not themselves make the cargo – it arrives in big ships or aeroplanes. There is only one conclusion to be drawn from all this – the cargo must be of supernatural origin and be sent by the gods.

But why should it come only to the white man? Presumably because he practises a powerful ritual which persuades the gods to send the cargo to them alone. At first it seems as if the white men are prepared to share this secret, for some of them gladly talk about their god. They explain that the old tribal ways are false, that the old effigies must be destroyed. The people believe them and attend the white man's churches. But in spite of this the cargo does not come to them. The natives suspect that they are being deceived. They notice that the religion the missionaries preach is ignored by most of the white men themselves and it follows therefore that these people must be using some other technique to influence the gods. So the natives ask the traders, who have these supernatural objects in abundance, how such riches can be obtained. The traders reply that if they want cargo, they must work in the copra plantations, earn money and then they can buy such objects from the white man's store. But this is not a satisfactory answer, for, hard as a native works, he cannot earn sufficient to buy anything except the meanest of the objects that he covets. The falsity of this explanation is also proved by the easily observable fact that the trader does not practise what he preaches, for he himself does no physical work whatever; he merely sits behind a desk shuffling papers.

So the native watches the white men even more closely. Soon he notices that the strangers do many senseless things; they build tall masts with wires attached to them; they sit listening to small boxes that glow with light and emit curious noises and strangled voices; they persuade the local people to dress up in identical clothes, and march up and down – and it would hardly be possible to devise a more useless occupation than that. And then the native realizes that he has stumbled on the answer to the mystery. It is these incomprehensible actions that are the rituals employed by the white man to persuade the gods to send the cargo to them. If the native wants the cargo, then he too must do these things.

So he erects imitation radio aerials. He puts a white cloth on an improvised table, places a bowl of flowers in the middle and sits around it as he has seen the white people doing. He dresses up in imitation uniforms, improvised from locally made cloth, and marches up and down. In the New Guinea highlands, the leaders of one cult claimed that a fleet of silver planes would land in their valley and the people accordingly began to build great storehouses to receive the cargo as an encouragement for the planes to come. Elsewhere on the island, it was said that a tunnel would open up in the mountainside and columns of lorries would drive out, loaded with material wealth.

The followers of a cult on Ambrym formed themselves into a militia, and set up guards on their villages who questioned travellers on their destination and the reason for their journey, and wrote down the answers in a register. They also set up notices by the road reading 'Halt' and 'Compulsory Stop'. Other people sat talking into empty tin cans, in imitation of radio telephones.

The first of these cults to be recognized sprang up in Fiji in 1885. In 1932, an essentially similar one developed in the Solomon Islands. With the increasing spread of Western materialism through the Pacific, the cults increased in number and frequency. Anthropologists have noted two separate outbreaks in New Caledonia, four in the Solomons, four in Fiji, seven in the New Hebrides, and over fifty in New Guinea, most of them being quite independent and unconnected with one another. The majority of these religions claim that one particular messiah will bring the cargo when the day of the apocalypse arrives.

On Tanna, the first signs of a cult were noticed in 1940. Rumours began to spread of a leader who called himself John Frum and who had spoken to the assembled headmen of villages in the south of the island. He appeared only at night by the flickering light of a fire and was said to be a little man with a high-pitched voice and bleached hair, wearing a coat with shining buttons. And he made strange prophecies. There would be a great cataclysm; the mountains would fall flat and the valleys would be filled; old people would regain their youth and sickness would vanish; the white people would be expelled from the island never to return; and cargo would arrive in great quantity so that everyone would have as much as he wanted. If they wished to hasten the arrival of this day, the people must obey John Frum's orders. The false teachings of the missionaries must be ignored. Some of the old customs which the missionaries had forbidden must be revived to show that the false Christian teaching was rejected. In compliance with these edicts, the people left the mission schools in great numbers.

In 1941, there was a new development. John Frum was said to have prophesied that when the day of the apocalypse came he would bring his own coinage stamped with the image of a coconut. The people should therefore rid themselves of the money that had been brought by the white man, for in so doing, they would not only remove the taint of the Europeans, but would hasten the departure of the white traders who surely would not wish to stay on the island when there was no more money to be taken from the natives. The Tannese then began a wild orgy of spending at the stores. People squandered the savings of a lifetime. Some men brought in as much as a hundred pounds, and golden sovereigns reappeared that had last been seen by Europeans in 1912 when they had been used as a reward to local chiefs for signing a treaty of friendship.

By May, the situation had become extremely serious. The mission churches and schools were deserted. Nichol, the dour British agent who had ruled unchallenged on the island since 1916, decided that the time had come for action. He arrested several of the leaders, identified one of them, Manahevi, as John Frum and had him tied to a tree for a day in an attempt to expose him as a perfectly normal human being with no supernatural powers. The prisoners were then sent to Vila where they were tried and imprisoned. People said that Manahevi was in fact only a substitute who had martyred himself in order to protect John Frum and that the real prophet was still on the island.

Soon after this, the first American troops came to the New Hebrides, and established their base at Santo. Stories spread through the islands of the great quantities of cargo that they had brought with them and of their extravagance and generosity. Soon it was being said on Tanna that John Frum was, in fact, King of America. Then came the startling and thrilling news that seemed to corroborate this – a battalion of African Americans had arrived. Physically they were very similar to the local people – they had the same black skin and frizzy hair, but there was one staggering difference – they were not poor, but as richly endowed with the cargo as the white soldiers.

Wild excitement overwhelmed Tanna. The day of the apocalypse was imminent. It seemed that everyone was preparing for

John Frum's arrival. One of the leaders said that John Frum would be coming from America by aeroplane and hundreds of men began to clear the bush in the centre of the island so that the plane might have an airstrip on which to land. Soon the situation was so serious that Nichol radioed Vila for more police. He also asked that an American officer should be sent to the island to help dispel the false rumours that were being spread.

The American came and talked to the assembled people, explaining that he knew nothing of John Frum. To emphasize his points and to impress the Tannese, he fired a machine gun at one of the notices erected by John Frum's followers, and shot it to pieces. Many of the people were so frightened that they fled to the bush. The sheds that had been built to receive the cargo were burned down at Nichol's orders, and several of the headmen most active in the movement were arrested and deported.

The missionaries tried to restart the school, but out of a population of 2,500 only fifty children attended. In 1946, John Frum was being spoken of again all over the island. The Tannese raided one of the trade stores and tore down all the price tickets from the goods that were on display. This was done, the people said, on John Frum's explicit orders. Once more, several of the leaders were arrested and exiled.

After this, there was a long period of calm. Very few people, however, thought that the movement was dead. Attendance at the mission school was still very poor, the old pagan rites flourished and there were always stories circulating about John Frum and predictions as to what would happen when he brought the cargo.

In an effort to regain their lost followers the Presbyterian church relaxed some of their more puritanical rules. There was no doubt that the way of life they had ordained for the Tannese was a strict and somewhat joyless one. As early as 1941, soon after the first large-scale rising, one of the missionaries on Tanna had written in his report for the Synod, 'We have taken dances from them and have done little to replace them or to meet the problem created by such a loss . . . We have clothed religion in black and sombre garments, rubbed the smile off its face as unseemly, suppressed the instinct to express our feelings dramatically as being evil and brought people to confuse Christianity with so-called respectability which is synonymous with drabness . . . We cannot expect to meet with success until we prohibit less and are more positively constructive. We must do all we can to make Christianity native Christianity and allow the Holy Spirit a chance to vitalize the native church instead of trying to force it into moulds.' Subsequently, an attempt was made to put such thoughts into practice. But it had little effect on attendances at the mission. In 1952, there was a further wave of activity triggered perhaps by a fall in the copra prices, which the Tannese believed had been engineered by the traders to deprive them of even more of the cargo.

The government, having failed to suppress the movement by arresting and imprisoning the leaders, now pursued a different policy. The cult was officially tolerated provided that it did no harm to anyone on the island, and no one's life was endangered. It was hoped that it might die a natural death, when the people found that none of John Frum's prophecies showed any sign of coming true.

It was the chance of witnessing if not the birth, then the very early stages in the development of a new religion, that drew us to Tanna. I hoped that, when we got there, we might be able to meet the leaders of the movement and discover from them how John Frum's orders and prophecies originated, and perhaps to persuade them to describe in detail the actions and appearance of their mysterious leader.

It took the best part of a day and a night for our ship, the *Concorde*, to sail from Vila to Tanna. She was an antiquated vessel, staffed by an elderly Anglo-French captain, a French engineer with only one arm, and six Melanesian deck hands. As night fell, a strong wind came up, and the *Concorde* began to roll alarmingly. Again and again black water came surging over the stern as one of the heavier waves overtook us. The captain stayed on the bridge with the helmsman, the Melanesians disappeared into the fo'c'sle, and the rest of us tried to sleep in the single cabin. Twice during the night, the one-armed engineer fell out of his bunk and landed with a splintering crash on the table in the middle of the cabin. When he was tipped out for a third time just before dawn, he did not bother to clamber back, but reeled over to the stove in the corner and began to heat up the contents of a gigantic saucepan. Within a few minutes a powerful smell announced that he was cooking a strong, rather stale, curry. Once or twice, when the ship executed a particularly severe roll, this unappetizing granular mixture slopped over and put out the burner, but the engineer, who seemed unaccountably happy and was whistling to himself without pause, scooped it up, poured it back into the saucepan and relit the gas. The steamy highly spiced odour that rose from it seemed to fill the entire cabin. It was impossible to get any fresh air for had we opened the scuttles the sea would have come flooding in with every roll and lurch of the ship. I lay on my back, bracing myself with my arms and legs against the side of the bunk to avoid falling into the puddles of curry and sea water that sloshed about on the floor. When the engineer, holding the saucepan high in the air, skidded acrobatically to the table and announced that breakfast was served, I found, to my regret, that I was unable to join him.

The *Concorde* dropped anchor in a small reef-enclosed bay at Lenakel on the west coast of Tanna. On the beach to meet us, and to collect the mail and the cargo that we had brought from Vila, stood the British and the French agents, a teacher from the Presbyterian mission school and Bob Paul, an Australian planter who had offered, when we had spoken to him by radio from Vila, to be our host. A tall thin man, with sandy hair, a small moustache and a deceptively mild manner, he owned more land on the island than any other European and was the only one to run a large plantation. For anybody who wished to talk to the Tannese about John Frum, he was the ideal host. To have stayed with a government official or a member of the mission would have branded us as opponents of the cult and we would have had little chance of persuading the local people to speak about their beliefs. Bob Paul, however, had always tried to be non-committal with regard to John Frum, neither disapproving nor encouraging the movement.

'Most unhappy people turn to religion in one form or another,' he said to us. 'The Tannese are extremely unhappy and confused at the moment. Why should we prevent them from trying to develop their own form of religion, so long as they don't interfere with anyone else?'

On one occasion only had Bob taken a hand in their activities, and this was at the time of the latest and most dramatic of all the John Frum risings, the affair of the Tanna Army. Bob told us about it as we sat in his garden by the sea, the blue Pacific creaming into breakers on the reef beyond.

'I first saw the Army when I went over to Sulphur Bay on the other side of the island to buy copra, and found, to my surprise, a party of men drilling in a clearing close by the village. They were wearing imitation American caps, long trousers tucked into sand boots something after the style of gaiters, and singlets with across the chest the letters TA, standing for Tanna Army, and beneath – USA. They carried very well made bamboo guns carved to resemble an American carbine with a long bamboo bayonet on the end of them. Their drill was quite smart too. Some of the boys had been in the police and had obviously passed on a bit of what they had learned. I didn't pay much attention at the time. They weren't harming anybody.

'Later, however, they became a bit venturesome and started

to march round the neighbouring villages scaring the wits out of the rest of the people. No one did anything to stop them, so they became more ambitious and started on a parade round the whole island, passing through every single village, saying that the Army had been founded by John Frum to hasten the day that the cargo would arrive and urging everyone to join them. Wherever they stopped, the locals had to provide pigs and cassava to feed them and there was no doubt at all that any Tannese who hadn't felt particularly enthusiastic about the movement so far, either joined the ranks pretty quickly or else felt frightened about what might happen to him.

'A day or so after they had started, I came across the Army marching down the road that leads to the Presbyterian mission. It seemed that they were on their way to parade through the mission and terrorize the few Christian Tannese who still remained there. It was to be the grand finale of their march

A cult gate and cross on Tanna

round the island. I went ahead of them in my truck and warned
the missionary. 'Well they are not going to come through here,
that's certain,' he said. So we parked my truck across the road
and stood in front of it. About a hundred of them with their
bamboo guns and pathetic uniforms came marching towards us.
When they got really close, we just told them to get the hell
out of it or there would be trouble. Fortunately, they turned
back and went home.

'After that the government thought they had better do something about the situation, so the District Officer and some police
boys went down to the Army's headquarters at Sulphur Bay to
have the whole thing out with the leaders. When they got there
they found that the Army boys had barricaded themselves in
and were standing on the other side with guns in their hands
– and not bamboo ones but real ones. Well, the District Officer
doesn't have any troops himself, only a few police boys, so he
cabled to Vila for reinforcements. Actually, things weren't really
bad – the boys in Sulphur Bay still let me go in to buy copra
even though they refused to admit the District Officer – but if
you judged from the hundreds of panicky telegrams that jammed
the radio waveband, you would have thought that we had our
backs to the wall. So in case any of my friends in the group
who might be listening were getting a little worried, I decided
to send a telegram myself. It read "Please send first opportunity
two heavy-duty peashooters, two bags of peas and one case of
putty medals".'

Bob told the story as a joke, but quite clearly any situation
in which people started threatening the government representatives with force was not to be minimized. Eventually the
government did send down troops, and the leaders of the Army
were arrested. They were deported, tried and put in gaol in Vila.
It might have been that the dummy guns and sham uniforms
were just being used for practice in preparation for the day when
John Frum would send the real things. It was also at least
as probable that these actions were yet another example of the

imitation of the white man's activities carried out in the vague belief that it was some form of magic.

Since that time, the movement had not been so active, but it was obviously far from dead and we did not have to walk far from Bob's house to find proof. By the side of the roads in the bush, on headlands by the coast, and on patches of savannah, we found the symbols of the cult — crude wooden crosses, painted red, many of them surrounded by elaborate fences of red stakes. Some were no more than a foot high, others as tall as a man. Scarlet gates were almost as abundant. Their hinges were functional and you could open them and walk through if you wanted to do so, but they had been built in isolation, leading nowhere from nowhere. They reminded me of the gates in our own cities which stand shut beneath a monumental arch while traffic swirls around them — gates that are only opened to allow royalty and their followers to pass through on some great ceremonial occasion.

On the top of a hill, a mile away from his store, Bob showed us a thirty-foot tall bamboo mast. A cross was tied to its top and a palisade had been put up around its base. Some orange flowers in jam jars had been placed at its foot, their freshness proving that they had only recently been put there and that therefore the mast was still venerated. When they had first built it, the local people had said that it was John Frum's radio mast which they had erected at his order so that he could speak to them and send them messages like those which came over the white man's radio.

As we drove along the slippery earth tracks that ran round the coast and across the centre of the island, we often encountered the Tannese trudging along the road, the women carrying heavy loads of sweet potato or cassava, the men with bush knives in their hands on their way to or from cutting copra in one of the plantations. They looked at us suspiciously and unsmilingly. Several times we stopped and asked one of them about the meaning of a nearby cross or gate. Always the answer was, 'Me no savvy.' Until the people had become more accustomed to our presence and had decided what our motives in visiting the island might be, there was little hope of getting any clear answer to our questions. Bob therefore spread the word through the men who worked in his trade store that we were neither missionaries nor traders nor government people but merely two men who had heard about John Frum and who wished to discover the truth about him.

John Frum's radio mast

After a few days, we felt that the news would have circulated sufficiently widely for it to be worthwhile for us to start visiting the villages. Outside each settlement there is a ceremonial assembly ground called the *namakal*. It is always shaded by a gigantic banyan tree. The huge heavily leaved boughs, the brown furry aerial roots that hang from them and the interlacing tangle of pillars that surround the trunk give an ominous brooding air to these places. Here, after the day's work has been done, the men of the village assemble to drink kava.

Kava is made from the crushed root of a type of pepper plant, *Piper methysticum*. It is not alcoholic, but it does contain a drug which is said to make you dizzy and unsteady on your legs when it is taken in excess or in a concentrated form. It is drunk in most of the Pacific islands to the east and everywhere it is regarded as being imbued with semi-sacred qualities. In Tanna it is drunk in an extremely strong form and prepared in a primitive fashion long since abandoned in most other parts of the Pacific. Several of the younger men sit and chew the roots, spitting out gobbets of masticated fibres. A mass the size of a man's fist is then put in a strainer made from the fibrous bract of a palm leaf and water poured over it into a coconut shell. The resulting opaque liquid, gritty and muddy brown, is swallowed in one gulp. Within a few minutes, the drinker becomes moody and irritable. The men sit around in silence. It is strictly forbidden for any women to come to the namakal at this time. Then, as night draws in the men drift back to their huts one by one.

The drinking of kava was banned by the mission both because of the unhygienic method of preparation and because of its intimate association with many of the ancient pagan rituals. The followers of John Frum had reverted to the practice, not merely because they enjoyed the taste and after-effects of kava, but because in drinking it they were making a deliberate act of defiance towards the mission.

Several times we went up to the namakal and sat as unobtrusively as possible, watching the preparation and drinking of the kava. Gradually, we came to know some of the men and talked in pidgin to them about trivialities. On our third visit, I broached, for the first time, the subject of John Frum. I was talking to an elderly sad-faced man named Sam. Fifteen years before he had been selected by the missionaries to be trained as a teacher, and he had taught for several years in the mission school. He therefore spoke easily understandable English. As we sat on our haunches beneath the banyan, smoking cigarettes, Sam spoke of John Frum, quietly and unemphatically.

'One night, nineteen years ago, plenty of the big men were having a meeting, drinkin' kava when John 'e come. 'E talk an' 'e say that by an' by 'e bring plenty cargo. The men will be happy and get everything they want and it will be good living.'

'What did he look like, Sam?'

'He white man, tall man, he wear shoes, he wear clothes, but he no speak English, he speak like man Tanna.'

'Did you see him?'

'Me no see 'im, but my brother see 'im.'

Slowly, reluctantly and with dignity, Sam told me more about John Frum. John had told the people to leave the school – 'Presbyterian church 'e no good; missionaries put in more-extra to the word of God.' John had told the people to throw away their money and to kill the cattle that the white man had brought them. Sometimes John lived in America, sometimes he lived in Tanna. But always and again and again, 'John 'e promise true. By an' by, white man 'e go, plenty cargo 'e come, an' everybody very happy.'

'Why has he not come, Sam?'

'Me no savvy. Maybe government man 'e stop 'im, but 'e come, some time. 'E promise 'e come.'

'But, Sam, it is nineteen years since John say that the cargo will come. He promise and he promise, but still the cargo does not come. Isn't nineteen years a long time to wait?'

Sam lifted his eyes from the ground and looked at me. 'If you can wait two thousand years for Jesus Christ to come an' 'e no come, then I can wait more than nineteen years for John.'

I talked with Sam on several other occasions, but each time, when I questioned him about the precise identity of John, how he moved about, or how he gave his orders, Sam contracted his brows and said 'Me no savvy.' If I pressed him further, he said, 'Nambas, big man belong Sulphur Bay, 'im 'e savvy.'

It was clear that Sam himself, though an ardent follower of the cult, was a disciple and not an innovator. The orders and edicts which he obeyed came from Sulphur Bay. Bob Paul confirmed that this village was indeed the main focus of the movement and told us that Nambas had been one of the chief organizers of the Tanna Army and had been imprisoned for a spell in Vila as a punishment for the part he played. Obviously we should have to go there, but I was anxious that we should not appear too eager to do so and that the news of our activities should have spread there before we made our visit. If we arrived unheralded and unexpectedly, Nambas's immediate reaction might be to deny defensively any intimate knowledge of the current working of the cult. If on the other hand, he knew we were paying attention to less important members of the movement, he might well be eager, from natural vanity, that we should take heed of him.

For several days we continued our journeys round the island. We went to see the missionaries and heard how an attempt was being made to wean the Tannese from their cult by starting a cooperative movement in which the full workings of trading were explained in detail. The people could see how their copra was sold, how much money it fetched and could themselves help to decide what cargo should be ordered from the lands across the sea. 'Look,' the missionaries could say to the followers of the cargo cult, 'our cargo comes. John Frum speaks false for his cargo does not come.'

The idea had only recently been put into action and it was too early to know for certain what success it would have.

I talked also to the Roman Catholic priest who had a small mission not far from Lenakel. Compared to the Presbyterians, his influence on the island was so tiny as to be negligible. Two years previously his church and his house had been totally destroyed by a typhoon and a tidal wave. Patiently, he had rebuilt it and continued his work. But his teaching drew little response from the Tannese. Only now, after six years of labour, was he about to baptize his first converts into the Catholic church, and he had only five of them whom he regarded as sufficiently prepared.

In his view, the most serious aspect of the movement was the educational one. 'For the past nineteen years,' he told me, 'hardly any Tannese child has attended school and when they cannot read or do sums, what chance have you of explaining the workings of the modern world to them? The longer the movement continues, the more difficult it will be to cure it.'

Later, he suggested to us that the cult had recently incorporated into its myths Yahuwey, the small but continuously active volcano that dominates the eastern side of Tanna. Even at Lenakel, twelve miles away, we could hear the rumbles of its explosions like distant rolls of thunder and on some days when it was particularly vigorous, everything in Bob's house became covered with a thin veneer of fine grey volcanic ash. To visit it, Geoff and I drove across the island from Lenakel, travelling along a muddy road that had been cut through the lush dank bush. The sound of the eruptions grew louder and louder until we could hear them above the noise of our car's engine. Then I noticed that behind the tree ferns lining the road the bush had been buried by a huge grey dune like some tip from a mine. The road twisted and we suddenly found ourselves in an empty Sahara of volcanic ash. Except on its very edges, where a few stilt-rooted pandanus trees were attempting to establish themselves, this great plain was totally barren and devoid of any living thing. Immediately in front of us, part of it was covered by a shallow blue lake. A mile away, beyond the lake, rose the rounded hump of the volcano itself, a thousand feet high. It was too squat to be graceful and not sufficiently high to be visually impressive, but of its menacing power there was no doubt. Above it hung a sullen yellow-brown mushroom of smoke and every few minutes the plain echoed with the sound of muffled explosions deep in its crater.

There were many indications that the followers of John Frum regarded this as a place of special significance. Among the pandanus at the margin of the plain stood several elaborate and solidly constructed gates and crosses, all of them painted scarlet. On the plain itself, we found sticks stuck vertically in the ash a few feet apart and stretching in a meandering serpentine line for half a mile to a gate which had been built on one of the hummocks of an old lava flow. On top of the volcano, we could just distinguish yet another cross.

Gates and posts leading across the lava field

It took us half an hour to trudge up the steep flanks of the volcano, picking our way through a litter of lava boulders that had been thrown out from the crater. Some had the glassy texture of congealed black toffee. Others resembled lumps of currant dough, granular with white felspar crystals. On this igneous slag-heap, only one thing grew – an orchid which raised on its slender stems pennants of delicate pink flowers. We reached the rim during a moment of relative quiescence, and I peered down into the throat of the volcano. Its sides were clogged and encrusted with ash, like soot in a flue, but I could not see to any great depth for the crater was filled by shifting billows of acrid white smoke. Suddenly there was a shattering explosion of terrifying magnitude and a cannonade of black boulders came rocketing

A sing-sing in the Wahgi valley

A Wahgi valley warrior, with bird of paradise feathers in his headdress

With the axe-makers in the Jimi valley

A green tree python

A Count Raggi's Bird of Paradise

A young Pentecost islander summons the courage for the ceremonial jump

The dive

Fishing at the blowholes in Tonga

Vaea, the Tongan chief, entertains us with a lavish feast

through the smoke high into the air above us. Fortunately, the volcano had discharged them vertically so that they fell directly downwards back into the crater, and there was little danger of any of them hitting us. The volcano's repertoire of noises was extremely varied. Sometimes it produced echoing sighs as of gas escaping at high pressure; sometimes electrifying detonations which reverberated around the crater. Most terrifying of all, it occasionally erupted with a long, sustained roar like the sound of a gigantic jet engine, which continued for minutes at a time until it seemed that our eardrums must split.

Geoff Mulligan filming the crater

After a quarter of an hour, there was a shift in the wind, the smoke eddied and the whole crater cleared. Six hundred feet below us, I could see at least seven vents glowing red hot. They were not simple holes but irregular gaps in the jumble of lava boulders. When one erupted, which it did quite independently

The cross at the crater's edge

of the others, scarlet spangles of molten lava shot into the air, some of them the size of a small car. They twisted, elongated into spanner-shaped lumps and divided in mid-air until at last they reached their apogee and fell back, to land with an audible thud on the sides of the vent.

On the highest point of the crater's lip, we found the cross. It stood nearly seven feet high. Once it had been red, but the volcanic fumes had corroded the paint and only traces of colour were left. The timbers of which it was made were stout and heavy and the task of carrying them up the steep sides of the volcano must have been a very laborious one. Why the leaders of the John Frum cult should have considered it so important to set up their symbol in this place was a question I hoped to persuade Nambas to answer if we finally managed to meet him in Sulphur Bay.

Perhaps the most impressive of all the John Frum monuments, however, was not this cross, but a trio of crude wooden carvings we saw in a small village that we drove through on our way back to Lenakel.

They stood beneath a thatched shelter, protected by an encircling fence. On the left squatted a strange rat-like creature with wings sprouting from its shoulders, enclosed by a symbolic square cage. On the right had been placed a model of an aeroplane with four propellers, outsize wheels and a white American star painted on its wings and tail. This surely must have represented the plane which would bring the cargo to the island. In the centre, behind a black unpainted cross, stood an effigy which could only be of John himself. He wore a white belt and a scarlet coat and trousers. His face and hands were white and he stood with his arms outstretched and his right leg lifted behind him in a travesty of a Christian crucifix. The figures were pathetically childish, yet they seemed deeply sinister.

The cargo cult shrine

At last we felt that the time was ripe for us to seek out Nambas. We drove from Lenakel to the ash plain around Yahuwey, across it, and then down a grassy track. The huts of Sulphur Bay village were grouped round a large open square in the centre of which stood two tall bamboo masts. This was where the Tanna Army under Nambas's leadership had once paraded and drilled. We drove slowly down one side of this square and parked beneath a gigantic banyan tree. As we got out, the villagers gathered around us. Most of them were dressed in scarlet singlets or shirts. One old man proudly wore at a rakish angle a battered steel helmet, no doubt a highly prized relic from the American occupation of Santo. The atmosphere was not a friendly or welcoming one, but neither was it overtly hostile. A tall elderly man with greying hair, an aquiline nose and deep-set eyes detached himself from the crowd and walked towards us.

'Me Nambas,' he said.

I introduced Geoff and myself and explained that we had come from across the seas to hear about John Frum, to discover who he was and to find out what message he preached. Could Nambas tell us about him? Nambas looked at me closely, his black eyes narrowed.

'Orright,' he said at last. 'We talk.'

He led me over to the foot of a banyan tree. Geoff, standing by the car, unobtrusively set up his camera. I sat down, put the tape recorder by my side and laid the microphone on the ground. The rest of the villagers clustered around us, anxious to hear what their leader would say. Nambas looked around him haught-ily. He obviously felt that there was a need to put on a good performance to confirm his position and authority with his supporters.

'Me savvy you will come,' he said to me loudly. 'John Frum 'e speak me two weeks ago. 'E say two white men 'e come to ask all thing about red cross and John.'

He looked around him triumphantly. As we had gone out of

our way to make sure that he knew of our arrival and plans, this news hardly surprised me but his people listening were visibly impressed.

'When John speak you, you see him?' I asked.

'No.' Nambas shook his head and then added, enunciating his words with the greatest care, ''E speak me 'long *radio*. Me got special radio belong John.' The Catholic missionary had told me about this radio. According to one of his converts, on appointed evenings an old woman with electrical flex wrapped around her waist would fall into a self-induced trance behind a screen in Nambas's hut and begin to talk gibberish. This Nambas would interpret to his followers, who were listening in the darkened room, as messages from John Frum.

'How often he speak you 'long radio?'

'Every night, every day, 'long morning time, 'long night time. 'E speak me plenty.'

Nambas

'This radio; is it all the same like white man's radio?'

''E no like white man's radio,' said Nambas mysteriously. ''E no got wire. 'E radio belong John. John 'e give me because I stop long time in calaboose at Vila for John. 'E give me radio for present.'

'Can I see this radio?'

There was a pause.

'No,' said Nambas foxily.

'Why not?'

'Because John 'e say that no white man look 'im.'

I had pressed him too far. I changed the subject.

'Have you seen John Frum?'

Nambas nodded vigorously. 'Me see him plenty time.'

'What does he look like?'

Nambas jabbed his finger at me. ''E look like you. 'E got white face. 'E tall man. 'E live 'long South America.'

'Did you speak to him?'

''E speak to me many time. 'E speak to plenty men – more than a hundred.'

'What does he say?'

''E speak, by an' by the world turn. Everything will be different. 'E come from South America and bring plenty cargo. An' every man 'e get every thing 'e want.'

'Will the white man get cargo too from John?'

'No,' said Nambas emphatically. 'Cargo come to native boy. John say 'e cannot give white man cargo because white man 'e got it already.'

'Does John say when he will come?'

''E no say *when*; but 'e come,' replied Nambas with quiet confidence. His listeners grunted their agreement.

'Nambas, why you put up red crosses?'

'John 'e say, you makim plenty cross. 'Im 'e mark for John.'

'Why do you put a cross on top of the volcano?'

Nambas leaned forward towards me his eyes blazing wildly. 'Because *man* stop inside volcano. Many man belong John

Frum. Red man, brown man, white man; man belong Tanna, man belong South America, all stop 'long volcano. When time come, man come from volcano an' bring cargo.'

'Me walk 'long volcano,' I said. 'Me lookim but no see man.'

'You no see 'im,' retorted Nambas scornfully. 'Your eye dark. You no see *anything* inside volcano. But man 'e stop. Me see 'im plenty time.'

Did Nambas believe what he was saying? Was he a mystic who had visions? Or was he a charlatan who was claiming special powers so that he could influence his people and make them do what he wished? I could not tell. If he were mad, then he had infected the whole of the island with his madness. Certainly it was not going to be possible to discover from him whether or not there had ever been an actual person named John Frum around whom the stories had developed. Nor, I now realized, did it matter. Nambas was the high priest of the movement, and historical facts and the material world had little relevance to his thoughts or his pronouncements.

I remembered the explanation of the cults that had been given me by the Lutheran missionary in New Guinea. It was obviously simplified – none of us, European nor Melanesian, work out our beliefs quite so logically – but nonetheless it closely matched the observable facts in Tanna. It seems that it is too much to expect a people to make, within the space of two or three generations, the transition from a Stone Age culture to the most advanced material civilization that the world has ever known without running the risk of their complete moral disorientation and mental dislocation.

We had visited Sulphur Bay on a Friday, and Nambas told me that John Frum had ordained that on this day each week the people should dance to do him honour. As evening came, a group of musicians with guitars, mandolins and drums made from tin cans, came moving slowly across the clearing beneath the banyan, playing as they walked. A group of women, wearing long grass skirts, surrounded them and began singing stridently.

Their song was not an old traditional chant but simple and repetitious, clearly derived from the American popular songs which were played incessantly on tinny gramophones in the trade-stores to attract customers. The people got to their feet and soon the whole clearing was full of the villagers jigging up and down in a mechanical stilted fashion. One or two of them added to the strangeness of the scene by collecting from the trunk of the banyan some small mushroom-like fungus which gave off a brilliant phosphorescent light. They stuck them on their foreheads and on their cheeks so that their faces were illuminated by an eerie green glow. The dance continued monotonously, the song being repeated again and again and the people dancing with a drugging insistent rhythm. Soon someone would produce some smuggled alcoholic drink and these people, believing that they were doing honour to their god of materialism, would carouse all night.

8

The Outer Isles of Fiji

F rom the New Hebrides, we flew eastwards to Fiji. In Suva, the capital, we made two quick alliances, first with the Public Relations Office and then with Broadcasting House. Our friends in both places tactfully told us that two Englishmen without a word of Fijian between them would not only find it very difficult to discover whatever it was that they were looking for in the more rural parts of Fiji, but would certainly, out of ignorance, fail to observe the numerous and complicated rules of Fijian etiquette with results that might well prove disastrous. The obvious solution, they said, was to provide guides, and this they did. Broadcasting House supplied Manu Tupou, a tall handsome Fijian who was one of their roving reporters. Although in his early twenties, he had a great knowledge of the traditions of his own people and this, combined with the fact that he was of noble blood and could claim relationship with many important chiefs, made him an ideal guide for us. Furthermore, his time would not be entirely wasted as far as Broadcasting House was concerned, for while he was with us he could make recordings which he could use in his own Fijian language radio programmes. From the Public Relations Office came Sitiveni Yanggona, a young Fijian also from a chiefly clan, who had relatives on some of the islands we were hoping to visit and who therefore would be an invaluable ambassador. Sitiveni – his name is the Fijian version of Stephen – later proved to be an accomplished guitarist, a talent which among the musical Fijians was almost as good an ambassadorial qualification as being connected with the aristocracy.

⸻

Where should we go? Nearly two hundred miles east of Suva, almost midway between it and the islands of Tonga, a mountain range rises from the ocean bed, the peaks of which project above the blue waters of the Pacific and form the coral-girt, palm-clad islands of Lau.

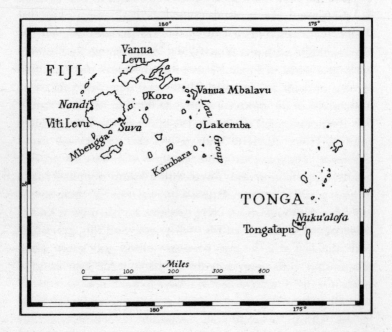

Manu and Sitiveni described them to us in rapturous terms. There, they said, the hibiscus and frangipani bloom as nowhere else and the palms produce the sweetest and largest coconuts of the Pacific; the islands have always been the home of the finest craftsmen of Fiji and only there do the old skills of canoe-building and kava bowl-making still survive. And of course, they added, it was universally agreed that the girls of Lau were the most beautiful in the whole of Fiji. Both Manu and Sitiveni, we discovered, came from Lau. Suspecting that perhaps they were a little prejudiced, we tried to get corroboration of their claims, but very few people in Suva, who were not Lauans, had ever been to the islands. Communications were difficult and the only ships that made the journey with any regularity were small and extremely uncomfortable trading boats that went out there to collect copra. Nonetheless, it seemed that Manu's and Sitiveni's eulogies were not entirely without foundation, for everyone who had even heard of the islands assured us that it was in Lau that the twentieth century had made the least impact and that the old Fijian customs had lingered the longest. Our minds were finally made up when we learned from Sitiveni's father, himself by birth a noble of Lau, that on the island of Vanua Mbalavu, in the north of the group, a strange ceremony was soon due to take place during which the sacred fish of an inland lake would rise to the surface and give themselves up to the villagers.

By good fortune, a government launch was scheduled within the next few days to leave Suva with a surveyor and take him to Vanua Mbalavu. He was going to assess the possibilities of building an airstrip for a New Zealander who owned a large coconut plantation in the northern part of the island. If we wished to see the fishing ceremony, we should have to stay at the village of Lomaloma in the south, but the launch could easily leave us there on its way and, fortunately, there was just enough spare room on board for the four of us.

The voyage took some time, for the crew of the launch anchored each night in the lee of some island as they were unwilling to risk sailing through these heavily reefed waters in the darkness, but on the evening of our fourth day out, we entered Lomaloma Bay. We scrambled ashore hastily, for the launch had to reach the New Zealander's plantation twelve miles to the north before nightfall. Our baggage was bundled out of the hold and dumped on the beach, the launch went hard astern and roared away. But we had not been left alone, for dozens of men, women and children had come down to the shore to meet the boat and there were many willing helpers to carry our luggage up to the village. Most of the men who walked beside us wore not trousers, but *sulus*, simple lengths of cloth wrapped around their waists like skirts, some red, some blue, all of them brightly coloured. The girls were also gaily dressed in cotton frocks and many of them had put flowers in their hair – scarlet hibiscus, or the elegant ivory-coloured blossoms of frangipani. I noticed that whereas most Fijians in Suva had frizzy hair, there were several people here whose hair was wavy and glossy, an indication of the influence of the Polynesian people of Tonga away to the east.

Lomaloma proved to be a pretty and very well-kept settlement. Many of its trim, thatched houses, or *mbures*, were surrounded by flower beds and between them stretched neatly clipped lawns. There was a school, two Indian-owned stores, a white-painted Methodist church and a small radio transmitter operated by one of the villagers. It had always been an important place. In the middle of the nineteenth century, the northern Lau islands were conquered by one of the greatest of all the warriors of the Pacific, the Tongan chief, Ma'afu. He made his headquarters at Lomaloma and established a large Tongan community there. One section of the village still remained proudly and independently Tongan. Later, after Fiji was ceded to the British crown, Lomaloma became the residence of the District Commissioners who ruled over the whole of Lau, and their office buildings, with the ships' cannon outside them, still stood. The administrative centre had later moved south to the island of Lakemba, in the middle of the group. Even so, Lomaloma still retained an air of dignity and importance which distinguished it from the more ramshackle and untidy Fijian villages of other islands, and it was still the home of the *mbuli*, the government-appointed chief who was responsible for the administration of the whole of Vanua Mbalavu. It was he who welcomed us and who was to be our host throughout our stay. He was a heavily built sombre man, deeply respected by the rest of the community. He seldom smiled, and when he did so, out of politeness to us, the expression seemed a painful one and vanished from his face with almost startling rapidity. He was a 'strong' man, we were told, and as an example of how he wielded his authority and backed up his discipline, one of the younger men described an occasion when the mbuli discovered a group of people making 'home-brew' – the highly alcoholic and illicit drink that is sometimes secretly made from mandioca, pineapple, sugar and yeast. He took the culprits out one by one and thrashed them, and none of these full-grown men dared offer any resistance.

He allocated to us a large beautifully built mbure that stood in the middle of the village close to his house. Its floor was covered by several layers of pandanus mats so that it was pleasantly springy underfoot and its magnificently constructed roof, the rafters and cross-stays neatly lashed with sinnet, was supported by four free-standing hard-wood columns nearly two feet in diameter. Normally this splendid building was used for community meetings, but now some beds were put in it and we were told to consider it our own house.

Although we were the guests of the mbuli, the work of looking after us fell to his womenfolk. Fortunately, he had a large number of them – his wife, a fat jolly woman; his cousin Hola, thin with protruding teeth and a recurrent bubbling laugh who did most of the cooking; and his two daughters, Mere (Mary) and Ofa. Mere was nineteen and the beauty of the village. Her hair was always carefully combed into the big globe now regrettably abandoned by many Fijians. She seemed very shy and seldom lifted her eyes from the ground when there were men present. Occasionally, however, if someone made a joke, or a saucy remark, she would look up and flash a small-toothed brilliant smile which every man in the village found very fetching. Ofa was two years younger and very like Mere, though she lacked her sister's poise and her face often clouded with childish uncertainties. Hola cooked in a special hut by the mbuli's house and Mere and Ofa would bring us our meals, serving them on a foot-high table, covered by an immaculate white cloth. As we ate, sitting cross-legged on the floor, the two girls would remain at either end of the table to brush away with fans any flies that might try to settle on the food. The dishes Hola prepared for us were delicious – raw fish in coconut milk, boiled chicken and yams, fish grilled on wooden spits, mandioca, sweet potatoes, bananas, pineapples and ripe juicy mangoes.

Our immediate neighbour was a fat cheerful man who had some congenital defect in his speech and was affectionately called in the village, Dumb William. But he was far from dumb, for although he could not articulate precisely, he produced a wide variety of extremely expressive noises and with the aid of swirling, stabbing, waving gestures and frequent rollings of his eyes, he could carry on elaborate and perfectly comprehensible conversations. Indeed, for us who could not understand more than a few words of Fijian anyway, he was one of the most easily understood of all the villagers. He came into our mbure almost every evening and regaled us with hysterically funny Rabelaisian stories about our neighbours.

William's proudest possession was a battery radio which, since his disability had also made him partly deaf, he played extremely loudly. But he did not listen very much to the radio programmes from Suva. The villages up the eastern coast of Vanua Mbalavu were connected by extremely antiquated telephones that once served Suva and which, when they were outmoded, were sold to the chief of Lau who had them installed in several of his islands. As there was only one line, winding the handle on the side of one telephone caused every other instrument in the island to ring, so to indicate for whom the call was intended, a kind of Morse code of rings was used. Lomaloma's telephone was placed in the mbuli's house and all day long it emitted an indecipherable jangle of rings. No one paid much attention or seemed to bother whether the call was intended for Lomaloma or not. Except for William. For him, the whole system provided an endless source of amusement, for he had discovered that by tapping the telephone wire and connecting it to the speaker of his radio set, he could enormously amplify the sound and listen to conversations between all the people of the island. He spent hours sitting by it with an absorbed expression on his face and thus became the village's major source of gossip and scandal. Because he spent so much of his evening in our mbure, and because we could understand his own private language of gurgles and gestures almost as well as anyone else could, we rapidly became very well informed about the private life of almost everyone in the village. As a result, we were not only able to share in scurrilous jokes with our neighbours and acquaintances but could even improvise a few ourselves. Within a few days we began to feel that we were no longer total strangers, but had become quite intimately integrated into the community.

The ritual fishing of Lake Masomo, the ceremony which had drawn us to Vanua Mbalavu in the first place, was due to take place three days after we arrived. Manu told me the legend of its origin, with continual interruptions and graphic embellishments from William.

'Once upon a time, a man on this island was working in his plantation when he saw two girl-goddesses from Tonga flying overhead. They were on their way to visit a relation who had married a Fijian man and were taking with them a present of some fish, neatly parcelled up together with water, in a big leaf of the wild taro plant. The man called up to them that he was thirsty and asked if they could let him have a drink. They ignored him and flew on. This made him very angry, so he cut a branch from a *ngai* tree and hurled it at them. But instead of hurting them, he merely knocked the gift from their hands. The water fell and formed Lake Masomo and the sacred fish of the gift have lived in it ever since. But they are taboo. No one is allowed to try and catch them except when the priests give permission.'

When the day of the ceremony arrived, some thirty of us from Lomaloma climbed aboard the village launch and sailed off northwards to join people in the settlements of Mualevu and Mavana whose priests, by tradition, controlled the rites. They too had their launches, and by mid morning we were in the middle of a small northward-bound convoy, travelling between the fringing coral reef and the high limestone cliffs that form the coast of this part of Vanua Mbalavu. After two or three miles the leading boat turned inwards to the entrance of a long narrow fjord that snaked deep inland between steep rock precipices. When at last the water shallowed, we went ashore and walked for another half-mile first through muddy mangroves and then up a steep rise. Beyond, we found Lake Masomo, a black sinister sheet of water no more than three hundred yards long, cradled in the hollow of the heavily forested hills. Some of the men from Mualevu had been working here for several days, felling trees and shrubs to make a clearing by the shore of the lake and building there half a dozen long shelters, simple frameworks of timber thatched with green leaves. Soon a hundred people gathered in the clearing. The women and girls began lighting fires for cooking and unpacking the taro and mandioca that they had brought with them wrapped up in leaves. Some of the men went into the bush to cut more branches with which to extend the shelters. Everyone seemed excited and as light-hearted as a bank holiday crowd at the seaside.

The rituals began with a series of kava presentations. First we ourselves, as strangers at the ceremony, gave kava to Tui Kumbutha, the chief of Mavana whose title, Tui, indicated that he was the most senior chief present. Then the various clans of the three villages presented kava to one another, and finally we all went up to a small shelter set fifty yards away from the rest of the huts to pay our respects to the head of the priestly clan who governed the whole ceremony. After he had accepted kava, he pronounced that the time was suitable for the rituals to commence.

Immediately, Tui Kumbutha despatched his orator to make the announcement public.

'Permission has been granted for the fishing to begin,' he called, standing in the middle of the clearing.

'*Vinaka, vinaka*,' we all replied, which means both 'Hear, hear' and 'Thank you very much.'

'Everyone here must take part. You must enter the waters of the lake, and, two by two, you must swim. It is forbidden for anyone to wear any clothing whatsoever except for skirts of *ngai* leaves. Anoint your bodies with oil, for otherwise the waters of the lake will bite you. You must swim until the priest announces that the time has come to take the fish. Only then may you take spears and gather the fish which will rise to the surface of the waters and give themselves up to you.'

The people needed no encouragement. While the men had been engaged in the kava ceremonies, the girls had been busy making heavy skirts from the long glossy leaves of the *ngai* tree, a branch of which the man in the legend had hurled at the flying goddess. The men took the completed skirts and slung them round their waists and then the girls helped them to anoint their bare chests and legs with coconut oil deliciously perfumed with the essence of crushed blossoms, until their magnificently muscled bodies glistened a golden honey-brown.

Most of the men had already cut for themselves short logs, stripped of bark, which were to be used as floats, and holding them above their heads and whooping with excitement, they ran down to splash into the lake. Manu and Sitiveni, already beskirted, came to tell us that both Geoff and I were expected to help in the ceremony. Unfortunately, Geoff had several ulcers on his leg which were giving a lot of pain and he decided that it would be unwise to swim, but there was nothing to prevent me from doing so. Hola had made a skirt for me, and when I had put it on, Mere oiled me thoroughly. Manu gave me a log float and we went down to the lake together.

Being anointed with coconut oil before the fishing ceremony

Entering the lake for the ceremonial fishing

The waters were shallow and extremely warm, but the pleasure of swimming was somewhat marred by the fact that the bottom was covered with a thick black ooze into which we sank up to our knees. However we soon learned to avoid it, even where the water was only two or three feet deep, by floating horizontally with our arms resting on our logs and kicking with our feet. Towards the centre of the lake the water was deeper, and it was possible to swim more actively without becoming covered in mud. Soon, with shrieks and giggles, the girls, also wearing skirts and their bodies shining with oil, came running down to join us. A few of them brought log floats of their own, but most swam over to the men and shared theirs. Then, in a long line, we all swam across the lake singing loudly, kicking out with our feet so that the waters behind us swirled black with ooze. Soon the unmistakable smell of sulphuretted hydrogen was rising from the water and, as I smelt it, I understood the way in which the ceremony worked. The gas had been produced by vegetable matter rotting at the bottom of the lake and until we had disturbed the waters, it had lain entrapped in the ooze. As it dissolved in the water, it formed a poison which forced the fish to the surface to 'give themselves up' as the priest had so mysteriously predicted. This also explained why the ritual stipulated that people should oil their bodies, for sulphuretted hydrogen, in solution, forms a weak acid which if it were sufficiently strong, could cause a rash on unprotected skin.

We swam for nearly two hours and then, one by one, we came out and went back to the encampment for an evening meal. But most of us returned as soon as we had eaten. In the cool of the evening, wearing only our skirts of leaves, it was warmer in the lake than out of it. A huge yellow moon rose above the mountains and spilled its light in a rippling avenue over the black water. We swam in parties, sometimes losing one another in the darkness and joining other groups, our shouts, laughs and songs echoing over the lake.

After an hour or so, when I was beginning to tire of swimming, I heard, mingling with our own songs, the distant sound of ukeleles and guitars. I waded out and found that back at the camp a *taralala* was in progress. This word derives from the English expression 'tra-la-la' which the dictionary defines as a phrase expressive of joy and gaiety, and its Fijian meaning is almost the same, for it is the name given to a happy informal dance. Couples, shoulder to shoulder, their arms around each other's waists, were shuffling back and forth with a simple rhythmic step, in the middle of a large ring of seated people. At one end sat the musicians and singers, and at the other, kava was being mixed and dispensed. The whole scene was lit by the flames of a small bonfire just outside the circle.

'Oi, Tavita,' called the mbuli's wife to me, using the Fijian version of my name by which I was known in the village, 'come and show us if you can dance.' I went across the circle to where Mere was sitting and to the accompaniment of whistles and cat-calls from Dumb William, we taralala-ed with the rest.

We sang and danced and drank kava late into the night. People came in from the lake to warm themselves by the fire and to join in the party and then one by one they drifted back into the darkness to swim again. When I went to my shelter, the music was still continuing as loudly as ever. I slept for only a few hours. In the morning, when I returned to the lake, there were still some twenty people in the water.

Then, at last, the fish began to rise. They were huge silver creatures and, as we swam, they leaped from the surface in front of our noses and flew in a silver arc through the air before they fell back with a splash. Many were swimming half-asphyxiated with their mouths on the surface.

I was floating idly at the end of the lake nearest to the camp, when I suddenly heard a shout behind me and twenty men came rushing down the path brandishing fish spears, long poles with five or six iron spikes radiating from the end. The priest had given the order for the gathering of the fish to begin. The

Girls catching the fish

men spread out in a line and began systematically to work their way down the lake. The air was thick with spears. Occasionally the half-poisoned fish, in an attempt to escape, zigzagged wildly across the surface of the water. Some were already so senseless that the girls were able to seize them by their tails. Ritual dictated even the small details of the handling of the fish. Normally a Fijian fisherman will thread his catch on a string which passes through the mouth and out through the gills, but in this case it was ordained by custom that the fish should be strung with the cord passing through their eyes, and all the men had armed themselves with small wooden skewers in order to carry them away in that fashion. Half an hour later, it was all over. I counted one hundred and thirteen large silver fish like oversized mackerel lying on the bank.

In the evening, we returned to Lomaloma and that night everyone feasted on *awa*, as the fish were called. I thought they

Bringing the fish from the lake

were delicious. Geoff, however, not having taken part in the ceremony, was perhaps a little less biased, as he maintained that the fish had the texture of cotton-wool and a taste reminiscent of bad eggs.

The practical value of the ritual was quite apparent. The fishing could only be successfully carried out if a large number of people cooperated – and therefore it had to be organized; and its practice had to be carefully restricted for if it were done too often, the fish might well be exterminated. The most convenient way of arranging all this was by turning it into a ritual administered by a priestly clan.

We had arranged before leaving Suva that a small trading boat which made a regular tour of the Lau Group should collect us from Lomaloma and take us down to the islands in the south, but it was not due to arrive for another week. The days which followed the fishing ceremony were among the happiest and most delightful that we spent during the whole of our journey in the Pacific. The daily life of the village, which initially had been disturbed and thrown out of balance by our arrival, gradually reverted to normal as our presence came to be taken for granted.

In the mornings, the village woke early. If it was a weekday, the people would spend their time on community work which had been decided upon the previous evening by the *turanga ni koro*, the headman. Perhaps a house had to be built, nets repaired or baskets woven. If it was a Saturday, families would be working on their own account in their cassava, yam or taro gardens. If it was a Sunday, no one would do work of any kind.

We became particular friends of Totoyo, a huge hairy-chested man with an incongruously high-pitched voice, who had the reputation of being one of the best spear-fishermen in the village. Sometimes we went out with him in his canoe and dived together over the reefs. He was a magnificent swimmer. Wearing tiny goggles that fitted close to his eyes, he would dive to fifteen feet in pursuit of a fish, remaining submerged for minutes at a time.

We now had to make arrangements to leave the island. By radio, we chartered a schooner to come out from Suva to collect us. The night before it was due to arrive, we held a big kava ceremony in our mbure. Geoff, fully recovered, sat next to me and Manu and Sitiveni sat on either side of us. At the other end of the ring sat the mbuli, his wife, Hola, the headman, Dumb William, Totoyo, Mere, Ofa and all the rest of our friends.

After we had all drunk kava, I walked across the ring and put in front of each member of the mbuli's family a small gift – cloth, perfume, jewellery and knives – which I had bought at the Indian store. Then, with Manu translating phrase by phrase I made a short speech. I thanked the people for their kindness to us, for their hospitality and for the open-hearted way in which they had received us into their community and said how sorry we were to leave.

*Manu with Mere and Ofa having
returned from fishing on the reef*

When I had finished, the mbuli began to make a speech in
reply. He had only spoken a few sentences when unexpectedly,
and in defiance of all custom, his wife interrupted him.

'I must speak. Do not be sad, Tavita and Gefferi,' she said,
with tears running down her cheeks, 'for you can never leave
Lomaloma. Now you are members of our family and we are
members of yours. No matter where you may go, you will
take something of Lomaloma with you. And as for us, we
will not forget you. However long it is before you return here,
this mbure is yours to live in for as long as you wish and we
shall always be ready to welcome you back to your second
home.'

I believed her as I listened. I believe her still.

The next day, a tiny speck appeared on the horizon in the west. Totoyo immediately pronounced it to be the *Maroro*, the ship we had chartered by radio. He could see very little of its shape but from the direction in which it was travelling, the time at which it had appeared, and the shipping news that he overheard daily on Dumb William's blaring radio, he was sure that it could be no other.

Slowly the dot increased in size until at last, through binoculars, we could see that she was a magnificent white-hulled schooner under full sail. Totoyo was right: it was the *Maroro*. Majestically she swung round between the two patches of ruffled water that marked the passage through the fringing reef into the lagoon. When she was no more than a hundred yards from us, she lowered her mainsail and dropped anchor. We said our last farewells and within an hour we had left Lomaloma.

The *Maroro* – her name is a Tahitian word meaning Flying Fish – was captained and part-owned by an Englishman, Stanley Brown, who had come out to the Pacific with the Navy during the war and had been so attracted by the islands that he had settled here for good. He was an ardent and skilful seaman and when he learned that we were two weeks behind our schedule, he suggested immediately that we should sail throughout the night, confident in the accuracy of his navigation to keep us clear of any reefs. As evening drew on, a stiff breeze came up. He stopped the engines, and we sailed on over the starlit sea, the shrouds straining, and the jib creaking, leaving in our wake a broad trail of luminescence.

We made very good speed. During the night we sailed south, past Lakemba, in the centre of the Lau group, and when dawn came, we continued westwards. Behind schedule though we were, we still had time to call at some other islands on our way back to Suva.

One day we landed on a small uninhabited atoll to gather coconuts. While I was wandering in the plantations, Manu came to me holding in his hand the largest crab I had ever seen.

Almost two feet across, it had a huge heart-shaped body, gigantic claws and a black fleshy pimpled tail curled up beneath it. In colour its shell was predominantly red-brown but its underside and the joints of its legs were flushed with blue. It was a robber or coconut crab and I handled it with the greatest care, for its claws looked quite capable of crushing one of my fingers if I gave them a chance.

A robber or coconut crab

Robber crabs are related to our own charming little hermit crabs that crawl around in the rock pools of the British coast dragging their winkle-shell home with them, but these Pacific monsters are so large and armed with such formidable defences that they do not require the protection of a shell home. Furthermore they have adapted themselves to life on dry land and only need to return to the sea for breeding.

The men told us that the crabs were a great pest in the plantations for they climbed the palms, cut down some of the coconuts and then descended to rip off the husks from the fallen nuts and break them open with their great claws to feast on the soft flesh inside. This story is widespread throughout the Pacific, but one which many naturalists dispute.

I placed Manu's crab on a palm to see if it could climb. Its long legs embraced the rough trunk, their sharp points easily finding holds, and slowly it began to clamber up, moving each of its six legs separately. There was no doubt whatever that it could ascend a palm if it wanted to.

I took it down before it climbed too high and put a piece of coconut in front of it to see if it would eat. The men laughed at me for doing so, saying that the crabs only fed at night. Certainly my specimen refused to take any interest in coconuts, whole or broken, old or newly picked. This, of course, proved nothing, but nevertheless, I found it hard to imagine how the creature, powerful though it was, would manage to split an unbroken coconut for itself.

We found others in the holes between the boulders above the shore. Soon we had five of the monsters warily promenading on the soft turf beneath the palms. One of the largest advanced slowly on a slightly smaller one. It reached forward with its pincer. The other crab did the same and the two claws met as if they were shaking hands. For a moment it seemed comic; then it became slightly horrifying. As the aggressor tightened its grip, chips of shell began to fly off the smaller crab's claw with an unpleasant splintering sound. The one that had been attacked brought its free claw forward and with dreadful deliberation fastened it to one of its opponent's walking legs.

We were watching a battle; but it was not one of cut and thrust, of bold dash and skilful parry, but a steady, inexorable tug of war. Only by their desperately waving stalked eyes did the crabs betray any emotion, or give any indication that living sentient beings occupied the huge armoured shells. I was reminded of the eyes of a soldier peeping through the steel slit in the front of a tank. The struggle continued for many minutes. I tried to disentangle the crabs, but picking them up seemed only to make them grip more desperately to one another, and they remained locked in soundless relentless combat. Then suddenly, the larger crab's leg that was gripped by the pincer of the smaller one, broke off high up at the joint close to the body. The raw white wound wept colourless blood. The pincers released their grip on one another and the mutilated crab slowly retreated. The victor walked backwards holding the amputated leg aloft in its pincer. Then it dropped the limb like a mechanical grab emptying its load. The battle was over.

The last island we visited before we had to return to Suva was Koro. When we had first arrived in Fiji, and had made arrangements for our journey through the outer islands, we had planned to spend two weeks in Koro, for the people of the village of Nathamaki, on the north coast of the island, are said to be able to summon at will from the depths of the ocean a sacred turtle and a great white shark. Such a claim is not unique; people in Samoa, the Gilberts and, within Fiji, in the island of Kandavu, are supposed to be able to do similar things but nonetheless the story seemed an extraordinary one. Our delay in Lomaloma meant that now we would only be able to spend twenty-four hours on Koro, but I was very anxious to do so in the hope that we might, even in this short time, witness the turtle-calling.

At dusk on the next night – a Sunday – we dropped anchor off Nathamaki and went ashore immediately to make our presentation of kava to the mbuli.

He had been expecting us several weeks before, for we had

sent word to him from Suva of our projected visit, but even though we were so late he appeared delighted to see us.

'You will surely stay here for at least a week,' he said.

'Unhappily, we cannot,' I replied. 'We must leave for Suva tomorrow night for we have passages booked on a ship to take us to Tonga.'

'*Oia-wa*,' cried the mbuli. 'This is bad. We hoped you would be our guests for many days so that we might do you honour and show you something of our island. And today is Sunday, so we cannot even welcome you with a big party and a taralala for it is forbidden by the church to dance on Sundays.' He looked round the kava ring mournfully and at the girls and the lads who stood clustered around the doorways of the mbure watching us.

'Never mind,' he said, brightening. 'I have an idea. We will drink kava for another four hours and then it will be Monday and all the girls will come in and we will dance until the sun comes up.'

With considerable regret, we declined this imaginative suggestion, but we promised to return early the next morning with our cameras so that we might film the turtle ceremony.

The next day dawned badly. The sky was filled with low misty clouds which stretched without a break to the horizon and rain squalls swept across the grey lagoon. We swathed our equipment in waterproofs, and took it ashore in the hope that as the day wore on conditions might improve.

The headman, who was going to perform the ritual, was waiting for us in his mbure, resplendent in his ceremonial pandanus kilt and bark cloth sashes.

Even though it was raining, he was anxious to go out and call the turtles. I explained that the weather was too bad to film. He looked extremely disappointed so I suggested that instead he should take us to the place where the ceremony was held so that we might decide where to position our cameras should the rain stop later in the day. He agreed, and together we went out into the drizzle. He led us along the beach and up a steep muddy path.

As we walked we chatted, for he had served in the Army and spoke excellent English.

'I think I will call the turtles anyway,' he said to me, casually.

'Please do not bother,' I replied. 'I only want to see the place.'

He walked on for a few steps.

'I might as well call them,' he said.

'I would rather you didn't. It would be infuriating if they came and we were unable to film them.'

He trudged on up the hill.

'Well I might just as well call them.'

'Don't do it for our sake,' I said. 'If they come this morning, they might not bother to return this afternoon.'

The headman laughed. 'They always come,' he said.

By now we were walking along the edge of a high cliff. The rain had stopped temporarily and a shaft of watery sunlight was glinting on the sea below. Suddenly the headman ran on ahead, stood on the bluff and began to chant at the top of his voice.

> 'Tui Naikasi, Tui Naikasi,
> God of Nathamaki,
> Who lives by the shore of our beautiful island,
> Who comes when called by the people of
>   Nathamaki,
> Rise to the surface, rise, rise, rise.'

We looked down to the sea five hundred feet below us. There was no sound but the rustle of the wind in the trees and the distant lapping of the waves on the shore far below.

> 'Tui Naikasi, rise, rise, rise.'

And then I saw a tiny reddish beflippered disc break the surface of the sea.

'Look,' I called excitedly to Geoff, pointing with my finger. 'There it is.'

As I spoke the turtle dived and was gone.

'You must never point,' said the headman reprovingly. 'That is tambu. If you do so, the turtle will vanish immediately.'

He called again. We waited, searching the sea. Then once more, the turtle rose to the surface. It remained visible for about half a minute, then with a stroke of its fore-flippers, it dived and disappeared. During the next quarter of an hour we saw eight more surfacings. It seemed to me that there were at least three turtles of varying size in the bay below.

As we returned to the village I pondered on what we had seen. Was it so very remarkable? If the bay was particularly attractive to turtles and there were always some cruising there, we should have seen them anyway for, being reptiles, they are compelled to rise to the surface to breathe. This would explain why the headman was so anxious to call them, for after all, it would have detracted from the miracle, to say the least, if the turtles had risen without anyone speaking a word.

Back at the village the mbuli entertained us to a splendid lunch of cold chicken, taro and yams. As we ate, sitting cross-legged on the matted floor, the headman told us the legend of the turtle-calling.

Many years ago, when Fiji was still uninhabited, three brothers and their families came sailing through the islands in their canoe. As they passed the tiny islet of Mbau, the youngest brother said, 'I like that place. I will live there.' So they set him and his family ashore and the two remaining brothers continued their journey eastwards until they came to Koro. 'This is a beautiful island,' said Tui Naikasi, the eldest of the brothers. 'I shall make this my home,' and he went ashore with his family. The remaining brother sailed on until he reached the island of Taveuni where he settled.

In the fullness of time, Tui Naikasi was blessed with many children and many grandchildren and when he came to die, he called his family around him and said, 'Now I must leave you; but if ever you are in trouble, come to the cliff above the beach where I first landed, call to me and I will appear from the sea to show that I am still watching over you.' Then Tui Naikasi died and his spirit was embodied in a turtle. His wife died soon afterwards and her spirit took the form of a big white shark.

Ever since then, before the people of Nathamaki embarked on a great voyage or their warriors set off on a raid, they would assemble on the cliff to feast and dance and finally to summon their ancestors before them, in the shape of a turtle and a shark to give themselves courage for the trials to come.

I asked an enormous man who was sitting next to me eating great quantities of yam, whether he believed the story. He giggled and shook his head.

'Do you often eat turtle meat?' I said, for it is a highly esteemed delicacy in most parts of Fiji.

'Never,' he said. 'For us it is tambu.'

He then told me of a curious event that had happened only a few months previously. Some of the village women, fishing in the lagoon, had accidentally caught a turtle in their nets. They hauled it into their canoe to try and disentangle it, but before they could do so a huge white shark appeared and charged them. They tried to drive it away with blows from their paddles but it refused to be frightened and dashed again and again at the canoe until the women feared that it might capsize them. 'We have caught Tui Naikasi,' one of the women said, 'and the shark, his wife, will not go away until we release him.' As quickly as they could, they freed the turtle from the folds of the net and tipped it back into the water. Immediately it dived and vanished, taking the shark with it.

By the time we had finished our meal, the weather had improved considerably and we decided to make an attempt to film the ceremony. From what we had seen during the morning, it would be extremely difficult to get convincing film of the turtle from the cliff top, so instead we went round to the bay by boat and landed on a huge rectangular block of stone standing in the water close to the cliff that the headman had told us was

Tui Naikasi's home. Ten minutes later, the tiny figure of the headman appeared at the cliff top. He waved to us, climbed into a big mango tree and began to call.

'Tui Naikasi, Tui Naikasi. Rise to the surface. Rise, rise.'

'If the turtle comes,' Geoff whispered to me, 'don't for goodness sake get excited and point at it. Just let me film it, before it disappears.'

'Tui Naikasi. *Vunde, vunde, vunde,*' called the headman.

I searched the sea with my binoculars.

'There,' said Manu, his arms resolutely crossed. 'About twenty yards away and a little to the left.'

'Where?' asked Geoff in an anguished whisper. The temptation to point was almost irresistible for I could see it distinctly, its head clear of the water as it gulped in air. Then the purr of the camera told me that Geoff had seen it as well. It lingered for almost a minute drifting lazily. Then there was a swirl and it had gone.

'Okay?' yelled the headman.

'Vinaka, vinaka,' we yelled back.

'I call again,' he shouted.

Five minutes later, the turtle reappeared, so close to us that I heard it gasp as it surfaced. As I watched it, Manu pulled my sleeve.

'Look down there,' he said softly, nodding towards the sea close by us. Only ten feet from the boulder on which we stood swam a huge shark clearly visible in the pellucid water, its triangular dorsal fin cutting the surface. Quickly Geoff swung his camera and filmed it as it cruised round the boulder. Three times it passed us. Then with powerful strokes of its long tail it accelerated and swam away towards the centre of the bay where we had last seen the turtle. Although we could no longer see its body we were able to follow its course by its dorsal fin. Then that too sank below the water.

I was very impressed. It might be possible to train both a shark and a turtle to come when called, but to do so one would have to reward the animals with food and this I am sure the people of Nathamaki do not do. Was it then merely a coincidence that both the shark and the turtle appeared when the headman called? To answer that properly, we should have had to remain in silence on the cliff top every day for perhaps a week, carefully noting the frequency with which sharks appeared in the clear blue waters of the bay and turtles came up to breathe. I was very sorry indeed that we were compelled to leave the island that night.

When we got back to the village, we found to our astonishment that the entire population had changed into ceremonial costume. As we arrived a group of girls ran towards us and hung garlands of frangipani blossoms around our necks. Behind them came the mbuli, grinning happily.

'Welcome back,' he said. 'We have prepared a big show for you, for the people feel you should see all our best dances before you leave.'

This was extremely embarrassing, for it was already late in the afternoon and I had promised Captain Brown that we would be back aboard the *Maroro* well before sundown so that he would be able to negotiate the inshore reefs and reach the open sea before darkness fell. But we could not be so rude as to refuse to watch the entertainment that had been prepared for us.

The mbuli led us to a mat laid out on the grass in front of his mbure. We sat down, then he shouted an order and a group of men and women nearby began to sing a rousing chant, accentuating the rhythm with claps in unison. A line of men, their faces blackened, holding spears in their hands, marched on to the grass in front of us and began a perfectly drilled war dance, brandishing their spears and stamping their feet. In the old days the words of the chant were usually a recital of the tribe's battle honours. These are still sung but the one we listened to was more modern and described the valour of the Fiji regiment which had served with such distinction and glory in Malaya.

As soon as the men had finished, their places were taken by children who performed a spirited club dance, stamping their feet and scowling ferociously in imitation of their elders. Verse followed verse as the children marched up and down swinging their clubs.

It was now getting quite late and I began to feel that I should have to ask the mbuli if he would excuse us leaving. Then thirty girls, garlanded and their bodies shining with oil, came from one of the mbures and seated themselves cross-legged in a line in front of us. They began a sitting *meke*, singing a delightful song and echoing its words by meaningful gestures of their hands and heads, their bodies swaying.

At last they ended amid great applause and laughter from everyone. I got to my feet, and with Manu's help, I thanked the people as best I could.

'And now,' I ended, 'sadly we must go. *Sa mothe*. Goodbye.'

As I stopped speaking, someone began to sing Isa Lei, the Fijian song of farewell. Within seconds the entire village took up the tune, singing with great fervour and in perfect harmony. The melody is a very sentimental one and it had never failed to raise a lump in my throat. Now it seemed more moving than ever, for this was in truth our farewell to Fiji. Everyone clustered round us, adding their garlands to those that already hung round our necks.

We shook hands with the mbuli and the headman and then we half walked and were half carried down to the beach. Still singing, the crowd followed us. As we pushed off into the lagoon several of the younger people swam after us.

When at last we reached the *Maroro*, the sun was already sinking into the sea in a glory of scarlet. Captain Brown started the engines. Slowly we moved across the lagoon towards the passage through the reef. We could see the people running along the beach to the headland close by which we had to pass, until several hundred of them had assembled on the green hillside. As we drew abreast of them we could hear yet again the melody of Isa Lei drifting across the water. Captain Brown replied with three hoots on the siren. The *Maroro* swung round, the crew hoisted the mainsail and we headed for the open sea.

Sitiveni, Geoff and Manu on the Maroro, *leaving Lau*

9

Royal Tonga

Geoff and I leaned on the rail of the promenade deck of the ungainly shabby merchant ship that we had boarded in Suva. Rain was beating down from the leaden skies with a depressing unvarying insistence, turning the surface of the sea into hammered pewter. For thirty-six hours we had wallowed our way eastwards through rough seas and heavy rain towards the islands of Tonga. Now the engines had reduced speed and we guessed that we were nearing our destination. Ahead of us we could just distinguish through the driving squalls, a horizontal grey smear that must be Tongatapu, the main island of the Tonga group.

We were met on the harbour jetty at Nuku'alofa by Jim Spillius, the anthropologist who had first written to me suggesting that we should come to Tonga. Standing on the quayside in the rain, he introduced us to Ve'ehala, a Tongan nobleman and Keeper of the Palace Records, with whom I had also corresponded about our visit. Jim drove the three of us along the empty flooded roads, splashing impressively through giant puddles. Eventually he turned into a road lined by elegant modern concrete houses, and stopped. Ve'ehala ran out through the rain, unlocked the door of one of them and beckoned to us to enter.

'This is your home for as long as you are in Tonga,' he said. 'A car is in the garage at your disposal. A cook and a servant will be here to look after you and your food will be sent from the Palace. If there is anything that you lack, you have only to let me know for it to be supplied.'

We spent most of the next three days talking with Ve'ehala, Jim Spillius and his wife, also an anthropologist, about the Royal Kava Ceremony, for it was essential that before we tried to film it, we should understand its significance.

The Royal Kava is the most important and sacred of all the surviving rituals of ancient Tonga and, in its enactment, it summarizes and reaffirms the social structure of the kingdom. In Tonga, as in all Polynesian societies, ancestry and rank have always been of paramount importance. In some other islands, before any ceremony may take place, a nobleman's spokesman will recite a long chant detailing his master's ancestry, which may stretch back to the legendary heroes of the creation, so that everyone shall know his qualification for performing the ritual. Although this custom is not followed in Tonga, lineage and precedence are nonetheless of consuming and vital interest, for nobles of royal blood govern the island, each inheriting with his title a section of the kingdom. But this is not a simple feudal system in which a lord extracts wealth from his serfs. The nobleman himself, though he has many privileges, has many responsibilities to his people and he must administer his villages, apportion land to his young men and often spend a great deal of his time and money in looking after their welfare. But although these titles are hereditary, the Queen must give her approval before a noble is confirmed in his rank and should he be considered unsuitable for the office that should by hereditary right be his, the royal confirmation may be withheld. If it is given, however, then the noble is installed at a Royal Kava Ceremony.

In essence, the ritual consists of an act of homage by the nobleman which is witnessed by all the aristocracy of Tonga who sit in a great circle. First, elaborate and munificent gifts are made to the Queen on behalf of the noble by his subjects. Then kava is mixed and served to Her Majesty and to every member of the circle. The order in which people are served and their position in the kava ring is governed by their lineage. But the determination of seniority and relative rank can be very complicated when aristocracy from all the islands of the group assemble, for nobility is transmitted by both the male and the female line, and temporary non-inheritable positions conferred by the Queen can confuse the position still further. But it is vital that there should be no mistakes, for in the kava ring relative ranks are made apparent to all and in time to come questions of important protocol may well be settled by reference to the last ceremony. It was for this reason that the Queen wished the entire ritual to be recorded on film.

The more we heard about it, the more I realized that the task of filming would be considerably more complicated than I had imagined. The ceremony itself would last over four hours. The kava ring would be a hundred yards across and except in the early stages we should not be allowed to step inside the circle. Furthermore, during the most important and sacred parts it would be unthinkable that we should move about, even outside the circle, as we should certainly deeply offend some of the older chiefs who in any case were somewhat suspicious of the whole project. In spite of this restriction of movement, it was vital that we should secure detailed close-up pictures of happenings at both sides of the ring and make recordings throughout the ceremony.

For all this to be achieved, we had to make detailed plans as to where we should place our cameras and microphones, when we should hurriedly move into new positions and, on the occasions when several things were happening simultaneously, which action should be filmed and which ignored. Furthermore, in order to put these plans into action, we should have to be able to follow every intricate detail of the four-hour ceremony which would be carried out in a language of which, so far, we knew not a word.

Jim and Elizabeth Spillius and Ve'ehala did their best to explain it all to us, but their task was extremely difficult for the whole ceremony was in reality a mosaic, each part of which was the responsibility of one noble or officer who was the authority on its protocol. As a result, not even Ve'ehala, keen student of Tongan ritual though he was, could give a definitive description of the entire ritual. There was, however, an ultimate authority on these questions, the Queen herself, and after each of our protracted meetings Ve'ehala would return to the Palace and seek an audience with the Queen so that he might be given answers to a long list of problems.

Ve'ehala coped with these trying problems magnificently. He was a young man, short and stout with a round face, and, mercifully, an extremely well-developed sense of humour. His laugh was memorable. It began as a giggle which gradually increased in intensity until his whole body was shaking and then, as he ran out of breath and was forced to inhale, it changed into a startling falsetto squeak.

Like nearly everyone else, he habitually wore Tongan national dress – a neck-tight tunic, a *vala*, the simple skirt like a Fijian sulu, and around his waist, belted with a long length of sinnet, a large mat of woven pandanus leaf strips, the *ta'ovala*. Ta'ovalas can vary enormously in size and quality according to the occasion. For an important ceremony, the mat might be a precious heirloom, extremely old, rich brown in colour and as finely woven and as pliable as linen. At funerals a rough tattered coarsely woven one would be appropriate. Ve'ehala, I suspect, had as many mats as an elegantly dressed Englishman has ties, but he usually appeared in comparatively new stiff ones which stretched from well below his knees to the middle of his chest. When sitting cross-legged on the ground, such a ta'ovala was obviously extremely useful, providing the wearer with a cushion on which to sit as well as an extended pocket in front of the chest where cigarettes, notebooks and pencils could be kept, but Ve'ehala found it something of an encumbrance when he had to sit on a chair around a table. Consequently, when we got to know him better he would sometimes take it off, and this he did, not by untying the sinnet belt and unwinding the whole mat, but by taking a deep breath so that the mat slipped to the ground and then, gathering his vala around his knees, stepping out of it, leaving an empty tube standing by itself on the floor.

Ve'ehala became the closest of our Tongan friends. He not only looked after our everyday wants, but he spent hours of his time telling us about Tongan legends and history. He was also an expert on the island's music and dancing, and a noted performer on the Tongan nose flute.

For the first few days, our time was monopolized by preparations for filming and we seldom left Nuku'alofa. It was a sunny unhurried town laid out on a neat but wearisome rectangular grid plan along the shore of a wide bay. The majority of its buildings were modern like the villa in which we lived, but almost as many had been built on traditional lines and were surrounded by kava and mandioca bushes. Apart from bicycles, the streets were almost free of traffic and the few cars that hooted their way through the crowds strolling idly down the middle of the roads belonged either to a Tongan Government official or a member of the small European community. Physically, the people were quite dissimilar from the Fijians of Suva, for they were not Melanesians but Polynesians, tall and handsome with golden-brown skin, flashing teeth, narrow noses and wavy black hair. Many of them walked barefoot and most wore valas and ta'ovalas, the only conspicuous exception being the girls of Queen Salote's School who were smartly dressed in immaculate bright blue tunics and straw hats that would have done great credit to the most fashionable English ladies' college.

The focal point of the town was the Palace, a white-painted timber building standing on the shores of the bay, that had been erected nearly a hundred years before by a New Zealand firm. It had two storeys, a feature which in itself was enough to give the building distinction in Nuku'alofa, and though its design was simple, it was ornamented with fretted edgings along the gables and eaves of its verandas which prevented it from appearing austere. It was the home not only of the Queen but of her son Prince Tungi, who was Prime Minister, and his family, and a great number of maids, musicians, dancers, cooks and servants who lived in separate buildings at the back. In one of its rooms, Privy Council was held, and on a side veranda kava was almost always being served to visiting notables. Processions of people bearing tapa cloth, fine mats, garlands, roast pigs and other gifts for the Queen were continually visiting it, and from its kitchens came the most exciting and reliable gossip in town. In the gardens, watched over by the burly Tongan policemen in khaki valas and bushranger hats who kept formal guard over the Palace gate, wandered another famous occupant, Tui Malilo.

Queen Salote's palace

Tui Malilo was a tortoise and, reputedly, the oldest living animal in the world. According to tradition, he and a female tortoise were presented to a Tongan chief, Sioeli Pangia, by Captain Cook in either 1773 or 1777. The chief later gave them to the daughter of the Tui Tonga. After sixty years, the female died and Tui Malilo went to live in the village of Malilo which gave him his name. Finally he came to Nuku'alofa.

If the story was true, he must have been at least 183 years old, exceeding in age another famous tortoise which was brought from the Seychelles to Mauritius in 1766 and which survived until 1918 when it fell through a gun emplacement. Unfortunately, however, Cook does not mention making such a gift in his journals, and even if he did present a tortoise there is no way of proving that Tui Malilo is the same animal. It may be that he was brought to Tonga at a later date by some other vessel, for sailing ships often carried tortoises on board as a ready and convenient supply of fresh meat.

Tui Malilo

However this may be, Tui Malilo was now extremely old. His shell was battered and dented by a series of accidents that had befallen him during his long life – he was trodden on by a horse, trapped in a bush fire and half crushed beneath a blazing log, and for many years past he had been totally blind. The loss of his sight prevented him from being able to forage for himself, so every day someone from the Palace brought him ripe pawpaw and boiled mandioca. Much of the work in the Palace gardens was undertaken by convicts, and this particular job was often carried out by a large and extremely amiable murderer.

Tongatapu, the main island on which Nuku'alofa stands, is extremely fertile. Much of it is covered by plantations of coconuts, the regularity of the rows in which they were originally planted disguised by their swerving grey trunks. But everything seemed to grow in abundance. The people cultivated some twenty different sorts of breadfruit. Taro grew luxuriantly, producing gigantic glossy leaves shaped like those of English arum to which it is related. The villages were not particularly tidy or well kept, but they never seemed shabby as African villages so often do, for the grass grew richly green between the huts, and flowering trees and shrubs blossomed in profusion. Everywhere hedges of hibiscus flaunted trumpets of blazing scarlet with pistils loaded with yellow pollen, and frangipani trees were almost as common, their bloated finger-like twigs sometimes bare but more often exploding into a spray of fragrant blossom.

Scenically, the most beautiful part of the island is the south-eastern coast. It seems that the whole of Tongatapu has been tilted, the northern side having sunk and the southern risen. As a result, the ancient limestone cliffs of the south are now some distance inland beyond the reach of the sea, and the rock platform, that the waves once cut at their foot beneath the surface of the sea, is now exposed above the level of the water. The Pacific rollers that crash on to this side of Tonga break against the outer edge of the platform and have eroded a series of pipes in the joints of the limestone. As each breaker surges in, these blowholes spout plumes of spray twenty feet high with a whistling roar, and water cascades into the shallow lagoons on the top of this platform. The spouting seawater is forced through the pipes at such pressure that it dissolves some of the limestone and this is later deposited to form a series of small terraces around the nozzles of the blowholes. The sight of the whole coast smoking when heavy seas are running and the feathery jets tumbling into the miraculously clear blue lagoons is extremely spectacular and the Tongans, who take a positive pleasure in scenes of natural beauty, often come down to the coast to hold feasts and watch the thundering blowholes.

Ve'ehala took us down there with Vaea, the nobleman in whose territory the blowholes lie, and gave us a feast. Together with some of the senior men of the nearby village of Houma, we sat in the shade of a few pandanus trees that formed a little thicket on the bare coral rock, and the women from the village brought us *polas* for the feast. Each pola consisted of a frame of plaited coconut leaves about six feet long, in the middle of which lay a small roast sucking pig flanked by two chickens, boiled yams, mandioca, sweet potato, red slices of watermelon, bananas, boiled Tongan puddings and young husked coconuts full of sweet cool milk. Garlands were hung around our necks and a group of musicians sang to us as we feasted, accompanying themselves on guitars and ukeleles.

After we had eaten, we went up into the village to watch the making of tapa cloth. Bark is first stripped from the thin stems of the paper mulberry tree and soaked for several days. Then the rough outer layer is torn away leaving only the white pliable inner cortex, and women, sitting in a line behind a log with a specially flattened surface, beat the strips with square-headed mallets. Each end of the log is slightly raised above the ground so that as it is struck it rings clear and an energetic team of tapa beaters produces a quick rhythmic tattoo of high-pitched notes which is one of the most common and characteristic sounds of a Tongan village. Beneath the blows of the mallet, the original three-inch strip soon quadruples its width. As it broadens, so

Women making tapa

Patterning the cloth

it thins. Then it is doubled and folded and beaten again until it has become a gauzy cream-coloured sheet eighteen inches wide and over two feet long.

When a woman has accumulated several hundred of these sheets, she invites her friends to help her make the final cloth. They use a long bench with a curved top on which are placed patterns made of creepers sewn on to dried palm leaves. The sheets of tapa are laid on top, three or four layers thick and stuck together with smears of a glutinous boiled root. Then they are rubbed with a cloth soaked in a brown dye so that the design from the patterns beneath appears on the cloth.

The finished tapa may be as much as fifty yards long with a bold and handsome design in richly varied russet brown, sometimes outlined later with black. It is used for skirts and for wall hangings, for sashes and for bedding, a single sheet of it being warmer than a thick woollen blanket. It is exported to Fiji where it is regarded as being much superior to the Fijian-made material, and it is used for ceremonial gifts, particularly in offerings made to the Queen.

At last the day of the Royal Kava Ceremony arrived. It was to be held on the *mala'e*, the ceremonial ground adjoining the Palace on the shores of the bay that is Nuku'alofa's equivalent of London's Horse Guards Parade. Geoff, Jim and I went down there in the early morning with all our equipment. On the side nearest the palace, in the shade of a line of magnificent Norfolk Island pines, a small thatched pavilion had been built which would be occupied by Queen Salote. As we arrived its floor was being covered by layer upon layer of tapa cloth.

Ve'ehala, carrying a staff and wearing an ancient and voluminous mat around his waist, appeared soon after. Then, one by one, the aristocracy of Tonga appeared on the mala'e. There were nobles from the island of Ha'apai, a hundred miles away to the north, and from Vava'u, yet another hundred miles beyond. Many were old men with close-cropped grey hair and deeply lined faces. Each was accompanied by his *mata'pule*, his squire or spokesman. Not for very many years had so many attended at one ceremony, for the Queen had let it be known that the record must be complete and no one had failed to appear. If it had not been for the fact that the positions in the circle had been the subject of great discussions for weeks past there would doubtless have been many heated arguments about the seating. Even so, Ve'ehala was called upon to adjudicate on a number of occasions. At the far end of the ring, opposite the Royal Pavilion, shrouded by leaves lest it crack in the sun, lay a gigantic kava bowl, almost five feet across, its surface coated with a thin film of pearly white enamel deposited over many years by the kava that had been mixed in it. Behind it clustered the *to'a*, people from the village whose noble was being installed.

Posted at the far end of the ground stood several policemen to turn away anyone who was not entitled to see the ceremony. Only the Spilliuses, Geoff and I of the European community had been granted permission to watch and it is likely that we were the first ever to have been given the privilege.

At last the circle was complete, arcing round from the pavilion to the kava bowl, nearly a hundred yards in diameter. The Queen alone was absent. Then the ceremony began. The people from the to'a brought the ceremonial gifts into the centre of the ring. The types of gift, though not the quantity of each, were specified by ritual. There were two gigantic tapa cloths, several hundred coconut leaf baskets, some full of mandioca, some of fish and some of chicken. Roast pigs were brought in whole, with their livers skewered to their chests; there were several different sizes, each with its own name, each with its distinctive type of preparation. The largest, the *puaka toko*, was hauled in on a platform of poles, the men singing an impressive tuneful chant. Lastly came the kava bushes, the largest of all, the *kava a toko*, also being hauled in accompanied by chants.

When all the offerings had been assembled in lines in the

ring, they were counted, men from the to'a lifting each up in turn, for it was important that all should know how much of each type of gift had been subscribed by the noble's people. All the members of the ring chanted thanks for the gifts. The counters retired to the to'a and silence fell. The stage was now set for the arrival of the Queen.

Counting the offerings at the Royal Kava Ceremony

She appeared from the Palace gardens, a truly regal figure, tall and statuesque, wearing a ta'ovala over five hundred years old and a wide thick sinnet belt.

The ceremony now became extremely sacred, *tapu*. First, one of the roast pigs was presented to her. With swift strokes of the knife, the carcass was dismembered and special parts of it were taken to particular nobles. Some were entitled to eat their share immediately, others were not permitted to do so. The Queen received the regal allotment of the liver. The kava toko was next taken down to the kava bowl where it was broken into pieces, and one section of it pounded. At a command from an official, Motu'apuaka, sitting outside the pavilion, all the offerings were then removed from the ring. With slow hieratic gestures, the

Mixing the royal kava

man sitting behind the bowl began to prepare the kava. Water was poured into the crushed root from hollow coconuts and then, using a large bundle of white hibiscus fibres as a strainer, he began the mixing. His actions were stylized and exaggerated, for all in the kava ring must see that the correct movements were being employed. Again and again he bent forward, gathered the fragments of root in the strainer and then lifted them to twist and squeeze the fibres around his arm.

At last the mixing was completed. At a call from Motu'apuaka, a coconut cupful was taken to the Queen. She lifted it to her lips. Then, one after another for the next hour and a half, everyone

Queen Salote drinking kava at the royal ceremony

drank in the prescribed order. When the last had been served, the Queen stood up and walked slowly back to the Palace. The Royal Kava Ceremony was over.

It had had none of the spectacular qualities of the Pentecost jump, yet curiously it had been more impressive. Whereas the earlier ceremony we had seen had been an athletic feat, in this, the atmosphere had been sacramental and very moving.

The time for our departure was now rapidly approaching. We spent our last days wandering through the villages and along the coast trying to record on film something of the island's magic that had captured both Geoff and me. It seemed impossible. The more we filmed the waving palm trees, the sparkling lagoon and the thatched huts, the more we realized that Tonga's special quality came not from the island, for we had filmed others that were more picturesquely beautiful, but from the people themselves. They were hard-working, devoted to their Queen and passionate in their attachment to the Church, but their over-whelming characteristic was contentment. In repose their faces always relaxed into a smile – a marked contrast to the furrowed foreheads and set mouths that had characterized the New Hebrideans. But happiness and contentment are not easy things to capture on celluloid.

One evening, we came home late and tired from filming all day in the blazing sun by the blowholes at Houma. As I entered our front door, I thought for a moment that we had come to the wrong house, for our living room was unrecognizable. Chains of hibiscus blossom hung from the walls and across the windows. A huge spray of cannas filled one corner and the mat-covered floor had been cleared except for the table which had been pushed to one side and loaded with pineapples, bananas, water-melons and roast chickens. As I stood, dusty and astonished, staring in the doorway, a young man from the Palace emerged from the kitchen wearing a brightly coloured vala and a flower behind his ear.

'Her Majesty understands that you have had a hard day's work,' he said. 'She has decided therefore that you should have a party.'

Behind me I heard an unmistakable high-pitched giggle. I turned and saw Ve'ehala resplendent in an enormous ta'ovala, quaking with delighted laughter. The music of guitars came from the room in front and a line of Palace dancing girls, grass-skirted and garlanded, advanced from the kitchen, singing as they came. Ve'ehala pushed us in through the door. Vaea was already there and within the next few minutes many more of our Tongan friends arrived. Soon the room was filled with singing, dancing, laughing people. It was past two o'clock in the morning before the last of them left us.

Had we found the people of paradise? Few of the Europeans we met in Nuku'alofa would have said so. To them the island was a backwater where nothing ever happened and they were bored. Ships only called at very long intervals so that you could not always get exactly what you wanted in the island's few shops and post from the outside world was often intolerably delayed. But perhaps their reactions were understandable, for they had come to Tonga to deal with matters that were quite foreign to the island's life – with electricity and the telephone service, with engineering and commerce – and they were the prisoners of their own professions, endeavouring to work as though they were part of an industrial community, when in fact they were living among a people to whom time, schedules, ledgers and the double entry system of accountancy seemed to be among the least important things in life.

But I suspect that to the Tongans themselves their island seemed the nearest approximation to paradise that can be found on earth. It is very fertile; there are always fish to be caught in the lagoon; each man has a plot of land of his own and can never starve. Life, indeed, is abundantly good. Flowers are beautiful, food sweet-tasting, girls pretty and music beguiling. The day has its duties but they are not so demanding that there is not ample time to enjoy its many pleasures.

Perhaps if I had stayed longer, I, like the other Europeans on the island, would have become discontented. I longed to find out.

BOOK TWO

Zoo Quest to Madagascar

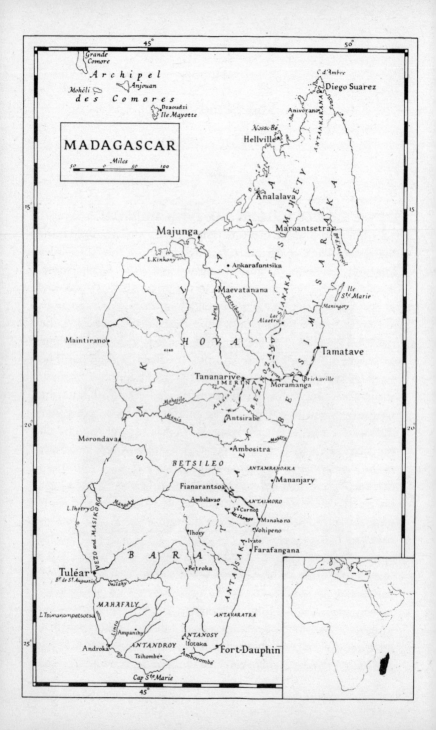

IO

The Island Attic

The island of Madagascar, on a map of the world, appears to be no more than a tiny insignificant chip splintered from the eastern flank of Africa. In fact it is huge – a thousand miles long and four times the area of England and Wales. Furthermore, in the nature of its animals, its plants and its people, it is almost as different from Africa as is Australia, four thousand miles away.

Geoff Mulligan and I flew to it from Nairobi. We left the coast near Zanzibar to begin our crossing of the sparkling blue Mozambique Channel that separated us from Madagascar. The small pyramids of the Comoro Islands, girdled in surf, materialized ahead, crept slowly towards us as we hung droning in the sky, passed beneath our port wing and disappeared astern. Then, less than two hours after leaving Africa, Madagascar loomed on the hazy horizon. We were approaching a new world. Nowhere in the forests and plains ahead would we find any of the creatures that teemed on Kenya's savannahs – no monkeys, no antelope, no elephant, no great carnivorous beasts of prey. In the short time that it had taken us to make the crossing, we had travelled back through fifty million years of evolutionary time. We were entering one of Nature's lumber rooms, a place where antique outmoded forms of life that have long since disappeared from the rest of the world still survive in isolation.

The fascination of lumber rooms does not depend solely on nostalgia. A wax cylinder from an old Edison phonograph may intrigue you because in its day it was new and revolutionary, and because in it you may perceive the seeds of the sophisticated apparatus of our own time. Sometimes among the attic's dust and cobwebs, you may discover a curious gimcrack gadget that left no successors and is now so outdated that its function is now a mystery. Lift the creaking lid of a forgotten trunk and you may pull out a bustle or a dress of such eccentric design that you marvel at the wild changes of taste and fashion. The same fascination, the same sense of entering the past, possesses anyone who begins to study Madagascar's animals. They too are survivors from a bygone age; they too, for us who are familiar with the highly evolved creatures that throng the rest of the world, are bizarre and strange. In them we may see our past.

Fifty million years ago Madagascar and Africa were one. The world, though old in geological terms, had not yet produced monkeys or apes, and the highest branch of the evolutionary tree, which would eventually lead to man, was occupied by creatures called lemurs. They already possessed many of the characteristics which later typified the monkeys. The form and proportion of their bodies were similar and they had human-like grasping hands and feet. Yet their faces were snouted and fox-like. Their nostrils, shaped like inverted commas, resembled those of a dog or cat. Their brains were relatively small and had not developed the complex lobes in the front part of their skulls that seem to be the seat of higher intelligence.

The lemurs, in their heyday, were a very successful group. Madagascar, which seems to have been their headquarters, was at this time connected with the other continents of the world and the lemurs prospered and spread widely, leaving their bones as fossils in the rocks of England, France, and North America. But some twenty million years ago, two great changes took place. First, Madagascar became isolated as an island; and secondly, more highly developed creatures emerged from the vast evolutionary ferment of Africa. With these animals, which included the bigger-brained monkeys and the large carnivores, the lemurs could no longer compete successfully for food and territory. As a result, most of the lemurs and their close relations outside Madagascar became extinct, only a few managing to survive as small unobtrusive creatures that found protection in the gloom of thick forests – the potto, angwantibo and galago in Africa, the lorises in Asia. But on the island itself, the main body of lemurs was safe, protected by the surrounding sea, a barrier which the more modern mammals of Africa could not cross. As a result, Madagascar's population of lemurs has continued to proliferate and has evolved into a great variety of forms.

Today there are over twenty distinct species. Some, in their size and habits, resemble mice, some squirrels, some civets. A group of them are monkey-like and one creature can best be compared with an ape. Yet although these animals are the representatives of one of man's early ancestors and are therefore of absorbing interest to zoologists, they are surprisingly little known. Only one or two flourish in captivity and can be studied in zoos. Many have never been taken alive out of Madagascar.

The peculiarity of the island's fauna does not rest solely on the presence of the lemurs. There are also many other odd creatures – hedgehog-like beasts called tenrecs, that have close relations only in the heart of the Congo and the Caribbean; snakes whose affinities lie not with African pythons but with the boas of South America; and forty-six genera of birds which live nowhere else in the world.

We stared down in fascination at the forests, the red muddy rivers, and the gaunt hills beneath us. Within the next few days we knew we should be seeing some of these creatures for ourselves. I found it hard to restrain my impatience.

We landed at Madagascar's main airport in the middle of the island. I am not sure what I expected to see on our drive from the airfield to the capital city, twenty miles away, but certainly it was not what we found. Though the sun was shining with tropical brilliance, the air was cool and fresh for we were in highlands, over three thousand feet above the sea. The treeless rolling hills were not cultivated with fields of corn or cassava as they would have been had this been Africa, but instead every fold and corner of the landscape was terraced into neat rice paddies. We might have been somewhere in Asia. The faces of the people standing by the roadside reinforced this impression for they had light brown complexions and straight black hair, like Malayans. On the other hand their clothes – broad-brimmed felt hats and sheet-like wraps of bright cloth worn over the shoulder – gave them the look of South American peones. The buildings in the villages through which we drove were neither primitive mud huts nor fenced kraals, but spindly red-brick two-storey houses with steeply pitched roofs and narrow first-floor balconies supported on thin square columns.

The names of the villages were frighteningly unpronounceable – Imerintsiatosika, Ampahitrontenaina, Ambatomirahavavy. I foresaw with gloom appalling difficulties in finding our way around the island if these words were typical of the place names. The task, though I did not know it at the time, was in the event even greater than I imagined, for Malagasy words are seldom pronounced as they are written. First and last syllables are usually ignored and whole rows of letters in the middle are either condensed or forgotten in a fashion so extreme that the standard examples of the perverse pronunciations of English place names seem laughably simple. One name at least has been rationalized for the sake of the stranger – Antananarivo, the capital, has always been pronounced Tananarive. Now it, at least, is spelt that way.

The city itself is perched on a series of hills which rise from a flat plain of rice fields circling the city so completely that during catastrophic floods a few years earlier the capital was transformed into an island accessible only by boat.

On the highest peak dominating the town stands a four-square building designed by a British architect in the middle of the nineteenth century. It was once the palace of Madagascar's last

Tananarive

Queen who signed a treaty of friendship with the French, and was later deposed by them when she did not fulfil its conditions.

From the end of her reign until a few months before we had arrived, when the Malagasy had regained their independence, the French had occupied and governed the island. French words sounded everywhere; French gesticulations were used as aids to bargaining in the markets. The pretty Malagasy girls had learned a great deal from French chic and walked on high heels, wearing the most elegant clothes with their long glossy hair upswept in sophisticated coiffures. The city's restaurants served excellent five-course meals accompanied by wines from Burgundy and the Rhône, and the streets breathed the subtle blended perfume of Gauloise and garlic that you can savour as well in Dakar or Algiers as you can in Paris.

Geoff and I planned in the next three months to film many of Madagascar's animals and, if we were allowed to do so, to catch a few examples to take back to the London Zoo. We knew that all lemurs were protected, but we hoped that we might be given permission to catch one or two of the more abundant species. Accordingly, we called on M Paulian, the Director of the Scientific Institute. He welcomed us hospitably and listened courteously to our plans and aspirations.

'I am sorry,' he said, 'but I must ask you not to catch any lemurs whatever. It is forbidden by law for anyone to kill one or even to keep one as a pet. Of course, we have not the staff to enforce such a law throughout the whole of Madagascar so our officials and those from the Forestry Department have been trying to persuade people that it is wrong to harm lemurs. Now, at last, we are beginning to have success. But if you now begin to catch the animals, and to get the people to help you to do so, they will believe that there is one law for the white foreigner and one for the native, and much of our work will be undone. I ask you, as a naturalist with a concern for wildlife, to do as I request and not to hinder our attempts to conserve these rare animals.'

There could be no reply but assent to such a plea.

'Film them by all means,' M Paulian continued. 'Such records will be extremely valuable, for few people have done so. I will give you permits to collect many of the other animals that are in no danger of extinction, and I will provide you with an assistant who can act as a guide and interpreter.'

M Paulian was even better than his word. Within a few days he had enabled us to hire a Land Rover, he had provided us with permits to enter many of the Forestry Reserves in the remoter parts of the island, and he had introduced us to Georges Randrianasolo, a young Malagasy from the laboratories who in the course of his work had travelled all over the island in search of birds and insect specimens for the Scientific Institute's collections. He was a short slim man with those spindly sinewy legs that look frail but are often a sign of extreme toughness. His eyes sparkled with enthusiasm when we outlined our plans to him. Clearly, he was as anxious to get started as we were.

II

Sifakas and Giant Birds

Three days later we were in our Land Rover driving down a metalled road. We had started. As we bowled down the open road, singing at the tops of our voices, our minds were full of the excitements and revelations that lay ahead.

Within an hour, the dynamo of our engine dropped off. Geoff fastened it back on with a bolt removed from the chassis and we were soon on our way again. It was, however, the first show of petulance by our car and highly indicative of its future attitude, for within a week or so it was to become extremely obstinate and alarmingly fragile. The bolt with which we fastened the dynamo was merely the first of a procession that were to migrate from the bodywork into intimate parts of the engine where they were to be forced into duties that no sane mechanical engineer would ever suggest they should perform. Had we known all this, perhaps we should have turned round and returned to Tananarive to look for another car, but in our euphoric mood the temporary loss of a dynamo seemed no more than a trivial interruption. We continued southwards, singing happily as though nothing had happened.

We drove three hundred miles that day through the rolling hills that form the spine of Madagascar. The roads were almost empty except for *taxis-brousse*, the little decrepit overloaded bush taxis that careered unsteadily between villages picking up anyone by the roadside who flagged them down. Although they were always so full that arms, legs and heads overflowed through their windows, we never saw them fail to pick up a possible fare. The people waited for them by the roadside, sitting on bundles or boxes, wrapped in their white togas, miles away from any visible settlement. If we had had room, we could have made a good trade ferrying passengers from village to village, but the back of our truck was packed almost to the roof with stores and equipment and it seemed impossible that anyone else could cram themselves inside. Impossible, that is, until we came across one of the taxis-brousse that had been so overloaded that its rear had subsided to the ground with a broken axle. It was then that we discovered that in fact we had room for two baskets of chickens, three men, a small boy and a lady who, by the most charitable estimate, weighed at least sixteen stone. We ended the day, and deposited our passengers, soon after dark in the town of Ambalavao. That night marked the end of easy driving.

When we continued southwards the next day, we travelled along a dusty pot-holed corrugated track that loosened our teeth in their sockets, made conversation inside the car well-nigh impossible, and caused the dynamo to drop off three times.

The scenery, however, was extremely spectacular. Mountains of bare rocks reared high on either side of the road, the grassy slopes at their bases strewn with grey boulders the size of houses. There were peaks shaped like cottage-loaves, like half-domes, like tremendous castellated ramparts. Georges named them all for us. The summits of many, he said, were used by the people as holy places in which to bury their dead. On one square-topped block, a whole tribe had once taken refuge in time of war, only to be starved into submission and then slaughtered by being thrown alive over the edge of the thousand-foot precipice.

There were few trees, for during the course of centuries the Malagasy have stripped their island of most of its forests, and soil erosion has bared the underlying rocks so that they stick through the shallow earth like the bones of a starving animal. In the past few decades, strenuous attempts have been made to replant the ravaged land, but the ground has so changed in character that the native trees can no longer flourish and the foresters have had

Mountains in central Madagascar

to plant instead eucalyptus saplings imported from Australia. Only they can thrive on the impoverished soil, but their uniform ranks make dull substitutes for the rich varied Malagasy bush.

On the third day of our southward drive, we had left behind even the eucalyptus, for we were entering the barren country of the south on whose parched sands only the most specialized desert plants can survive.

Great areas of the land had been planted with parallel lines of sisal, a Mexican plant the fibres of which are used for making rope. Each bush is a fearsome rosette of huge fleshy spears from the centre of which sprouted a tall mast bearing sprays of flowers, but for the most part the sand was colonized only by prickly pear and desiccated leafless thorn scrub.

Then suddenly there was a dramatic change. On either side of the road rose rank upon rank of slim unbranched vegetable pillars thirty feet high, each heavily armoured with spines and

South of Ambalavao

clothed with spiralling lines of small, oval leaves. A few of these stems were crowned at their tips with tassels of withered brown flowers. Though these weird plants resemble cactus, they are quite unrelated and belong to a group – Didierea – which is found nowhere else in the world but in this part of Madagascar.

These forests were our destination, for Georges was confident that in them we should find the first of the creatures we were seeking, the most monkey-like of all the lemurs, the sifaka.

Georges had suggested that we should stay that night in a village he called Fu-tak. Having now accustomed myself to the idiosyncrasies of Malagasy pronunciation, it was no surprise to find it marked on the map, north of the town of Ambovombé, as Ifotaka. It lay in the centre of a tract of Didierea bush, a small hamlet of tiny rectangular wooden hutches set in a grove of tamarind trees.

We set out early the next morning to look for the sifakas. The forests were unpleasant places in which to work. The spines of the Didierea trunks and the thorn bushes that grew between them caught in our clothes and tore our flesh. In many places our way was barred by half-fallen stems, so entangled in the underbrush that it was impossible either to step over them or to stoop beneath them. To pass them meant cutting a way through with knives, an action we were unwilling to take because of the noise we should undoubtedly make. Avoiding them often involved long detours which made it almost impossible for us to keep a straight course.

For an hour we picked our way through the dense, vicious forest. Ahead I detected a thinning in the Didierea palisades and I made gratefully towards it, hoping to find a reasonably open space in which to rest and take stock.

Geoff Mulligan in the Didierea forest

I slowly pushed aside a thin barbed branch with the tip of my knife and was about to step into the sunshine when I saw in the middle of the clearing, standing beside a low flowering bush, three small white figures. They were busily plucking the petals from the bush and with both hands cramming them into their mouths. I stood frozen and for a half minute the creatures continued feeding. Then Georges, coming up behind me and unaware of what I had seen, trod on a twig. As it cracked, all three animals looked round towards us and immediately they were off, leaping along the ground with their long hind legs together and their short arms held in front of them, like people competing in a sack race. Within a few seconds they had bounded across the clearing and disappeared into the Didierea.

Geoff had been standing by my shoulder and, for a moment, neither of us spoke, unwilling to break the spell of this enchanting vision.

Georges grinned happily.

'Sifaka,' he said. 'I told you they would be here and we will find them again for they have not gone far away.'

Quickly we fastened the camera on to its stand, fitted the long lens, and followed them into the bush. The assembled equipment was not only very heavy but extremely difficult to negotiate through the thorn thickets, the legs of the tripod continually catching in the matted branches. Fortunately, we did not have to carry it far, for within a few minutes Georges, who was scouting ahead, held up his hand. As quietly as possible, we crept towards him. He pointed and there, among the swaying Didierea stems, we glimpsed a patch of white fur. Cautiously we advanced, Georges and I holding aside the thinner branches to allow Geoff to carry his equipment through in silence.

At last we found a vantage point from which we could gain a relatively clear view. The sifaka, clinging to the top of a Didierea stem, was well aware of our presence, but it did not seem to be particularly alarmed. Perhaps it felt that it was much less vulnerable thirty feet up in the air than when it had been down on the ground and had first seen us.

A sifaka

Step by step, we moved the camera towards it until there was little point in approaching any nearer for Geoff was already able to take close-up shots of the animal's face through the telephoto lens. Its thick silky fur was snow white except for a russet brown patch on the top of its head. It had a long furry tail which it held curled up between its legs. Its face was bare of fur, jet-black and scarcely monkey-like, for it had a distinct muzzle. Its arms were considerably shorter than its legs, which explained why it had moved on the ground in an upright position. As it stared down at us with its blazing topaz eyes, it let out a curious grunting sneeze that might well be written down as 'sheefak'. This call, of course, is the origin of its name and though the word 'sifaka' is most usually pronounced by European zoologists as a trisyllabic word, the Malagasy, as is their habit, do not pronounce the last 'a' so that the name on their lips approximates very closely indeed to the animal's call.

I felt a sense not only of excitement but of privilege, for this creature does not flourish in captivity and very few naturalists had seen it alive. Because of this, although its detailed anatomy is well documented, not a great deal was known about its natural history. One thing all authorities were agreed upon is that the sifaka is a phenomenal jumper. Some anatomists claimed that it achieved its great leaps by gliding with the aid of a fold of skin which stretches between its upper arms and its chest.

Sifaka jumping between the Didierea stems

We were now in a good position to test the truth of this, for the sifaka ahead of us was on the brink of another open patch in the Didierea. If it were to retreat any further, it would either have to jump down into a lower tree or leap across to the next Didierea stem over twenty feet away. I guessed that it would prefer to leap if the distance was not, in fact, too great. We moved our cameras a little to one side so that we should get the best possible view and then Georges walked boldly towards the animal. It glared down at him, wide eyed, sneezed three or four times and then lost courage. It gathered itself together and with a tremendous spring of its powerful hind legs, it launched itself into space. As it shot through the air, it brought its hind legs forward so that both its hands and feet were ready to grasp the vertical stem ahead. As a result its body was upright, its tail streaming out behind. It landed with an audible thump and embraced the branch with its arms. As the stem shook with the impact, the acrobat looked back at us over its shoulder. There could be no doubt. It had achieved this prodigious leap solely by the tremendous power of its hind legs and without the aid of gliding of any kind. Already we had learned something.

The local people had a great deal of information to provide about the sifakas, but it was difficult to sort out fact from fancy. They said the animals have a knowledge of medicine and that an injured sifaka will plaster special leaves over its wound to ensure rapid healing. A female sifaka, according to another story, when she is about to give birth, will pluck the fur from her chest and forearms and build a soft cradle, weighting it down with pebbles so that the wind does not blow it away. This may possibly be true for some observers have reported that females with newborn babes seem to have very little fur in these places. On the other hand, as we discovered later, the youngsters cling to their mothers' bodies from a very early age, as do the young of apes, so that nest of fur so painfully produced could only be used for a very short time.

One charming belief certainly has a foundation in reality. In the early morning, the sifakas have the habit of climbing into the tallest tree and sitting there with their arms upraised, facing east, so that the first warming rays of the sun strike their chests.

The sifakas peered at us

The people say that they are devout religious creatures and are worshipping the sun. Partly because of this, the sifakas are held to be *fady* – taboo, and certainly in the old days, no one would have dared to harm them. Unfortunately for the animals, the old beliefs are rapidly dying, even in this, one of the remotest parts of Madagascar.

They were very trusting animals and as long as they were aloft in the branches and we did not move too abruptly, we could approach quite close to them without their taking to flight. Day after day we filmed them. They slept and spent most of their mornings in the Didierea forests high up on the waving stems, sunning themselves and feeding. During the hottest part of the day they descended to a lower level in the branches where they were less conspicuous and there they dozed, lolling about in the most unlikely and seemingly perilous positions, sometimes leaning against a trunk with their feet dangling, sometimes

hunched with their knees drawn up to their chins, and sometimes, most comic of all, lying full length along a bough with
an arm and a leg hanging free on either side.

Every afternoon at about four o'clock, one family of five
came close to the village to feed on the long bean-like fruits
that hung from the tamarind trees. They ran gaily up and down
the branches hand over hand like sailors clambering up rope
ladders, often venturing rather hesitantly on to the outermost
twigs to grasp particularly tempting fruit. For an hour or so,
they would sit munching contentedly above us with the sinking
sun turning their white fur the colour of honey. Then as darkness approached, they would leave and return to the security of
their Didierea fastnesses.

But one evening, two of them, a pair, lingered behind. The
female seated herself on a horizontal branch, swinging her legs
and combing her fur with her teeth. We saw the male approach
her from behind. She showed no sign of being aware of him.
Suddenly he sprang at her, almost knocking her from the
branch, and expertly put a half-nelson on her. She rolled over,
slipped out of his grip and caught his head in the elbow of
her left arm. He wriggled round, wrapped his arms round her
waist and squeezed her. She opened her mouth wide and
soundlessly. I could have sworn she was laughing. For five
minutes they tussled with one another. Then abruptly, they
stopped and, sitting beside one another, they peered down at
us forty feet below them. We did not move. The female suddenly
swung round and caught the male's upper arm with the long
grasping toes of her left foot, and the wrestling match entered
the second round.

This was not a true fight, for although they sometimes closed
their jaws on one another's arms or legs, they never bit one
another. They were playing.

Young animals often play, seemingly to learn and practise the
skills they will need when they are adult. A puppy will shake a
shoe as he will later shake a rat; a kitten will pounce on a ball

of wool practising the actions that will be necessary to catch a mouse later in life. Adult animals in captivity also develop games, largely it seems as an outlet for their energies which are not fully occupied. But examples of full-grown animals playing for pure enjoyment in the wild are rare. There is seldom time for recreation in the merciless world of nature.

But the sifakas did not seem to be faced by the problems that harass most animals. They had no need to search for food – mangoes, tamarinds, flower petals and succulent green shoots were plentiful and easily found. Neither were they perpetually haunted by fear or the need to hide, for they have no natural enemies. And there was a further, more fundamental factor in their lives – they lived in families.

If you watch a troop of monkeys, you are soon aware that the social structure of their community is based on a strict hierarchical system. Each monkey is well aware of its position. It cringes to its superiors, it bullies mercilessly those who are socially beneath it. As a result, you seldom if ever see two adults engaged in a game which has no purpose but pleasure.

We discerned no such system among the sifakas. Their family life seemed to be based on affection. During the many hours that we watched them, we never saw a squabble and many times, as on this occasion, we saw them playing or caressing one another.

It was an enchanting sight and we sat beneath their tree watching them for over an hour. At last, the sun began to turn red. The female broke away from her mate's grasp. With her left leg she deftly kicked her tail away from the branch, like a Victorian lady swinging her long train into position behind her. The male followed her and together they wandered back through the branches towards their dormitory in the Didierea.

From Ifotaka and its weird forests of Didierea, we drove west-wards into a country even more parched and dry. Often the wheels of our car were a foot deep in sand. If we travelled slowly we lost impetus and sank to a halt in the thicker drifts, spouting plumes of sand from the backs of the wheels. If we travelled at speed, we slid uncontrollably from side to side in a way that would have been very unnerving had there been anything to hit on either side of the road other than thorn bushes, euphorbias or sisal plants. In between the tracts of sand, we changed into the low-ratio gears and roared our way over steep ridges of rock in a series of thumping jolts and crashes.

The car, understandably, did not take kindly to this treatment so inappropriate to her age and condition. By the time we had reached the small town of Ampanihy, she could go no further. A shock absorber had been torn off her chassis, the bolts in one shackle had sheared and, because of a puncture, we had put into use her spare tyre which was a laughable patchwork of thin pitted rubber and naked canvas.

For a day we worked on her. Geoff's mechanical ingenuity was taxed to the utmost and I, in the course of recounting our troubles to an interested crowd of spectators and advisors, greatly increased my vocabulary of French mechanical terms. Georges scoured the markets and the Indian-owned stores and returned with a varied selection of rusty nuts, bolts and antique sparking plugs. Some of these we used immediately so that we might restore a few of the bolts doing service in the engine and the suspension to their rightful places in the bodywork. The remainder we kept as spares.

When at last we had patched her up, we set out again towards the south-west corner of the island. We camped a few miles from the coast at a point marked on our map with a blue line and the words Linta Fleuve. We had expected a river. We found a river-bed half a mile wide, flanked with low cliffs, but filled only with dry hot sand.

We had come to these deserts for one particular reason – to search for the largest eggs in the world, eggs which may well have given rise to the legend of the rukh.

Our camp

Arab folk tales are full of references to this gigantic creature. The Crusaders returning to Europe in the Middle Ages brought back some of the stories; and the most widely known reference occurs in the saga of Sindbad the Sailor, who, as is related in the Arabian Nights, found an egg as big as a house. Unknown to him, it belonged to this monstrous bird, the rukh. Some of his companions cracked it and in revenge the rukh flew above their ship, darkening the sun with its wings, and dropped boulders upon them, eventually sinking their ship.

To Marco Polo, in the thirteenth century, the rukh was no legend but a real animal and he described it in detail.

'It was for all the world like an eagle, but one indeed of enormous size; so big in fact that its wings covered an extent of thirty paces and its quills were twelve paces long and thick in proportion. And it is so strong that it will seize an elephant in its talons and carry him high into the air and drop him so

The rukh, from Linschoten's Voyages, 1595

that he is smashed to pieces; having so killed him, the bird swoops down on him and eats him at leisure.'

Polo never claimed to have seen this monstrous creature, but in proof of its existence he described its feather which had been sent to Kublai Khan, his master. It was ninety spans long and the quill two palms in circumference. This impressive object seems to have been a withered palm frond, no doubt rare and unfamiliar in thirteenth-century Pekin. Polo, however, went further. Although he had not visited the area, he had reliable reports that the bird lived in the islands 'south of Madagascar'. At first reading, this makes little sense, for there are no islands south of Madagascar for several hundred miles, but the reference is not as meaningless as it seems. Polo describes 'Madagascar' as being rich in camels and a great centre for trade in 'elephants' teeth'. Neither detail is true of the island we today call Madagascar. It is likely that Polo was in fact referring to Mogadishu on the north-eastern coast of Africa where there are certainly plenty of camels and ivory. If this is so, then 'south of Mogadishu' must refer to Madagascar and its satellites, Réunion and Mauritius. Furthermore, his informants may have had a good reason to believe that the rukhs lived hereabouts, a reason that the world of European learning did not become aware of until 1658, over three centuries later.

In that year, a Frenchman, Sieur Etienne de Flacourt, who had been appointed by his king Director of the French East India Company and Governor of Madagascar, published the first book on the island. It is a remarkably detailed work and contains lists of the plants, minerals, fish, insects, mammals and birds. Among them is this entry: 'The vouron patra is a giant bird that lives in the country of the Ampatres people (in the south of Madagascar) and lays eggs like the ostrich; it is a species of ostrich; so that the people of these places may not catch it, it seeks the loneliest places.'

The report was an unsensational one and at a time when every voyage produced stories of fresh wonders and discoveries, it attracted little attention and was soon forgotten. But in 1832, another Frenchman, Victor Sganzin, saw one of the eggs of the 'vouron patra'. The people were using it as a water bottle. It was astonishingly large – over a foot long, six times the size of an ostrich egg. Sganzin managed to buy one from the natives and sent it back to Paris by merchant ship. Unfortunately, the vessel was wrecked and sank at La Rochelle and the egg was lost. It was not until 1850 that Europe saw these strange objects – three of them and some fragments of bone that were brought to France by a sea captain named Abadie.

For several years there was a great controversy in learned circles about the identity of the bird that laid these gigantic eggs. Some authorities stoutly maintained that the creature must have been some sort of eagle, as Marco Polo had described. Others thought that it was a huge penguin, or a giant rail. The question was finally decided beyond doubt when some enormous bird bones were recovered from a swamp in central Madagascar. From them it was quite clear that the bird was ostrich-like and flightless. It had stood nearly ten feet high and the scientists named it Aepyornis.

Although it was not the tallest bird that ever existed – some species of extinct moas of New Zealand stood a little higher – it was very stockily built and was almost certainly the heaviest of all birds, weighing, according to some estimates, nearly one thousand pounds.

Flacourt had been correct, and the fact that he had described the giant bird as being a species of ostrich, coupled with his ignorance of its bones or of comparative anatomy which might

A reconstruction of the Aepyornis

otherwise have led him to such a conclusion, must surely mean that his informants had actually seen the living creature. Now, sadly, the birds are certainly extinct, for enormous though Madagascar is, no part of it is so little known that it could still conceal a creature the size of an Aepyornis. Nonetheless, there are still gigantic eggs to be found and I hoped that we might discover, if not an entire egg, then at least a small fragment of one in the sands around the dry Linta River.

———

We had pitched our tent beneath a cuphorbia tree which grew close by the only source of water for many miles around – a thirty-foot-deep well. People came from far distant settlements to draw up brimming buckets for themselves and the herds of cattle and goats they brought with them. The beasts were kept in the shade of a thorn scrub thicket a hundred yards away and allowed down a few at a time to suck greedily at the water that had been poured out for them in open concrete tanks beside the well.

Geoff and I began our search for the egg fragments. The sun blazed ferociously from the cloudless sky, roasting the dunes. The surface of the sand was so hot that walking barefoot on it would have been, for us at least, acutely painful, and the glare reflected from it was so bright that we had to screw up our eyes. Hour after hour we plodded on, the sand yielding with each step so that walking was doubly exhausting.

Barren though the desert seemed to be, we found many signs of life – the sinuous track of a snake, the trail of a lizard whose tail had left a thin wavy groove between its footprints, chains of short-shafted arrows left by small birds as they had pattered over the sand.

Spiders had draped the branches of the low thorn bushes with their webs and in some miraculous way had suspended empty snail shells from the lower edges to serve as hanging weights, keeping the silken nets taut. Beneath one bush, we found a handsome tortoise nearly two feet long, its chocolate-brown domed carapace starred with radiating lines of yellow. These creatures, we knew, are revered by many tribes. If a man meets one, he places a small offering on top of its shell and goes on his way, delighted by the encounter, for he regards it as a good omen. But the meeting did not have any particularly good effect on our fortunes and we trudged back to camp, hot, parched and empty-handed.

In the afternoon, after the worst of the heat of the day had subsided, we tried again. After two hours, I at last found something. Three small objects the size of a ten-penny piece and twice as thick. On one side they were dull; on the other, pale yellow and with a distinct grain. There could be no doubt, they were pieces of a gigantic egg. While we sat in the scanty shade of a fleshy-leaved bush, examining our finds, and spitting on them to clean their surface, a small mop-headed boy, dusty and naked except for a necklace of blue beads and a loin cloth, came

Fragments of Aepyornis eggs

towards us driving a herd of goats. I called him over and showed him our treasure.

'I look for big egg,' I said in French. 'These – small pieces – no good. I look for big pieces.'

He stared at me, completely nonplussed.

'*Œuf*,' I said earnestly. '*Grand œuf*.' But no flicker of expression passed over his impassive young face.

I knew my French was poor, but I doubt if he would have understood a true-born Frenchman. He obviously spoke only his local Malagasy dialect. I tried once more. I waved my hands graphically to indicate the shape and size of the object I was seeking. But it was no use. The boy looked past me, noticed that his goats were straying, hurled a stone at them and ran off.

Small though the fragments were, we were delighted with them. Back at camp, I showed them to Georges with considerable pride. Although for modesty's sake I did not put it into words, I hoped that I was able to suggest that I had been remarkably sharp-eyed to have discovered these tiny pieces in the empty wastes surrounding the camp.

When I awoke the next morning, a tall gaunt woman wrapped in a sheet was standing in front of the tent staring at me through the mosquito netting. On her head, she carried a large basket. She touched her forehead and her heart with her right hand in the Arab gesture of greeting. I struggled out of my sleeping bag, trying to gather my wits sufficiently to embark on the long conversational battle in mangled French that I was sure would be necessary in order to discover what she wanted. I should not have worried. The woman had no need of words, her actions spoke for themselves. She simply took the basket from her head and poured on to the ground a cascade of egg fragments.

I looked at them, flabbergasted. Not only was it clear that the little herd boy the previous day had understood precisely what I had been doing out in the desert and had spread the news to his village, but also it was equally evident that, far from being sharp-eyed in finding my three fragments, I must have been almost blind. This woman had collected at least five hundred in a few hours.

I tried to thank her and gave her a reward. She touched her forehead again as a sign of thanks and strolled gracefully away, with the splendid erect bearing that comes to all people who habitually carry burdens on their heads.

By now, Georges and Geoff were also awake. After running our fingers through the huge hoard in wonderment, we set about making coffee. Before the kettle boiled, a second woman arrived. She too carried a basketload of egg fragments.

'It's a good job that lad *didn't* understand your French,' said Geoff. 'You might have offered him five francs a piece, and if you had, we would have been bankrupt by now.'

We had clearly been more successful than I had believed possible in asking for egg fragments. But now, when we tried to spread the word that we did not want any more, we were quite unable to stop the avalanche of shell that poured into the camp. Every hour a fresh contribution arrived and by the end of the day the pile beneath the euphorbia tree was over a foot high. It was astonishing evidence of how abundant the Aepyornis had once been. The shells of all birds' eggs are composed of calcium carbonate, but whereas most are paper thin and therefore quickly reduced to powder, the massive thick shells of Aepyornis are not easily destroyed. Thus, as each generation of Aepyornis chicks were hatched, the egg fragments were left scattered through the land to accumulate in great numbers.

My original aim had been to find a piece or two. That had seemed to be a sufficiently formidable task, but now that we had discovered how common they were, I became more ambitious. It was too much to hope that we might find a complete unbroken egg, for after all only the rare addled or infertile ones would remain whole and many of these, in the course of subsequent centuries, must have been smashed. But all the pieces brought to us by the women were relatively small. I now hoped that we might find a really large piece which would provide, from its curvature, some idea of the size of the original egg.

The next day, Geoff and I decided to search separately in order to cover more ground. Now we knew exactly what to look for, we saw pieces everywhere and I returned to camp with my pockets bulging. I found Geoff sitting not far from camp in the bottom of a deep hole with piles of freshly excavated sand all around him. He had reasoned, very sensibly, that if he could not find a really large piece, the next best thing was to make an intensive search of a single promising site in order to assemble a dozen or so fragments that might have come from one individual egg and would therefore fit together. He had been remarkably successful and showed me proudly fourteen pieces that he had discovered within a foot or so of one another. We took them back to the tent, washed them and began trying to piece them together. Two fragments at least belonged to one another.

It was while we were trying to find a third piece to join on to them that the little herd boy reappeared. He strolled in nonchalantly, carrying something wrapped in a grubby scrap of cloth. He put it down on the ground and untied the knots. Inside lay about twenty pieces, some quite tiny, some the size of small plates and twice as big as any we had seen before. Georges was away from camp pursuing his birds, so I tried to question the boy myself. Had he gathered them from several different places, or had the whole collection come from one spot? I could get no answer. I paid the lad a large reward and he trotted back to his goats by the well without a word or a smile.

We spread out the pieces on the sand, outside-up, and stared at them. It was as though we were playing with a jigsaw. With an ordinary jigsaw you at least know that all the pieces belong to the same puzzle, that all of them are in front of you and that they all fit together to form a complete picture. This was more difficult and far more exciting. Were these pieces from several eggs? Were there enough to make a reasonably complete whole?

After a few minutes of trial and error I spotted two sections whose angular edges echoed one another. They fitted together. I fastened them with adhesive tape. Then I saw another pair, and a fifth piece that fitted on to the first two. At the end of an hour, we had two large cups. I held one in each hand and carefully brought them together. They matched perfectly. Only a few small sections were missing.

The complete egg was of astonishing size. In length it was almost exactly a foot. Its girth was 27 inches; its longest circumference, measuring over the two ends, 32½ inches. The smallest fragments had fitted together on one side, the lines of the joins radiating like the spokes of a wheel from a central point. This might have been the spot where a blow had landed and shattered the egg in comparatively recent times. I preferred to imagine, more romantically, that it was the place where the young Aepyornis chick, which must have been an extremely powerful little creature, had hammered its way out into the world with its beak.

Geoff Mulligan with the completed egg

Why had the birds become extinct? The most likely explanation was a change in climate. Madagascar has certainly got drier through the centuries. The parched bed of the wide Linta River was an indication of the change. The huge weight of the Aepyornis, together with the proportions of its bones, have led some scientists to suggest that the birds inhabited swamps: when drought overtook the island, the birds lost their natural habitat and perished. But the eggs must surely have been very valuable as food for the local people. So it may well be that hungry human nest-robbers were responsible for the elephant bird's ultimate extinction.

Which came first, the fabled rukh or the knowledge of these wondrous eggs? Perhaps the Arabs, sailing across the Mozambique Channel in their dhows, had seen the shells being used as containers for fresh water in the canoes of the fisher folk of the Madagascan coast and the myth grew from such a seed. Perhaps the legend was a widespread fancy flourishing independently in the Arab world which Marco Polo sought to substantiate later by linking it with the reports from Madagascar. No one can say.

For me, the deducible reality of the Aepyornis was as strange and exciting as any rukh, and as I held the complete egg in my hand, I had no difficulty in imagining the time when the bed of the Linta River was filled with a brown eddying flood and gigantic birds, nearly ten feet tall, waded magnificently through the swamps.

12

Flamingoes, Tenrecs and Mouse Lemurs

I cradled our precious reconstructed egg in my lap as we lurched and rattled our way back from the Linta River over the stone-strewn hills and through the Didierea forests, back northwards to Ampanihy and then westwards over better roads towards the Bay of Saint Augustine and the town of Tuléar.

Along the coast, both to the north and the south of Tuléar, lie several salt lakes which we had been told in Tananarive were the haunt of flocks of flamingoes. The first we visited was away to the south and had the unpronounceable name of Lac Tsimanampetsotsa. To reach it, we had to take a ferry across the Onilahy River, just south of the town, and then drive for a day through interminable dunes of sliding sand. The lake was a mile-long stretch of corrosively bitter, milky water and in the middle of it, far beyond the range of our lenses, we saw a group of a hundred or so flamingoes – tiny, angular shapes moving slowly through the heat haze. This was a great disappointment. Not only was it impossible to get near them, but the size of the flock was insignificant compared with the vast concourses, hundreds of thousands strong, that frequent the salt lakes of East Africa.

We talked to some of the people living in a small village by the lakeside, asking them whether the birds ever nested here, for although they were unfilmable now, if they should be breeding later on in the year, it would be well worth coming back with inflatable rubber boats and waders to protect our legs from the biting alkaline water and try to get pictures of them as they stood by their small mud nests. One or two of the older men said that, in years gone by, the flamingoes had nested on the salt flats at the northern end of the lake, but it was many years now since they had done so. I was unsure how much reliance to place on this piece of information. It sounded a little like the compromise that such people often politely make, with the kindest motives, between the news that they realize will make the stranger happy and the actual facts.

The next lake we decided to inspect was Lac Ihotry, the largest of those that lay to the north of Tuléar. The road that led us there, though uncomplicated by a ferry, was none the less not a simple or straightforward one. For many miles we travelled through sandhills. Then we veered inland and found ourselves crossing rolling plains studded with brown, conical termite hills as thick as concrete spikes in a tank trap. As we journeyed farther north, the vegetation became less sparse and soon we were among baobab trees, taller and more splendid than any I have seen in Africa. Their tremendous cylindrical trunks rose sheer for thirty or forty feet before producing little flat-topped sprays of twiggy branches so absurdly small in comparison with the bloated boles that they recalled a child's disproportioned attempt at drawing a normal tree. In Africa, people account for the baobab's ludicrous appearance by explaining that, in the beginning of time, the first baobab offended God and that He, in order to punish it, plucked it from the ground and thrust it back upside down, with its roots in the air.

Looking at them from a distance, it was difficult to appreciate fully their true size, for our eyes, as though refusing to admit the existence of a tree so outrageously gross, seemed to place them closer to us than they really were, thereby minimizing their size and making them more acceptable to our imaginations. It was only when we came across one that had fallen and lay prostrate by the side of the road that I fully comprehended their gigantic dimensions. The iron-grey flank dwarfed our Land Rover as it would have been by one of those vast steel boilers that are sometimes hauled through a town at dead of night, filling the entire road on their way to a shipyard.

The baobabs grew thickly around Lac Ihotry and it was between two of them that we caught a glimpse of pink. We drove on urgently and beyond we found the lake covered by a garrulous, honking, sublimely beautiful horde of flamingoes. I estimated that there were ten thousand of them, but there may well have been double that number.

We pitched camp by the lakeside, close to a village of fisher people, and on its muddy shore we erected a rectangular hide of hessian for our camera. Day after day, we crouched in this suffocating, airless enclosure, watching the birds as they dabbled through the tepid waters. There were two species mingled in the flocks – the Great Flamingo, standing over four feet tall, with a predominantly white body streaked with deep pink only

Lesser flamingoes

221

in its wings; and the Lesser Flamingo, a somewhat shorter bird, with a heavier black bill, and with its pink colour, though still concentrated on its wings, suffused more generally through much of its feathers.

In the mornings, the birds distributed themselves evenly over the southern end of the lake. Nowhere was it more than a foot or so deep and the flamingoes strode about in a dignified manner, lifting their thin pink legs high in the air, with their long necks sinuously drooping and their bent bills in the water. With pumping movements of their throats, they sucked water through the plates that line the interior of their beaks and so filtered out the tiny particles of food, expelling the excess water through the sides. The two species, though they employed the same type of filtering mechanism, dredge at different levels, the Lesser seeking the microscopic algae floating in the top few inches of the water, the Greater plunging its head deeper to collect small crustaceans and other tiny animals.

They fed in this manner until towards midday. By then the heat reflected from the surface of the lake was so intense that the air shimmered and the images of birds feeding more than a few yards away from us became blurred and quavering. Filming was impossible and we gladly left the sweltering hide and took refuge in the camp. Even there, the heat was inescapable. Seldom did the slightest breeze blow through the leafless trees and when it did it brought no relief for it was as hot and as dry as the breath from an oven. At this time the flamingoes themselves seemed to do little. Most of them had stopped feeding and were standing motionless by their reflections in the glassy waters.

By three o'clock, the temperature had fallen sufficiently for us to be able to get shimmer-free photographs and we would return to the hide, for by now the birds were behaving differently. No longer were they dredging, but they were leaving the feeding grounds. As each party took off and spread their wings, they revealed to the full the ravishing beauty of their red and black primary wing feathers, their reflections staining the waters of the lake the subtle, soft pink of a blush. They flew with their long legs trailing behind them, their necks outstretched, and landed in the slightly deeper water at the northern end of the lake. There some of them formed long queues, three or four individuals deep, that wound snake-like for several hundred yards. Others assembled into tightly packed companies and stood with their heads high, jostling and pushing one another. At a distance their thin legs were invisible, so that their clumped bodies coalesced to form a static, roseate cloud, suspended a foot or so above the surface of the water.

What were they doing? Were they preparing for a migratory flight? Or was this, perhaps, some form of mass courtship, preparatory to pairing? The more we watched them, the more I realized how little we knew about these beautiful flocks.

———

When the sun dropped behind the baobabs on the horizon and its reddening rays lost most of their heat, the pink of the flocks dissolved in the splendour of flame that lit the sky and shone in the waters of the lake. The big brown buzzards and white-naped crows perched in the tree tops, preening themselves, and for an hour or two it was sufficiently cool to make walking a pleasure. At this time, both we and the villagers went down to the lakeside to draw water from holes that had been dug a yard or so from its margin. This water, having been filtered through the ground, was far less bitter than that in the lake itself, but even so it was muddy and unpalatable. It was our only source and we drank great quantities of it to replace the liquid our bodies had lost as sweat during the day. For medical reasons, we boiled it scrupulously and dropped chlorinating tablets into it, but though we added coffee powder or fruit cordial to it, we never succeeded in doing anything more than lightly veiling its essential nastiness.

During these pleasant evenings, we temporarily turned our

attention from the flamingoes and wandered among the baobabs and the thorn scrub that grew between them, peering in hollow trees, searching among the branches for nests and turning over rotting logs to see what other creatures we could find.

There were several kinds of birds – scarlet weaver finches, larks, hoopoes, helmeted guinea fowl and flocks of little Madagascar lovebirds with sober grey heads and green bodies – but none of them occurred in any great numbers. Even on the lake itself there were few species other than the flamingoes – one or two solitary egrets, a small company of red-billed duck, and in the evenings, particularly, a cluster of long-winged elegant Mascarene swift-terns. We found no snakes, nor did we discover any mammals until one evening I turned over a log and saw, curled up asleep in a snug little chamber lined with crisp brown leaves, a tiny little spiny tenrec.

A spiny tenrec

It was no more than six inches long, with minute eyes, a wet, pointed snout liberally supplied with long whiskers and a back entirely covered by short spines. It looked, in fact, exactly like a miniature hedgehog and had I not known from prior reading that no such thing as a true hedgehog occurs in Madagascar, that is exactly what I should have supposed it to be.

Its internal anatomy, however, makes it quite clear that the tenrec is a very different animal and though, like the hedgehog, it is a member of the great group of Insectivora, it has several features which bear a marked similarity to the marsupials. Many zoologists, indeed, regard it as one of the most primitive of all true mammals. Like so many of the creatures of Madagascar, the tenrecs do not occur naturally anywhere outside the island and their only close relatives elsewhere in the world are the giant water shrew which lives in the forests of West Africa and an extraordinary beast called the solenodon which is restricted to the islands of Cuba and Haiti.

There are many different kinds of tenrec in Madagascar and by no means do all of them cloak their true identity beneath a mantle of spines. Some are small, hairy creatures, black, striped with yellow. Some are mole-like, some shrew-like and others burrow in the dykes of the rice paddies and swim about in the canals and flooded fields like water rats. One of them has the odd distinction of having forty-seven vertebrae in its tail, more than any other mammal. The largest of them all, a creature the size of a rabbit and sometimes known as the tailless tenrec – unhelpfully for several of the other kinds have no tail – has a stiff, bristly fur with a few small spines buried in it at the back of its neck.

As we were later to discover when we caught other species, the tenrecs vary their behaviour with their armoury. Our small, spiny tenrec was able to roll himself up into a ball, not quite as perfectly as a hedgehog, but nonetheless sufficiently well to serve as an adequate defence against dogs or any other creatures seeking a meal of flesh but not relishing a mouthful of prickles. He spent most of his day in this attitude, but during the evenings he would uncurl and trot about, whiffling his little nose in the air to savour the signs and stimuli which assuredly his tiny eyes failed to give him. If we touched him then, he would jerk up his shoulders and make a very creditable effort to impale our fingers on his prickles. If we disturbed him still further he might rarely snap his little jaws at us, but more usually he would bring his head and his back legs together and frown deeply in an attempt to bring forward the spines on his scalp to meet those on his rear.

Because of this habit of his, he is prohibited food for any Malagasy man who might pride himself on his courage, for the people believe that to eat his flesh would inevitably infect them with the cowardice that they consider this kind of tenrec displays when he takes no positive acts to defend himself but merely curls up in a ball.

The big tailless tenrec, on the other hand, lacking prickles, will snap and bite at the least provocation. As a result, there is no taboo which ordains that he is unsuitable eating even for a Malagasy soldier and indeed he is much hunted for his flesh. Paradoxically, the very efficacy of his bite has stimulated a superstition much to his detriment, for women will seek his lower jaw bone, which is armed with an extraordinary number of sharp white teeth and several more than are carried by most mammals, and hang these around their children's necks as charms to ensure that they grow up with good strong teeth.

We found five more of the engaging little spiny tenrecs and kept them all together in a wire-fronted box lined with straw. Their normal food, we assumed, is insects and earthworms and we provided them with both. But we also gave them small fragments of raw meat which during the night they gobbled greedily and on which they thrived.

Our delight in them was observed by some of the men who visited the camp to sit and watch us as we went about our strange activities with the butane gas cooker, the tape recorder or the camera. Empty tins, discarded pieces of film and unwanted bottles they took eagerly away and in due course we would see these objects reappear down at the wells serving as water carriers, cups, or, when they had no functional value, converted with a piece of string into necklaces for the children.

One evening three of the men came to the camp with something in return – a wriggling bundle tied up in a shirt. When I unknotted one of the sleeves and peered down it, I saw, not one but a large number of small, furry creatures with round, lustrous eyes and long tails. The men could not have brought us anything better for these were the smallest of the entire lemur clan – *Microcebus*, mouse lemurs.

Mouse lemurs

When at last we had managed to transfer them to a cage, we found that we had twenty-two of them. They cowered in the back of the box, blinking nervously. The men had found them in hollow trees and quite evidently they were nocturnal creatures that hated the daylight. We cut strips of sacking, hung them over the front of the cage and left the mouse lemurs to settle down in the darkness. That night, however, we saw them at their best as they frisked around the cage in the moonlight.

They closely resembled the bush babies of Africa, though they were smaller than any of them. Indeed they are the tiniest of all the group of Primates for, excluding their furry tails, they were only about five inches long. Their large, slightly protruding eyes had been a warm yellow during the day, but now in the darkness, in order to increase their powers of vision, their irises had opened wide and their eyes became a deep liquid brown. Their large ears were paper thin, like those of a long-eared bat, and they kept them in constant motion, twisting and quivering them to catch every tiny sound.

Charming and appealing though they looked, they were savage little creatures. When, each evening, we put into their cage grasshoppers, stick insects and beetles, they fell upon them with chirping squeaks of delight, seizing the insects in their tiny hands and munching the soft abdomens, like children eating corn on the cob.

We had been given permission to collect these creatures alone among all the lemurs, for the Malagasy do not hunt them for food and they are happily in no danger of extinction. Nor were we ostensibly setting a bad example of breaking the embargo on taking lemurs of any sort, for the people do not recognize them as belonging to that family, but regard them merely as a curious form of mouse. Together with the tenrecs, they formed the nucleus of the small collection of animals that eventually we were to take back to the London Zoo.

We had now been in the south of the island for over a month, longer in fact than we had allowed ourselves in our schedule. If we were not to cut short our visits to other parts we should have to leave. We broke camp, and drove back through the baobabs to Tuléar.

13

The Spirits of the Dead

Throughout Madagascar, the people worship their dead. Although, for over a century, Christianity has been preached energetically and with a devotion that many times led to martyrdom, the cult of the ancestors has remained the most potent element in tribal beliefs. It is from the dead, the people say, that all good, wealth and fertility ultimately come. If the ancestors should be displeased and unhappy, then they may neglect to supervise the welfare of their descendants and poverty, sterility or sickness will overwhelm a family. Accordingly, great care and attention must be paid to the ancestors. The precise form in which a tribe expresses its reverence, however, varies widely. As we drove east from Tuléar on the first stage of our journey back to Tananarive, we entered the territory of the Mahafaly people and here we found, standing isolated in the loneliest stretches of the harsh desert, the gaunt magnificent homes of the dead.

Each tomb was a square rock-faced construction which provided the communal grave for all the members of one family. The finest we saw had sides some thirty feet long and four feet high. On its level, rubble-covered surface had been erected row upon row of beautifully carved posts, their shafts cut into geometrical designs of lozenges, squares and circles, their tops sculpted into the images of the humped long-horned cattle that are the main wealth of the people. Lining each wall lay the horns of the many cattle that had been sacrificed during the funerary rites, their curving points projecting outwards as though in protection of the corpses that lay buried in the centre beyond them. Around the horns had been placed offerings for the use of the dead in the afterworld – mirrors, chipped enamel dishes, and metal suitcases, hot and buckling in the sun.

A tomb of the Mahafaly people

Georges told us of the innumerable taboos that govern the siting, design and construction of these impressive monuments. Many factors dictate that a tomb must be built in a remote place: the sight of it will arouse painful and bitter memories; if its shadow were to fall on a house, it would assuredly bring with it the taint of death; furthermore, the spirits of the ancestors wander away from the corpses during the night and, if the tomb were close to a village, they might inadvertently return to the dwellings of the living and claim the occupants.

The exact siting of the tomb is also a matter of great concern. Malagasy houses are accurately orientated so that the door faces west. If a tomb were similarly placed then the dead might become confused and afflict the living with their presence. The tombs therefore are built deliberately askew to the cardinal points of the compass.

During the laborious process of building, many other detailed customs must be observed. A great number of cattle must be sacrificed and their blood used to wet the huge rock slabs that will form the doors. If during the heavy labour of hauling these stones into position a man should injure himself so that his blood mingles with that of the slaughtered cows, it is taken as a sign that the tomb's thirst for blood is not yet quenched and that it will soon be claiming more occupants.

The taboos involved at all stages are so numerous that building presents an extremely complex problem to the people. If it is done ignorantly and rules are broken, then the tomb may become a cruel malevolent object with an insatiable appetite. But if all the rituals ordained by tradition are scrupulously observed, then it will provide a restful home for the dead and will call only to the aged who are tired of life.

On our second day of driving we turned north and soon reached the stark denuded mountains that form the heart of Madagascar and are the home of the Merina, the tribe that for centuries ruled and dominated the island. Once again I was struck by the great difference between these small, delicate-featured, light-skinned people and the taller, darker, frizzy-haired people of the southern deserts.

There seems no doubt that the Merina are relatively recent occupants of the island and that they came from the region of Malaya and Borneo. The physical resemblance between them and the Indonesian people is in itself convincing, but there are many other clues which confirm this origin, which at first sight seems so unlikely. Georges and I had amused ourselves during the long hours of driving by trying to compare the smattering of Malay that I had learned in Indonesia some years earlier with

Malagasy words. Most of the words I could remember meant nothing to him, but some bore a strong resemblance – an island is *nusa* in Malay and *nosi* in Malagasy; *maso*, an eye, in Malagasy is *mata*. A few were virtually identical in both languages – *anak*, a child; *masak*, ripe; *ini*, this; *mati*, dead.

The valiha player

There are also other elements in the culture of the Merina people which stem from the East. In one village where we stopped for lunch, I saw an old man, wearing a white robe and a trilby hat, sitting playing a *valiha*. It was a yard-long piece of bamboo with fifteen wire strings stretched along its length between two collars that encircled each end. He played to us for some time, his fingers plucking lightly at the strings and producing a soft rippling music amplified by the resonating tube of bamboo. Nowhere in Africa can you find anything resembling a valiha; yet in Thailand, Burma and other parts of the East, similar instruments are common.

As we approached the capital, we passed several small groups of people walking along the road headed by men bearing flags and carrying in their midst a long wooden box slung by a pole. When I asked about them, Georges' reply was a gruesome one. They were carrying corpses.

We had returned to the mountains at the end of the dry season. In a week or so the rains would break and the people would plant out the young rice seedlings in the flooded paddy-fields. This is a time of great ritual significance. Bodies of people who had been buried away from their ancestral land were being disinterred and carried back to the villages where they belonged, and throughout the hills of Merina the stone doors of the family tombs were being opened, for this was the season of the festival of *famadihany*, the turning of the dead.

A few days later, outside a hamlet some fifteen miles from Tananarive, we attended one of these ceremonies which the French call *retournements*. The tomb was smaller and less elaborate than those of the Mahafaly people, a simple square structure, its sides of cemented boulders, its door, already open, placed in a smaller square attached like a porch to one side. No one yet had entered the underground chamber to which it led.

Some fifty or sixty people sat on the grass nearby, surrounded by their saucepans, cooking pots and baskets of food, for many of them would spend the whole of this day and the following one by the side of the tomb.

The women wore bright cotton frocks, a few carried parasols; the men were dressed more variously, some in striped garments like nightgowns, some in smart city suits. A little farther away, shielded from the sun by a newly built shelter of branches and leaves, a band of clarinets, cornets, euphoniums and drums was playing raucously. It is extremely important that the music shall be loud for it might be that the spirits of the ancestors have left the tomb temporarily and they must be called back so that they may appreciate the festival being held in their honour.

Little happened for several hours. One or two people rose to their feet and, largely ignored by the crowd around them, danced a few swaying steps.

In the middle of the afternoon, three of the older men, headed by the senior members of the family to whom the tomb belonged, descended into the dark grave chamber, each taking with him a woven pandanus mat. When they emerged, they were carrying in the mat a corpse swathed in a white sheet. Unceremoniously, they hurried through the seated people and laid their burden on a specially built platform of branches a few yards away. One by one, the bodies were taken out and placed side by side in a row.

Removing the bodies from the tomb

Women holding the swathed bodies

There was no note of gloom or sorrow in the behaviour of the onlookers. They chatted loudly; they laughed. Whatever their private feelings might be, it is forbidden for the people to remain mute or to weep at this time, for the dead after their long months of silence in the tomb want to hear the voices of the living. Their emergence from the grave must be a gay occasion, lest grief should lead the ancestors to believe that they are not welcome on their return to the community.

Now that the worst of the heat of the day had passed, the band had left their shelter and were sitting on the grass playing with renewed vigour. The music was lively, its rhythm accentuated by thumps on a bass drum, its melody carried by the wailing clarinets. The dances became more formal and elaborate. Most of the family took part in a slow quadrille between the bier and the open mouth of the grave. At the end of each dance, the performers turned to face the corpses and made obeisance to them.

With darkness, most of the crowd returned to their homes, but the family remained to keep vigil over their forebears lying on the trestle in the moonlight.

The next day we returned. Once more the people danced in a desultory way for several hours. Then at about three o'clock, the band stopped and a hush spread through the crowd. In silence, the head of the family displayed to the people a magnificent silken sheet, broadly striped in red, blue and green with small glass beads woven into its fabric, a *lamba mena*.

Many sheets or lambas are made locally for everyday use, but these special lamba menas are extremely expensive objects and so sacred that it would be unthinkable for one of them to be used for any purpose other than this ceremonial one.

The headman called out to the crowd to witness the fine quality of the sheet, for it was all-important that everyone should realize that proper respect was being paid to the dead.

Now everyone clustered around the corpses and one by one they were taken away. Groups of women sat holding the swathed bodies across their knees. The slightly forced gaiety that had prevailed until now, disappeared, as the women communed with the spirits of the dead, caressing and patting the bodies. Some spoke to them, comforting and beseeching them to be happy. A few openly wept.

The men meanwhile began to tear strips from the lambas to serve as bindings for no other material could be used for such an important purpose. The women surrendered the corpses and each was rewrapped in a new gaudy shroud. Many of the bodies were little more than dust, mingled with the mouldering remnants of the lambas of past ceremonies. The smell of damp decay hung in the air.

The men completed their work briskly, handling the remains roughly and without particular reverence.

When all the bodies had received their new lambas, they were replaced on their platform, and the family began once more their stately quadrilles. There was little of the frenzied passions of Africa in the steps and gestures of their dance. Instead, the sinuous movements of their arms, their fluttering fingers, and the controlled poise of their bodies recalled the style of the dancers of Bali and Java.

The festival was drawing to a close. Everyone present – children, women, old men – gathered around the communal bier and, waving their arms above their heads, danced a final salute to the dead. Then, one by one, the bodies were hoisted on the shoulders of the people and carried in procession three times around the tomb. On their last circuit, they were handed down to the men standing on the steps of the grave and returned to darkness.

It is a point of honour among the people of Merina that this ceremony should be performed regularly. Only the sons of dogs, they say, would permit their ancestors to lie forgotten and uncared for in the tomb. The dead wish to be entertained with dances and feasts, and to see once more the herds and the fields that they once tended and tilled. Nonetheless, it is an extremely expensive occasion, for a great deal of food must be provided, lamba menas are costly and musicians' fees are high, and even though many families devote most of their income to the famadihany, few can afford to carry it out each year.

Poverty or sterility; the appearance of one of the dead in the dreams of the living; the addition of a new corpse to the tomb; all these will demand the performance of the rite, no matter how recently it has been carried out. Any family which allowed more than five years to pass without turning the corpses would be regarded not merely as dishonourable and shameful, but stupid. For the ceremony is a logical one. If the ancestors live on in spirit and if they control the destinies of the living, then it is only sensible that the living should repay their debt and do honour to the dead.

Yet perhaps this is not the only motive lying behind the ceremony, for there are several aspects of it which point to an additional origin. It is usually held at the end of the dry season when the rice fields that have for so long lain dry and barren are about to spring once more into life. Furthermore great emphasis is placed throughout on fertility. Older accounts of the festival describe how childless women may take portions of the corpses' shrouds as potent charms to cure their sterility.

Perhaps the festival is akin to the many that were once held in springtime all over Europe and are still practised in many other parts of the world, during which animals and gods are sacrificed and then resurrected symbolically in the belief that, by the powers of sympathetic magic, the grain on which the whole of the prosperity of the community depends will also once more spring to life after the dead months of winter and keep famine from the earth.

In Tananarive, we handed over our ravaged Land Rover to a garage. It would be a week or so before it could be fully repaired and overhauled. Georges had to attend to some work in the Scientific Institute. Geoff and I were alone once more. We decided to take an aeroplane to Diego Suarez, in the north. There, we might find many things of interest, but in particular, after seeing the retournement, we wanted to visit a sacred lake just south of Diego which is the focus of perhaps the most famous of all Malagasy ancestor cults.

The port of Diego Suarez stands on the shores of a bay that notches the north-eastern coastline. Fifty miles south of the town lies the sacred lake of Anivorano. It is not large, a placid expanse of lead-coloured water girdled by wooded hills. According to legend, a prosperous village once stood on this site. Its inhabitants had the reputation of being extremely unfriendly towards strangers. One day, a wizard from a neighbouring tribe passed by. It was hot, he was thirsty and he asked for a drink of water. Everyone refused him. At last, an old woman had pity and gave him a cupful. After he had drunk, he thanked her and warned her to leave the village immediately, taking her children and belongings with her, adding that she must on no account mention her departure to anyone.

After she had gone, he went to the middle of the village and put a curse on its inhabitants. Because they had been so mean with the water which they possessed in abundance, their village would be drowned and they would be turned into aquatic monsters. Then he left. Soon after, there was a great cataclysm, the village was submerged beneath a lake, and the people were transformed into crocodiles.

The descendants of the old woman live today in the village of Anivorano, a mile from the lake. Just as, in times of trouble when poverty or pestilence threatens, the Merina people will open the family tombs and commune with the dead, so these folk visit the lake and make offerings to their ancestors, the crocodiles.

We sought out the village postmaster, who, we had been told, was the most influential man in the community. He sat behind his desk, large and cheerful, and was most accommodating when we asked about the ceremony. He suspected that the women might be holding a *fête* in two days' time for the benefit of one of them who was childless. He would speak to the family conducting the rite and, with luck, he might persuade them to allow us to witness it. Needless to say, in return for the privilege of being present, we would be expected to make a substantial contribution towards the costs. A cow had to be sacrificed and cows were, of course, expensive. Furthermore, a great deal of singing was involved and this was thirsty work. Could we perhaps bring along a few dozen bottles of lemonade with maybe a bottle of rum to add a little strength? In view of the villagers' legendary past, I felt we could hardly refuse them a drink.

It was evident that a regular stream of visitors from ships putting in to Diego Suarez had made the people of Anivorano well aware of the commercial value of their lake and its legend.

However, we accepted the postmaster's suggestions and two days later Geoff and I returned to the village with our cameras.

We found the postmaster down by the shores of the lake with several other men and a wretched cow tethered to a tree. Nearby sat a group of women, with brightly coloured cloths draped over their heads in Arab fashion. We produced our bottles of drink. The women fell upon the lemonade; the postmaster commandeered the rum.

The poor cow was swiftly and expertly dispatched. One of the men collected some of its blood in an enamel plate, took it down to the lakeside and swilled it in the water.

The women began a strident chant, clapping their hands rhythmically. Within seconds, a small black hump broke the surface of the lake some fifty yards from the shore. It was a crocodile.

The women sang even more loudly. One of them threw back her head and let out an ululating yell, vibrating her tongue. A man advanced gingerly down the slope towards the lake and lobbed a hunk of meat down to the water's edge. A V-shaped wake flared from behind the crocodile's head as it slid smoothly through the water towards us. Another smaller yellowish head surfaced close by on the right.

A second gobbet of meat landed with a splash in the water. Within a few minutes, the larger crocodile had grounded on the shore and lay with its scaly back and long-keeled tail half out of the water.

I was anxious that we should walk down a little closer to them so that we could get a better view, but the postmaster restrained me.

'The women,' he said, 'they will not like it.'

'Who is worrying about the women?' said Geoff, eyeing his heavy camera and thinking, no doubt, of his chances of making a quick retreat.

The second crocodile drew up alongside the first and the pair lay watching us balefully with their heads resting on the mud.

The crocodile swallowing the sacrifice

'Sometimes', said the postmaster, 'they come right up on to land for the meat, but we had three *fêtes* within the last month, so perhaps they are not very hungry.'

The big crocodile lurched forward and with a sideways movement of its head, seized a lump of meat a foot long and slid backwards into the safety of deeper water. It raised its head vertically, displaying a formidable row of white conical teeth, and with three convulsive snaps of its jaws swallowed the meat.

The women yelled appreciatively. The yellow crocodile, emboldened by the example of the first, grabbed its share. Several more pieces of meat complete with hide were thrown down, some landing halfway up the bank, in the hope that the beasts might be lured right out of the lake. But there was enough by the water's edge to satisfy them. After half an hour, they had eaten their fill and, with a surge, they twisted around and swam slowly and quietly away towards the centre of the lake.

From a zoological point of view, the ceremony was unremarkable, proving only that crocodiles can be trained to expect food when they hear a certain sound. As a genuine Malagasy custom, it seemed to have little value, having been reduced almost to the level of a tourist attraction.

Yet nonetheless, there could be little doubt that once it had been a true and deeply felt rite. Everywhere else on the island, crocodiles are loathed and feared, for every year they are responsible for the deaths of human beings. As a result, they are hunted mercilessly. Only here are they protected and fed, and originally there could have been few other reasons for this other than a religious belief.

I am sure they are respected today as a not inconsiderable source of revenue; but I suspect that for many of the people of Anivorano they still also possess the supernatural aura that surrounds the incarnations of the dead.

14

Chameleons, Herons and Lemurs

We decided that for our next trip, we should visit the north-western sector of the island where live species of lemurs, lizards and many other creatures that are found nowhere else. The ideal centre seemed to be the forest of Ankarafantsika, some seventy miles inland from the port of Majunga. Happily Georges was able to join us once more, for he wanted to catch some small reptiles that occur in the forest for the Institute's own collections. And so less than a week after we had returned to Tananarive we were on the road again, with a fresh load of stores and film, in a rejuvenated Land Rover.

The journey was a dramatic one for that evening as we drove through the mountains in the dusk, we crested a pass and looked down into a valley laced with lines of orange flame like an illuminated seaside town. The people were burning the coarse moorland grass and scrub, so that when the rains came the new succulent shoots would be easily found by the searching muzzles of their herds. Great areas of the hillside were blackened and scorched. In several places the advancing frontiers of the fires straddled the road and we had to drive for many yards flanked by flames licking fifteen feet into the air, a menacing roar drumming in our ears and our nostrils filled with pungent smoke.

We reached Ankarafantsika on the afternoon of our second day of driving and Georges directed us to a hut in the middle of the forest. It was quite large and had several rooms, but it was semi-derelict, its thatch sagging into holes, the mud of its walls flaking away from the wooden stakes to which it had been plastered. Half of it was occupied by a young Malagasy forester and his wife and we, with his permission, moved into the large vacant room at one end.

Madagascar is the ancestral home of the chameleon family. It was here that these strange reptiles first evolved and from here that they spread throughout Africa and into the continents beyond. Even today, the island still contains more different species than occur in the world outside its shores, and among them are

A helmeted chameleon

the largest and the smallest, the most vividly coloured and the most bizarre of all the many members of this varied family. One of them, *Brownia*, is a minute, stumpy-tailed creature which lives on the ground and measures no more than one and a half inches. It is almost certainly the smallest of all living reptiles. Another kind, the giant of the group, grows to over two feet in length and feeds not only on the insects which form the major part of the diet of its more normally sized relations, but on young mice and nestling birds. Intermediate between these two extremes of size are a great number of species that bear extravagant ornaments on their heads – peaked helmets, crests like roosters, horns like unicorns, skinny flaps at the back of their necks or twin scaly blades on the ends of their noses.

Georges was emphatic that several spectacular species were abundant in the forest around our hut. Perhaps they were, but they were nonetheless very hard to find. This was not because of their celebrated ability to change the colour of their skin to match their surroundings, but because of their habit of remaining completely motionless among the tangled branches where the irregularity of their silhouettes made them extremely difficult to detect. Indeed, the colour of a chameleon's skin varies not so much with its background as with its emotions and with the intensity of light. Pick up a grey one and it will turn black with rage; tease a mottled green one and in its anger it may suddenly become striped with yellow or orange. In general, the brighter the sun, the more brilliant are their colours, and at night-time or in a closed box, most of them turn almost white.

These startling changes are produced by differently coloured sets of pigment cells embedded in the warty skin. When they are contracted, they are invisible – as they are when the animal is in the dark – but under the stimulus of bright light, or some excitement, one or more sets of them are expanded so that their colour – red, black, orange, green, yellow – suddenly becomes apparent.

Catching a chameleon, once you have found it, is easy enough, for it is incapable of moving at any speed. All you need do is to take a stick, hold it parallel and a little above the branch that the chameleon is walking along, and it will obligingly and unwittingly leave the safety of its own tree and clamber on to your stick, so that you can bring the beast down without even touching it. This is particularly useful when the animals are up in the highest, thinnest twigs, far beyond arm's reach.

But next, you have to detach it from your stick and put it in a cage. This is a little more alarming, for as you pick up the reptile by the back of its neck, it hisses in a most ferocious manner, opens its mouth very wide to expose the brilliant yellow lining of its throat, and sucks in air so that its body becomes inflated and grows appreciably in size. At this moment, it looks so formidable that you may have to calm yourself with the thought that chameleons are quite harmless and that, although they will not hesitate to give you a sharp nip if they can, it is only the very biggest of them that have enough strength in their jaws to break your skin.

Perhaps, however, it is not their jaws but their eyes which are most unnerving. Each eyeball is almost entirely covered by scaly skin, often brilliantly coloured, leaving only a small peephole in the centre. The entire eye, as a result, resembles the high-powered lens of a microscope. The chameleon is able to revolve these strange organs through a wide range of angles so that although the animal may be facing away from you as you hold it, it can nonetheless keep you fixed with a disconcerting glare over the back of its neck. Even more extraordinary, these eyes move independently, so that while the animal stares at you with one eye, it may be focusing the other straight ahead in order to grab with its forelegs the door of the cage into which you are trying to put it. How the animal is able to correlate in its brain the constantly changing images received by its two swivelling eyes defeats the imagination.

After a day or so of searching, we became more skilled at

spotting them as they sat in the bushes and trees, and soon we had assembled a collection of over a dozen – so many, in fact, that the problem of feeding and housing them became a major one. I pondered on this and eventually devised a method which I thought would neatly solve both difficulties at the same time.

In the hut, I had noticed an old galvanized-iron bath. I dragged it out and cleaned it. In the middle of it, I erected a tall, dry, twiggy branch, piling boulders around its base so as to hold it firmly in an upright position. On the twigs I tied one or two pieces of raw meat and I filled the tub with water.

Geoff had been washing by the lake while I had been doing this and when he came back, my creation was complete. It stood in front of the hut like an over-extravagant Japanese flower arrangement. Understandably, he was a little puzzled, so I explained to him the cunning ingenuity of it all.

'The two factors we have to bear in mind,' I said, 'are first, that chameleons live on flies; and second, that they cannot swim. Put them on this branch and as the only way of escape is through the water, they will have to stay there. Thus we have a cage which is not only spacious and secure, but a thing of beauty. Furthermore, the thought of escaping will not occur to them, for this is a chameleon's paradise. The raw meat will attract hordes of flies, thereby providing a constant source of food for them and relieving us, at the same time, of the tiresome business of having to search every morning for hundreds of grasshoppers.'

Geoff expressed suitable admiration. Together, we took out the chameleons from their many and various cages and put them on the branch. They clung there, goggling angrily at one another and we sat down proudly to watch them explore the amenities of their new home.

One or two of them walked down the branch, inspected the water and retreated. So far, it was as I had predicted. But then they assembled at the top of the branch and marched in a line along a stout, horizontal twig that projected more than two feet beyond the edge of the bath. One by one, they leaped off the end, like divers leaving the crowded high-board of a swimming pool. I was astonished. Never before had I seen a chameleon show any signs of being able to jump. They landed with a soggy thud on the ground and proceeded to make off with an air of wounded vanity, lifting their thin legs high in the air and waggling their torsos in their efforts to produce an unaccustomed turn of speed.

We fielded them one by one and replaced them on the branch, but it was quite clear that my elegant construction was a total failure as a cage. Nor was it any more effective in providing them with food. I had not previously bothered to study the conditions necessary to make meat attractive to flies – in the past it had seemed that any piece of meat left out in the open was covered with them in a few seconds. But not a single insect came to the succulent morsels that dangled from the branch.

'The sun is baking the meat and drying it up,' Geoff said. 'You should have put it in the shade.'

Laboriously we shifted the bath and the branch to a new position beneath a tree. But no flies appeared.

'It's too windy,' suggested Georges. 'They never come unless it is calm.'

We moved everything into the lee of the hut where it was both shady and protected from even the slightest breeze. This was no more successful. Finally, I smeared the meat with honey. When this failed as well, I gave up. We put the chameleons back in their individual cages and once more set about the laborious business of catching grasshoppers and crickets for them in the meadow of grass down by the lake.

Although collecting sufficient insects was a very time-consuming task, the rewards were high, for a chameleon taking its meal is a fascinating sight. When you first place a cricket within a foot or so of one of them, the reptile merely swivels its eyes. But as soon as the insect moves one of its legs, or strokes its antenna, the chameleon immediately becomes alert. Slowly it advances on the cricket, swaying groggily back and forth. This movement may help it to estimate the exact range, which is of great importance. When the chameleon is satisfied that its quarry is within capturing distance – and this may be as much as a foot away – it leans forward, slowly opens its mouth and then, as swift as an arrow, the long shaft of its tongue flashes out, the sticky pad at the end of it hits the insect and the tongue retracts bringing the cricket with it. Then with dreadful deliberation, the chameleon champs its jaws until with a great gulp it swallows its spiky, struggling mouthful.

Chameleon catching its prey

The chameleon's tongue is a remarkable piece of apparatus. In shape it is a tube which normally is kept contracted in a fat coil at the back of the throat. When its owner decides to use it, however, it suddenly contracts the rings of muscle that encircle the tube so that in a fraction of a second it is converted from a short, stubby object into a long, thin shaft.

As long as the insect is some distance away, the tongue is an extremely efficient weapon, but at closer ranges, it has its limitations. On one occasion, a small morsel of grasshopper became stuck to the upper lip of one of our largest chameleons. It irritated him enormously and for nearly five minutes he tried to manipulate his huge tongue so that he could curl it up and retrieve the fragment. His efforts to do so were hilariously ineffective. Eventually he had to give up all hope of recovering the piece, rubbed it off on a twig and abandoned it.

A helmeted chameleon

We fed our chameleon collection every morning, and often we were watched in horror by the forester, his wife, or other passing visitors. They were all appalled at our foolishness. These creatures were not only poisonous, they said, but also extremely evil. To touch one was madness. Nothing we could do would convince them otherwise. On our return from Ankarafantsika, we were able to turn this belief to our own benefit. We had to spend several nights in small towns in the centre of Madagascar and one morning, when we came out of our hotel, we found to our dismay that thieves had burgled the car, smashing one of the windows in order to unlatch the door. Fortunately they had ignored all the valuable and irreplaceable cameras, film and recording apparatus, and had stolen only our food and an exceedingly disreputable pair of suede shoes. However, we could not properly repair the window, so it was impossible thereafter to lock the car effectively. The solution was simple. We took out each evening the largest and the most virulently coloured of all our chameleons and sat him on one of our camera cases in the middle of the mound of baggage that filled the back of the car. We left him there, glowering ferociously and revolving his eyes. No one ever interfered with our car again.

It was in the forest proper, the wild, profuse, close-knit tangle that began beyond the ordered ranks of eucalyptus and kapok plantations, that we went to search for brown lemurs, the creatures which for us had been one of Ankarafantsika's main lures. Supposedly they were very common, but at first we could find little sign of them. We soon discovered the reason. In the centre of a clearing in the forest a stout post had been driven into the ground. From it ran three poles, like the spokes of a gigantic, horizontal wheel, their farther ends resting among the trees at the edge of the clearing. Three thin, springy saplings had been lashed to the central stake, pulled down so that the nooses that hung from their ends spread wide and invitingly over the top of each pole and then fixed in this position by a simple trigger. The way in which the device would work was easy to imagine. Brown lemurs are essentially tree-living creatures and they loathe coming down to the ground. Faced with the prospect of crossing the clearing during their perambulations through the forest they would choose to run along the horizontal poles. As soon as they put their heads through the noose, their forelegs would release the trigger, the curving sapling would swing back and the lemur would be snatched into the air. It would remain dangling there until the hunters came to cut it down and slaughter it for food.

Since all lemurs are protected by law, the trap was an illegal one and we willingly helped Georges to destroy it. Its discovery, however, had told us one thing. The poachers, whoever they were, must certainly have studied the habits of the lemurs and set their trap where they knew that the creatures were likely to appear. The best place for us to look for the animals was obviously in the immediate neighbourhood. We set up the camera, sat down and waited.

We did not have to be patient for very long. Within an hour, I heard a chirring grunt and looking up among the tracery of boughs, I saw a small, brown creature, with a black face and an amber-coloured underside, peering down at us and wagging its tail indignantly. It was the size and shape of a large polecat, though more heavily built. Soon there were a dozen of them in the branches staring at us suspiciously. We made no movement, except when Geoff changed lenses to get closer pictures. After ten minutes or so, they seemed to lose interest in us and trooped off, running along the branches with the agility of squirrels. At jumping, however, they were far less adept, bracing themselves visibly for the effort and landing heavily on all fours. Several of them were females encumbered with puppy-sized babies riding piggy-back. As they left, a youngster, perhaps a year old, which until

Georges with an illegal trap

then had been scampering about independently, tried to clamber on the back of one of the adults. Presumably the full-grown one was a female, but she objected violently to this illegal hitch-hiking and turned round to give the young one a clout across the side of his face. For a moment or two they sparred, while other members of the group ran past them. The female, as though anxious not to be left behind, turned away. In a flash, the youngster clasped her around the chest and as they vanished into the leaves beyond, he seemed to be firmly in the saddle.

However, the troop had not gone far, for we could hear them

crashing riotously in the branches not far away. Geoff unscrewed the camera from the stand and followed them. It seemed best to let him go alone, as two of us would only cause unnecessary disturbance. He returned after about ten minutes and for a moment I thought he was extremely ill with a sudden attack of fever. His face was white and the whole of his body was trembling uncontrollably. He had no idea what was the matter with him, but Georges knew immediately. He had unwittingly blundered into a bush that was covered in poisonous stinging hairs. Georges rushed him down to a stream and helped him to wash. It was a full hour before he was completely recovered. Before we left that day, the three of us went back to find this venomous bush which Georges identified for us so that we could memorize its seemingly innocuous appearance and avoid others like it in the future.

Once we had discovered the whereabouts of the brown lemurs, filming them was not difficult, for they were inquisitive creatures and, provided that we did not tax their tolerance by going unreasonably close, they allowed us to watch them for hours on end. From their four-footed gait and the general appearance of their long, lissom bodies, one might have judged them to be related to weasels, or perhaps to mongooses or civets. Only their human-like hands and feet reminded one that they were closely related to monkeys.

As they rollicked through the trees, chirring brazenly at one another, thrashing their tails from side to side in their excitement, it seemed that they feared no one. A troop of them passing through the forest had the air of a piratical, swashbuckling gang on its way to cause havoc among the gentler and more reticent inhabitants of the trees. Yet in fact they were almost entirely vegetarian. Once, it is true, I saw one with his head deep in a wild bees' nest that hung from a branch, burrowing energetically and then sitting back to lick his sticky fingers, but their staple food was leaves, flowers, the green bark from young twigs and, above all, fruit. Every day they came to one of the tallest trees in the centre of the forest to gorge themselves on the succulent yellow mangoes that hung from it. In the end, it was by this tree that we waited regularly for them, and there that we succeeded in getting the most attractive and animated pictures of them, feasting, squabbling and chasing one another through the branches. They were a joy to watch and I was indeed truly sorry when, as we counted the tins of film, we found that we had exposed sufficient to run for over an hour and that the time had come for us to turn our attentions to other things.

15

The Dog-Headed Man

Among the dragons, mantichores, hydras and unicorns that the natural history writers of the sixteenth and seventeenth centuries pictured so imaginatively and described in such detail, there strides the cynocephalus, the dog-headed man. He is represented standing upright, wearing a shaggy coat, with enormous human-like hands and feet, his body tailless and proportioned like a man, but his face fanged and snouted like a dog.

Marco Polo claimed that he lived in the Andaman Islands – 'I assure you all the men of this island have heads like dogs, and teeth and eyes likewise. In fact in the face they are all just like big mastiffs.' Aldrovandus, the great Italian encyclopaedist, writing at the beginning of the seventeenth century, described a particularly intriguing characteristic of the beast. According to some authorities, he wrote, the dog-headed man has the habit of soaking himself in water and then rolling in dust. This performance, repeated again and again, eventually provides him with an armour which is both tough and magical, for spears thrown at him by his enemies not only fail to wound him but bounce back and infallibly strike the attackers.

Not all the unlikely stories of the early naturalists were entirely without foundation and as the world became better known, the monsters concocted from the hearsay of previous centuries were traced to their sources in actual animals, the existence of which was vouched for by first-hand reports, eyewitness drawings and skins and bones sent back to the curio cabinets of Europe. That unlikely creature the camelopardal, with its absurdly long neck, proved to be based upon the giraffe; the long horn which had been supposed to demonstrate the existence of the unicorn was shown to come from the narwhal; and the mermaid, though the legend of her existence persisted longer than most, was eventually linked with the sea cow. The cynocephalus, too, was explained. It was equated with the baboon.

The cynocephalus, as illustrated by Aldrovandus, 1642

This identification has always seemed to me to be very unsatisfactory. It is undeniable that a baboon's head is very dog-like, but surely even the most misanthropic person would not regard the stocky body of the baboon as human-like. The beast is essentially four-footed, with a tail, short or long according to the species, and bears little resemblance to the old drawings of the cynocephalus which is usually shown standing erect with legs as long as its torso and without a tail.

Of course, the legend may not have been inspired by anything more than a nightmarish imagination as was obviously the case with the cyclops, or the human headless monsters who had eyes and mouths in the middle of their chests. No one can prove conclusively that any one actual animal was the inspiration of such a widespread story as the dog-headed man, which is found in the accounts of Arab navigators, as well as in European literature. Nonetheless, the fact remains that one of Madagascar's lemurs matches very closely the old drawings. This is the largest of the whole group, a relation of the sifakas and the only lemur without a long tail – the indri.

Before we left London, I had tried to find out as much as I could about this extraordinary animal. The plain facts of its anatomy were not difficult to discover. It stands over three feet high. Although at first sight is seems to lack a tail it does, in fact, possess a short stump hidden in its dense silky fur, but, in the words of one account, 'this is sensible only to the touch'. It has a short naked black muzzle and large ears, and its hands are huge, six times as long as they are broad. In colour it seems to be variable, some writers calling it black, others parti-coloured black and white, and yet others describing its thick woolly coat as being brilliantly coloured – velvety black, with a white patch around the buttocks extending in a triangle up the back, the sides of its torso yellowish and its thighs and upper arms washed with a delicate grey.

But the details of its habits and behaviour were much more difficult to discover and the authorities often seemed to contradict one another. Some said the animal was active only in the daytime, others that it was, 'like other lemurs', nocturnal. As we had already found that many lemurs are active by day, we could discount this version. It was reported to proceed through the forest trees by prodigious leaps of its hind legs, yet the only museum specimen I could find on exhibition was mounted hanging from a branch by one hand as though it were an ape. Most books affirmed that it was almost exclusively vegetarian; yet a few added that it was tamed by the local people and used to hunt birds, which seemed an astonishing activity for a creature which is supposed to live on leaves and flower petals.

But none of these descriptions was a first-hand observation, which was scarcely surprising for the creature had never been brought alive to Britain, the only record of a captive indri being a report of ten which were sent to Paris over twenty years previously, all of which died within a month, presumably because the zoo authorities could not provide an acceptable substitute for their highly specialized diet of leaves.

To find a detailed eyewitness account of the indri in the wild, I had eventually to turn to an account written in 1782 by a Frenchman, Sonnerat, who was the first European ever to describe the animal. He says that the indri is almost entirely black, that its eye is white and sparkling and that it has a call like that of a crying child. 'The word "Indri",' he continues, 'in the Madagascan language, means "man of the woods"; this animal is very gentle; the people of the southern part of the island take the young and train them for hunting as we train dogs.'

Here at least I had traced the origin of the hunting story. Sonnerat, however, was a notoriously gullible observer. When he went to New Guinea to collect seeds of spice plants, he happily confirmed the legend of birds of paradise feeding on celestial nectar. His statement that indris were used for hunting birds was therefore not wholly reliable, to say the least, yet it had been repeated in dozens of books without further corroboration for nearly two hundred years. Even the name he gave to the beast was apparently misapplied, for in fact the word 'indri' does not mean 'man of the forest' at all. The correct Malagasy name is 'babakoto'. Presumably Sonnerat's guides had pointed to the strange creature high up in the trees and had called out 'indri', for this word means simply, 'Look at that.' Sonnerat took it to be the creature's local name, noted it down as such, and the world of science, abiding by the rules of priority, had called it by that name ever since.

But if the reference books I consulted were meagre and often contradictory with facts about the indri's natural history, they were extremely generous in providing information about local beliefs concerning the animal. These were numerous and varied. One described the hazards facing a newly born infant indri: when a female is about to give birth, she clambers down to the ground and finds a quiet sheltered spot, while her mate sits close by in a tree. As soon as the babe is born, she throws it to the male who catches it and tosses it back. To and fro the infant is thrown. If it survives this strange treatment, it is cared for there-after with the greatest affection by its mother, but if one of its parents fumbles and lets it fall to the ground, it is abandoned.

Another story was a warning to would-be hunters of the indri: if you throw a spear at the animal, it can catch the weapon in mid-air and hurl it back at you with great force and unfailing accuracy – an interesting parallel with Aldrovandus' story about the dog-headed man.

All authorities, however, seemed agreed that many of the local people held the creature in superstitious awe and quoted folk tales to show why this should be so. One story provided a charming parallel in fable to the current zoological beliefs as to the indri's place in the evolution of the higher mammals. It tells of a man and a woman wandering in the forest. After some time, the woman gave birth to an enormous number of children. When they grew up, some, being industrious by nature, began to clear the forest and plant rice. The others continued to live only on the roots and leaves of wild uncultivated plants. The first group, as time went by, began to fight among themselves. They were the ancestors of human beings. The others, horrified, took refuge in the tree tops so that they might continue to live in peace. They were the first indris. Thus mankind and the indri are related, having a common ancestor. To hunt an indri as one might hunt an ordinary animal would obviously be unthinkable, so the people left it unmolested. The indris, according to legend, recognize this relationship for they often help mankind. Once they howled a warning to a village of the approach of robbers. On another occasion a man, having climbed a forest tree to gather wild honey, was set upon by the bees and badly stung. Half-blinded, he slipped and fell. But as he tumbled through the branches, he was caught by a huge indri. The beast silently helped him down to safety and then disappeared into the forest.

We had not yet had a chance of seeing an indri for they live only in a restricted part of the forests of eastern Madagascar, between the Bay of Antongil in the north and, to the south, the river Masora, which empties into the sea halfway down the east coast. This limited distribution is in itself peculiar. Although the bare tree-less mountains of the central plateau form an obvious barrier to the animal's spread westwards, there seems little reason why it should not live farther north and south. The eastern forests extend almost unchanged in character in a long strip parallel to the coast for a hundred miles or so beyond the indri's territory in both directions, and indeed both sifakas and their nocturnal cousins, avahis, with which the indri shares the middle section of the forest, are found throughout the entire length of the strip. Perhaps there is some tree providing fruit or leaves essential to the indri's diet which grows only in this central part, but if this is so, no one has so far discovered what tree it is.

The indri's territory was easily reached, for both the road and the railway, which link Tananarive with the big east coast port of Tamatave, cut through the middle of the forest, running alongside one another for much of the way. The railway had only a single track except at the small village of Perinet about halfway along its length, where, for a few hundred yards, it split into double track so that the eastbound train from the capital and the westbound train from the port could draw up alongside one another before continuing their journeys along the single line. To provide refreshments for the passengers, the railway company thoughtfully built a huge hotel. Hardly anyone ever stayed at it, we were told – why should they, it was in the middle of nowhere – but it did have rooms if we wanted them. It was the obvious place from which to begin a search for the indri.

We left Tananarive by the Tamatave road, making good speed in our rejuvenated truck along the best metalled road in the whole of the island. For the first hour we travelled through the bare uplands of the central plateau. The spring rains had already flooded the rice fields that terraced every fold of the hills and the people were busy paddling in the muddy water planting out the young rice seedlings. The road, after forty miles, zigzagged down the steep scarp that ends the plateau and we descended several hundred feet into thickly forested hills. After three hours' driving, we at last reached Perinet. The village itself was tiny, a cluster of shacks grouped round the railway line. Hidden away in the surrounding forest lay a bauxite mine, a lumber camp and an intermittently occupied training school for forestry officers, but these were invisible from the village itself which was dominated by the hotel, a brick building with two enormous frowning eaves resembling an inflated Swiss chalet. It seemed capable of accommodating a hundred or so travellers, but when we arrived no trains were waiting outside and the vast dining hall was empty and silent.

Our footsteps echoed with embarrassing loudness on the polished wooden floor. We coughed apologetically once or twice. After several minutes, a door opened at the far end of the hall and, to our surprise, there emerged the figure of an extremely glamorous girl. She wore a chic but flimsy silk housecoat that barely succeeded in covering her ample figure. Her lips were heavily reddened and her lashes blackened with mascara, but she was clearly not yet fully awake, although it was approaching midday, for as she tottered towards us on her stylish high heels, she was blinking sleepily and doing her best to complete her upswept coiffure.

Jeanine, however, as we were to discover later, was no ordinary hotel-keeper. Until a few months previously she had been a mannequin in Tananarive and the proprietress of a very fashionable bar and guest house. But she had been forced to leave the capital because of what she darkly referred to as '*un grand scandale*'. She had retreated to the seclusion of Perinet as mistress of its hotel, but she loathed it and regarded her exile with the deepest despair. Each evening of our stay she revealed to us, over cognac, further intimate details about the nature of this '*scandale*', illustrating them with photographs from her scrapbook. The political repercussions, it seemed, would have been catastrophic unless she had left the capital.

All this, however, we did not learn for some time to come. Now Jeanine seemed too sleepy to talk and required a great deal of reassurance that we had not come to Perinet by mistake, that we did not intend to catch the midday train either to Tananarive or Tamatave, but of our own free will were hoping to take rooms in her hotel for a fortnight or so.

When we at last convinced her on these points and had unloaded our belongings, we drove farther down the road to visit the resident Forestry Officer who had a house close by the training school. He was a florid-faced elderly Frenchman, with closely cropped hair. Our conversation was not very profitable, mainly because he had lost his dentures and it was difficult for me to understand exactly what he said. It seemed that he was in poor health and as a result unable to show us personally the parts of the forest that were most likely to harbour the indris. Instead, he recommended that we should enlist the aid of Michel, one of his Malagasy deputies who was in charge of the breeding and rearing of tilapia fish in a range of ponds half a mile away.

We found Michel, a young cheerful man wearing a pith helmet the size of a small umbrella, supervising the draining of one of his ponds. Babakoto, he told us, were quite common hereabouts and he often heard them singing in the forests close by. If we wished, we could go and look for them straightaway, and abandoning the emptying pond he led us up a muddy

The rainforest of eastern Madagascar

puddled track that wound into the forest. It had been cut many months before by teams of foresters to enable them to drag down logs of valuable hardwood, but so far the work of felling the trees had not yet been started and the bush was still quiet and undisturbed.

As Geoff and I followed Michel into the twilight of the forest our spirits sank. If this was typical of the places in which the indri chose to live, it was no wonder that the animal had so seldom been seen by naturalists, for this was the thickest bush we had encountered so far. Beneath the roofs of leaves formed by the crowns of the highest trees, sheaves of bamboos waved and creaked, curving tree ferns spread their parasols of gigantic fronds, palms reared fans of tattered glossy leaves, and rank upon rank of spindly saplings reached upwards in an imperceptibly slow race to the light. Orchids squatted on the rafter-like horizontal branches of the taller trees and clambered around the trunks like ivy. Everywhere lianas looped from tree to tree, binding the whole forest into a dense matted tangle. The chances of filming successfully here seemed remote. Not only was it dark, but the vegetation was so thick that, unless we were very lucky, it would be impossible to get a clear filmable view of any creature that was more than a few yards away.

The forest nonetheless was obviously extremely rich in animal life. From a small stream that trickled between huge moss-covered boulders came the flatulent honks of frogs. Over one of its deep brown pools, some yellow-headed weaver birds were busy constructing their retort-shaped nests from the ends of a dangling palm leaf. High in the trees, sun birds were searching for flowers from which to drink nectar, attracting our attention with their high-pitched whirring calls. In the confused chorus of birdsong, we recognized many of the notes we had learned elsewhere in the island. Somewhere here, if only we could see them, were drongos, white eyes, warblers, parrots and pigeons. I had stopped walking and was standing trying to disentangle in my mind this babel of sound when the songs of the birds were suddenly drowned by a chorus of spine-chilling unearthly howls.

'Babakoto,' said Michel triumphantly.

The noise was deafening. Sonnerat's description of a crying child, though far from adequate, was as good a simile as I could think of to characterize its quality, but it had not warned me of its volume. Even a gang of the lustiest children could not have produced a tenth of the sheer noise. Several individuals were singing in chorus, each producing a weird wail, sliding up and down the scale in caterwauling glissandos.

So loud was it we could not believe that the animals were more than a few yards from us. Desperately we tried to look through the palisades of trunks and the series of leafy curtains which must have been concealing the creatures from us. We could see nothing of them, not even the tiniest patch of black fur, not the flash of an eye, not even a movement among the branches or the glossy leaves that might betray their presence. Then, as abruptly as the wailing had started, it ended and, like the hum of a concert-hall audience between movements of a symphony, the crickets, the frogs, the flycatchers and the parrots took over, sounding feeble in comparison with the tremendous chorus that had just ceased.

But we were jubilant. We now knew for ourselves that the indris were really here. Michel furthermore was encouraging.

'Always,' he told us as we walked back to the fish ponds, 'they sing at the same time. They have the habit to come to the same place at the same time each day. Tomorrow they will be here again. Come with your cameras a little earlier. Perhaps then you will have better luck and catch sight of them. If they don't sing, then call to them with their voice, and often they will reply.'

It seemed good sense and we returned happily to the hotel. That evening over the cognac, in the echoing barn-like dining room, we reported our good fortune to Jeanine. She smiled emptily and brought the conversation back to the intricate and sophisticated scandals of Tananarive and plied us with questions about the latest Paris fashions.

We returned up the track into the forest the next morning as Michel had advised, taking with us our equipment. But we neither saw nor heard anything of the indris. We did our best to imitate their wailing calls but no reply came back to us from the trees. We made an attempt to explore the immediate neighbourhood but five minutes was enough to convince us that there was little to be gained in doing so, for the bush was so thick that it was impossible to proceed more than a few yards without making so much noise that any indris nearby would have heard us and be scared away. There seemed nothing else to do but to have patience and pertinacity. Day after day we returned to exactly the same place. Again and again after waiting two or three hours we whooped our counterfeit calls. Though we came to know every bird that haunted the neighbourhood, we saw nothing of our main quarry.

Searching for indris in the eastern forest

Six days we did this. On the seventh day, we were beginning to lose patience. We waited for a full three hours without seeing or hearing anything of them. I was wondering whether to try to call them once more when Geoff touched my arm.

'You know,' he whispered, 'I reckon there's a female babakoto hidden in that tree over there. She's got a baby on her knee and she's saying – "Now watch those two extraordinary animals down there. They have the habit of coming to the same place at the same time each day. Always they sing at the same time. In a minute they will do so."'

I did not have the heart to repeat yet again my inadequate imitation of an indri's call.

16

The Creatures of the Forest

To be candid, I was beginning to lose faith in the possibility of our ever seeing the indris. Michel had said that they were regular in their habits, yet though we had plodded again and again up the track beyond the fish ponds into the forest, lugging our recording machine, camera and long telephoto lens, we had never heard them calling again except in the far distance. Perhaps, on the single occasion they had sung in this part of the forest, they had strayed for once off their usual daily path; or, more likely, our presence there day after day had frightened them and made them choose another part of the bush in which to sleep and feed. Maybe we should explore.

On the other side of the road, the loggers had cut another similar track into the forest which seemed just as promising and indeed our first foray up it produced a minor success. I had left the path and was making my way towards a fallen tree lying in a pool of sunlight flooding through the rent torn in the canopy by its fall. As I cleared aside the wet waist-high shrubs to see, cautiously, where I was putting my feet, I found that I was about to step into the middle of a collection of shiny olive-green objects, the size of golf balls. There were almost two hundred of them. When I picked one up, a split opened along one side revealing some twenty pairs of frantically waving legs. The creature straightened itself out, unfurled a pair of knobbly antennae and proceeded to walk determinedly up my arm. It looked like a giant version of the little wood-louse that lives under stones in an English garden. In fact, however, this resemblance was deceptive for it was not a member of the woodlouse family, but a strange species of millipede. Why so many should have gathered together in one spot I could not imagine but I was quite sure they would make a splendid display in the London Zoo's Insect House, so we filled our pockets with them and took a hundred or so back to the hotel.

Jeanine was predictably horrified. I assured her that these millipedes were completely harmless and passed their lives doing nothing worse than nibbling at rotting vegetation, but when the one I had put on the table came to life and displayed its numerous legs, she let out a piercing scream and bolted for the kitchen.

We housed the whole collection in a large wooden box covered with wire netting and filled with wet moss and decaying wood pulp. The safest place to keep them for the night seemed to be the corner of my bedroom and I did not imagine that they would be anything but the most peaceable of companions. But as soon as I turned out the light and prepared for sleep, they awoke and began clambering energetically over one another, rattling their legs on the wire, rasping against the rough sides of the box and noisily champing the wood pulp. The resultant clamour was disturbingly loud, but lazily I decided against getting out of bed and carrying the whole box down to the truck outside. Instead I buried my head beneath my pillow and eventually succeeded in getting to sleep.

When I opened my eyes soon after dawn the next morning, it was abundantly clear that the millipedes were much more versatile escapologists than I had supposed. The chicken wire had presented them with no problems whatever. Thirty or forty lay around the floor of my room, rolled up and asleep like huge glinting marbles. I opened my door and found that almost as many had crawled beneath it and now lay scattered along the length of the passage. I could imagine only too clearly the nature of Jeanine's reaction if she should see them. Fortunately, it would be some time before the first of the hotel staff arrived and many hours before Jeanine herself was due to emerge for coffee, so I was able to gather them up and replace them without anyone else knowing that they had been wandering around the hotel throughout the night.

They spent the next night in the truck with a double thickness of wire netting over their box. It was not, however, the end of the incident. I had not dared to confess what had happened to Jeanine, but when the maids began to discover millipedes in the linen store, the pantry and the bathrooms, I thought she would deduce where they had come from. I need not have worried. She accepted this hideous invasion of her hotel as simply another proof that life away from the lights of Tananarive was nasty, brutish and primitive.

The millipedes were not our only acquisitions. A few days later, the Forestry Officer drew up outside the hotel in his large smart saloon car. He was on his way to a meeting in a town twenty miles away, but as he set out he had met some men on the road carrying a newly caught tenrec. Remembering us, he had bought it from them for a few francs and, as he had no cage or sack handy, had put it loose in the boot of his car. It was not, he said, a little hedgehog tenrec, but the tailless tenrec – the true *tandraka*, a big hairy creature the size of a rabbit, and this particular one was very lively and extremely ferocious. As we stood contemplating the back of his car it became clear to us that there were a number of risks to be run before the creature inside, which was presumably awaiting us with teeth bared, was truly ours.

When we had assembled a pair of gloves, three sacks and an empty cage, the Forestry Officer cautiously lifted the boot lid an inch. I tried to peer inside but it was too dark to see anything. He widened the crack to two inches. Still I could see nothing. Warning us to pounce bravely and without hesitation, our friend threw up the lid. Geoff and I lunged forward. But there was nothing visible on which to pounce. Gingerly we removed the toolbag, the jack and finally the spare wheel. The Frenchman was mystified. The boot was undeniably empty.

The tailless tenrec

Then we heard a scrabbling deep inside the chassis somewhere between the front and rear mudguards. The poor tenrec had gone to a very metallic earth in the very vitals of the car.

By this time we were surrounded by a crowd of curious sympathizers and there was no lack of helping hands when I suggested that the only way to reach the beast was to unscrew the panels lining the interior. The invisible tenrec spurred us on by rattling around in his cavern, though it was difficult to locate the exact place from which the sound was coming. Two men, who had failed to secure front-line places inside the car with screwdrivers, began to investigate the possibilities of removing one of the doors, a procedure they clearly anticipated with the eager relish of children taking a toy to pieces, but one which could not conceivably contribute in any way towards the recovery of the wretched tenrec. At this point the Forestry Officer called a halt to the dismemberment of his car. He was, he said, somewhat tired of the whole business and he proposed to forget about the animal lodged in the chassis and to drive on to his meeting.

I pointed out that this would be most unwise. We had demonstrated in the most convincing fashion that the tenrec was irrecoverable in its present position except by the wholesale use of an oxyacetylene cutter. If he drove off and subjected the beast to an hour or so of jolting in a car getting hotter and hotter under the blazing sun, the poor creature might well die. And if it did that, his car would be quite unusable for a week or so before the smell wore off. A far better plan would be to shut the boot, leave the car and join us for coffee in the hotel. Maybe the tenrec, left in peace, would clamber out of its doubtless extremely uncomfortable refuge in the chassis and return to the comparative space of the boot, for assuredly there must be some route, however devious, between the two places or he could not have got there in the first place.

The Forestry Officer, though clearly considerably put out by this complete dislocation of his day's plans, saw the force of this argument and agreed.

Two hours later we quietly opened the boot again. The tenrec was sitting at the back nonchalantly washing himself. He was the size of a large guinea pig with an absurdly long tapering nose, immense whiskers, beady eyes and enormous hindquarters that ended abruptly and vertically. We pounced and within seconds he was in one of our travelling cages. He drank long from a pot of water and then addressed himself with enthusiasm to a pile of fresh chopped steak that I had purloined, with the cook's connivance, from Jeanine's kitchen.

Although we already had back in Tananarive Zoo the spiny tenrecs which we had caught by Lac Ihotry, we were extremely glad to have this different species, for whereas our first captures looked like nothing more unusual than miniature hedgehogs, this one, the tandraka, was a very different animal and, while it was true to say that his appearance was somewhat nondescript, it was also equally true that he bore no resemblance to any other familiar creature whatever. Furthermore, tandrakas have one particular claim to distinction – they produce more babies in one litter than any other placental mammal. Fifteen infants is not an unusual number, an exceptional litter of twenty-four has been recorded and one pregnant female, on dissection, proved to have thirty-two embryos in her womb.

To the Malagasy, however, the tandraka's main quality is that it makes succulent eating. They hunt it with dogs, particularly during April and May, at the onset of the Madagascan winter, for the tandrakas hibernate and at this season they have accumulated such large stores of fat that their bodies are almost spherical. So highly are they valued that they have been introduced to the nearby islands of Réunion and Mauritius and turned loose to proliferate and provide the inhabitants with a regular source of excellent meat.

When we had asked among the Perinet villagers for tandraka, they had shaken their heads and had declared that the beasts were still sleeping, inaccessible in their deep burrows. Our specimen was obviously one of the first to emerge and we were worried that the shock of being caught, then suddenly thrust into a strange metal container full of intricate and doubtless unpleasantly hot bolt-holes and finally being unceremoniously pounced upon, might prove too much for him after so many months of tranquillity, but happily he showed no ill effects. By the time we got him back to London and handed him over to the Zoo, he had increased considerably in both size and girth, but he never lost his passion for trying to cram his paunchy body down even the smallest suspicion of a hole.

The forest around Perinet was rich in reptiles. We collected three spectacular chameleons, monsters nearly two feet long, with virulent green bodies, rust-red eyeballs and two horns on the end of their snouts. Although they seemed garishly coloured, they were surprisingly difficult to see as they ambled in slow motion through the forest shrubs or stood poised on a branch with that stone-like immobility that only a reptile seems able to achieve. They were, however, conspicuous creatures in comparison with the lizard in which I was most interested, the Uroplatus or frilled gecko. We knew that these reptiles occurred somewhere in the eastern forests, that they clung to tree trunks, and that they were so well disguised it was almost impossible to find them. When searching for such animals the best policy is to recruit some of the local men or, even better, small boys to help in the hunt, for their eyes are always much sharper than those of city-bred foreigners. But when I explained what creature it was I wanted, even the most eager and helpful men in the village refused to assist. The beast was evil and it would be madness to interfere with it, they said. It had the unnerving habit of jumping on to a man's chest and clinging so tightly that it could only be removed with a razor. Furthermore, anyone who touched it would certainly die within a year unless he slashed with a knife the part of his body that had been contaminated and so washed away the evil with blood. Even Michel, with his scientific training in forestry, was not entirely impervious to these stories, for while he scoffed at such superstitions and agreed that Uroplatus was an inoffensive little lizard, he explained that he himself could not catch one for us, for after all, he said, you can never tell about these matters and it would be silly to take unnecessary risks.

We had therefore to search unaided. As we walked through the forest, we thumped every tree with our fists in the hope that we might startle a gecko, make it move and so reveal its presence. But we had no success.

It was only after three days of desultory trunk-thumping that we found one. It was clinging to the bark, head down, no more than two feet from my eyes and had it not made a slight movement of its head, I should never have noticed it, so perfect was its camouflage. It made no further movement as I reached up with my hand, relying for its safety on its disguise. I gripped it with my thumb and forefinger around its neck, and gently detached it.

A frilled gecko disguised against a tree

It was about six inches long. Its grey blotched body matched almost exactly the colour of the bark on which we had found it and its eyes, in many creatures glittering tell-tale clues, were disguised by tatters of skin that overhung the eyeball and broke up its circular outline.

But these two devices, by themselves, were not sufficient to account for its near invisibility. As wartime experts in camouflage realized, an object will always be easily discovered if it casts a shadow. They solved this problem by draping a net around the sides of a bomb dump or a factory, and pegging it to the ground like a flaring skirt so that the building appeared to have no vertical walls and was reduced to a shadowless hump on the surface of the land. The Uroplatus employed a similar device. An irregular flap of skin hung around its chin, and continued as a ragged fringe along its flanks, and its tail was edged by a long flange on either side. When the gecko pressed itself flat against the bark of a tree, the lower edge of these membranes seemed to melt into the bark and the animal became transformed into an incon-spicuous swelling on the rough surface of the tree trunk.

There are several kinds of Uroplatus and later we acquired a different species, nearly three times as big with extremely thin legs and a most extraordinary eye, the pupil of which appeared to have a grooved surface like a peach-stone. But it too had the flanges and frills which provide such a perfect disguise for these strange creatures.

—

Although the men in the village were aghast at our temerity in catching a Uroplatus, they raised no objection to our doing so. I feared, however, that they might protest strongly if we were to catch any boa constrictors, for many Madagascan tribes believe that these snakes are the incarnations of their ancestors.

The origin of this superstition is not difficult to understand. The people, during the retournement ceremonies, must be well aware that worms issue from the decaying corpses. As boas are often found in the dank gloom of the sepulchres, what is more natural than to suppose that these snakes are simply the fully grown form of the worms and that they bear within them the spirits that once inhabited the bodies from which the worms came.

Merina people dancing
beside the tomb

One of Madagascar's
more ferocious-
looking chameleons

A frilled gecko clinging head–down on the trunk of a tree

A sifaka

Looking for indris in the Madagascan rainforest

A ruffed lemur

Magani working on a bark painting

Mimi figures on the wall of a rock shelter near Nourlangie

Barramundi fish painted in the X-ray style near Nourlangie

A spear fisherman on the coast near Maningrida

Among the Betsileo who live in the southern part of the central plateau, the belief is particularly strong. If a boa is found close to a village, the people receive it with great veneration. They gather around it, searching for some sign that will enable them to identify the human spirit it contains. If the snake is particularly sluggish or has a scar or a wart on its flank or its head, then this may provide the clue by which the anxious villagers can link it with some person, long since dead, who possessed just such characteristics.

They question the snake, calling out the name of the person they suspect it to be. If the reptile shakes its head from side to side, as snakes so often do, then this is taken as confirmation of the identification and the animal is reverently carried to the house it occupied during its human incarnation and there presented with gifts of honey and milk. Sometimes a chicken is sacrificed before it, so that it may lap the warm blood with its flickering tongue. The chief of the village then makes a speech, welcoming the spirit back to its home, explaining that the people are glad that it has visited them.

In some villages, the family concerned build special cages in which they will place the snakes they consider to be their parents or grandparents. In other areas, the reptile is allowed to make its own way back to the forest.

For us, who wanted to catch boas, these superstitions could have been a severe obstacle, for clearly we might deeply offend the people if we unceremoniously dumped such a sacred creature into a sack and proposed taking it away with us. We were relieved to discover, however, that in Perinet these beliefs were not held. But though the villagers did not consider the boas to be the incarnations of their ancestors, they nonetheless regarded the creatures as being almost as evil as the Uroplatus and nothing would persuade them to have anything to do with the snakes, let alone catch them for us.

Fortunately, we did not need their help, for the boas were common, easily found and simple to catch. One we discovered beneath a pile of logs close by Michel's fish ponds, and two more we came across in a marshy patch of ground in the forest, lying in a swirl of coils, their broad flanks slowly heaving as they breathed. They were so sluggish that all we had to do was to grasp them by the back of their necks and drop them into a sack.

Collecting snakes in the forest

They are not venomous, but kill their prey by squeezing, and one might have supposed that they would be related to the typical and similar constricting snakes of Africa, the pythons. But in the perverse way of all Madagascar's animals, their affinities are not with any African snakes, but with the boas of South America.

In fact, the anatomical difference between boas and pythons is not large. Both groups are primitive members of the snake tribe, lacking highly developed poison fangs and still possessing the rudiments of hind limbs in the region where a pelvis once existed. Indeed a naturalist presented with the skeletons of a boa and a python would be hard put to it to tell one from the other, the main difference between the two being a small bone in a python's skull which is absent in the boa. Nevertheless, the distinction is a major one, for whereas all pythons lay eggs, all boas give birth to their young alive, and as if to give clear demonstration of her affinities, the female that we had caught by the fish ponds produced four lively ochre-coloured babies soon after we brought her back to London.

Picking up a boa

My hotel room was now well stocked. The chameleons sat goggling at one another on the curtain rail, the Uroplatus hung upside down on a piece of bark in a tall cage next door to the tandraka, the millipedes – during the day – slumbered in a big box in the one corner and the boas occupied a slowly moving sack in the other. Although we had not caught any, we had seen several kinds of lemurs – brown lemurs like those we had watched in the mango trees in the forest of Ankarafantsika near Majunga; sifakas, which here are called *simpona*; and a gentle lemur. This last was new to us and quite enchanting. I came face to face with it one morning as I was walking by myself. It was sitting on an inclined liana only about two feet from the ground, holding on firmly with both hands, a little grey furry creature the size of a small monkey, with a flattened face, a brown cap and a long tail. In wide-eyed horror it stared at me. I could almost hear it repeating, 'Oh my goodness me.' For a full half minute it stayed where it was and then tried to dash away. But gentle lemurs are quite incapable of moving at speed, and the best it could produce was a panic-stricken amble along the ground. Away it went, occasionally looking back over its shoulder at me. I stood quite still until it had disappeared.

The forest indeed was by far the most abundantly populated area that we had visited in the whole of Madagascar, and every day we found fresh creatures to fascinate us – moths, beetles, snakes, little lizards, black parrots, flycatchers, strange frogs – but one animal eluded us. We still had not found the indri.

17

Babakoto

We had been asked by an ornithologist friend to record the song of the Madagascan magpie robin, for he had predicted that it would have a call so sweet and complexly beautiful that it might be considered to be among the finest produced by any bird. The robin, a small velvet-black bird with snowy spots on its wing and gleaming white outer tail feathers, was not an easy bird to see, for it was shy and unobtrusive and seldom left the cover of the lower forest bushes. Its song was indeed beautiful, a sweet thin trilling melody, and once we had learned to recognize it we began to appreciate just how abundant the birds were, for though we could not see them, we often heard their carolling in many places in the forest.

We made our first attempt to record them one morning soon after dawn, taking with us a special parabolic reflector, an aluminium dish over two feet across, which acted as a kind of sound searchlight, concentrating the sensitivity of the microphone mounted at its centre into a narrow beam so that it was possible to record a sound a considerable distance away and at the same time cut out most of the other noises from the surrounding forest. We had selected for our recording one particular cock bird, bolder than most, that habitually sang from among the leaves of a bush not far from the track we normally followed.

When we arrived, we found him already calling lustily. Quickly, I plugged the microphone cable into the recorder and carefully aimed the reflector at the bush. Unperturbed, the little robin continued to pour out his long chains of silvery notes. As I brought the reflector into line with him, the needle on the recorder dial began to echo each throb of his song with a quiver. For several minutes the spools revolved and the tape moved steadily across the recorder head. Then suddenly, a deafening eerie wail pealed out from the trees beyond, so loud that the recorder needle thrashed hard against the stop pin of the dial and clung there shuddering. It was the indri, louder and closer than the first time we had heard them. Geoff snatched his camera. I swiftly turned down the volume control so that the recording should not be distorted, and with my binoculars frantically searched the green tangle ahead. The invisible singers – for there were several of them – continued their bawling unabated. But no matter how hard we looked, we could see nothing of them. To be baulked this way a second time was doubly infuriating. I walked up the track, moving as slowly as I could manage in my excitement, to try and find a vantage point from which the creatures would be visible. Though I strained my eyes, I could find no sign of them.

The calls stopped and simultaneously a tall thin-trunked tree some thirty yards away shuddered and I caught a momentary glimpse of a body sailing through the air. The indri had left. Once more we had failed.

'Well,' said Geoff, as we walked back disconsolately to breakfast, 'at least we have got a recording to prove that the creature does really exist and that – once upon a time – we were within a few yards of it.'

It was then that I thought of using a trick which is often employed by ornithologists to locate the birds that they wish to study. Cock birds sing both to attract their mates and to proclaim their sovereignty over the territory they inhabit. If, therefore, you play a recording of a bird's voice, hen birds may be drawn to it and cock birds may come to dispute angrily with this new intruder in their territory. The method, however, works with other creatures besides birds. I had employed it one night several years earlier to lure a large croaking toad into the range of my flash-light camera. Now we had the recorded voice of the indri. Perhaps they too would respond to their recorded calls.

I did not have a great deal of confidence in the idea. For one thing, the volume of noise produced by the speaker of our battery-driven recorder was so feeble in comparison with the original sound that at best it could only resemble the song of a far-distant group of indris. But we had tried every other method and failed, so we might as well try this.

For the next few days, we patiently played the recording in several parts of the forest but without result. Then one morning, soon after dawn, I put down the recorder by the side of the track we habitually followed at a point that seemed particularly suitable. The ground fell steeply from the path towards a lush dell containing only a few thin trees and carpeted by a plant with wide spear-shaped leaves. On the far side of it a small stream swung in a curve, cutting a swathe through the forest so that, from the track, we looked down into a green, relatively clear amphitheatre.

Geoff set up his camera and fitted our most powerful telephoto lens to it. As soon as he was ready I turned on the recorder. For a minute or two the tinny counterfeit calls echoed thinly among the unresponsive trees. I had almost decided to give up and try elsewhere when the voice of the recorder was completely drowned by stentorian trumpeting hoots. They were totally different from the indri calls we had heard before, and I could not imagine what creature was producing them.

Then I saw one of the singers in a tree in the middle of the dell – a big furry lemur, particoloured black and white, sitting on a branch some thirty feet from the ground. His chest, fore-arms and legs below the knee were white and he appeared to be wearing a black cape around his shoulders, a pure white cap and sooty black socks and gloves.

My heart sank. This could not be an indri. The skins we had seen in the Scientific Institute in Tananarive had been almost entirely black except for a small triangular patch of white on the back which spread from hip to hip and pointed up the spine. What was more, the hoots were entirely different from the wails that Michel had identified for us as those of the indri.

'It's only a ruffed lemur,' I whispered disgustedly to Geoff, 'and we can easily get really close-up shots of the one in Tananarive Zoo.'

A ruffed lemur

Nonetheless, we started filming, for he was a most beautiful creature, and anyhow good pictures of a wild free individual would be far more valuable than that of a captive animal. Furthermore, we were ideally placed, for the ground fell so steeply from us that we were almost on the same level as the animal as he sat some twenty yards farther down the slope, thirty feet up in his tree.

The recorder continued its indri wails. The beast glared

indignantly at us with bright yellow eyes. Once more he hooted his irritation and another trumpet came from a tree on the left. I turned and saw two more of the animals sitting with their necks craned forward, staring at us in puzzlement. The first one reached up and pulled himself on to the branch above. I made a mental note that his movements were not like the other members of the Lemur genus, such as the ring-tail or the brown lemur, which are all essentially four-footed in their gait. This was a surprise, for the ruffed lemur is an extremely close relation. This creature, I said to myself, moves more like a sifaka. And then, as the animal seated himself once more, I blinked in surprise.

'Where's he put his tail?' I muttered to Geoff. 'He should have a very long black one.'

'Perhaps it's curled up between his legs,' Geoff answered.

I continued staring at the animal through my binoculars. The animal stared back at us, threw his head back and hooted once more, showing the bright red inside of his mouth. Then he raised one of his long hind legs and grasped the tree trunk in front of him, almost on a level with his chest. He did *not* have a tail. I was quite sure. Stupidly it took me several seconds to come to the only possible conclusion.

'Geoff,' I said quietly, 'that is an indri.'

There could be no doubt. There is only one tailless lemur. I then recalled the book that said that, though the indri was predominantly black, its colouring was 'variable'. This must be the explanation for the disparity between this creature and the skins I had seen. The difference in the voice could also be accounted for. The animals were not replying to the song with a similar chorus, but were so startled by it that they were responding with alarm calls. To that extent, my trick with the recorder had not worked, for no doubt they would have hooted in the same way if I had been playing a Wagner overture. Nonetheless, we were too jubilant to worry about such a trivial detail. We had found them and Geoff had already exposed a full

The indri

four hundred feet of film. Rapidly, he changed magazines, dismantled the long telephoto lens which had only taken in the animal's head and shoulders and replaced it with a shorter lens to take shots of the entire creature. I stopped the tape machine, plugged in a microphone, and recorded the repeated indignant trumpetings which the indris continued to make, as though outraged by our presence. Cautiously, Geoff stepped off the track on to the slope to try and get shots from a different angle, but this was too much. With a gigantic bound, the first indri leapt away, springing from trunk to trunk so rapidly that he appeared to ricochet from one tree to another. The other two followed him down into the thick forest beyond the stream. Within seconds they were out of sight.

Michel had been emphatic that the babakoto followed the same path through the forest each day. If he were right, then the animals might be in the same place the next morning. We were up before dawn to see. They were there, and as we had not needed to play the recorder to find them, they were undisturbed and oblivious of our presence. The big male, the first we had seen, was feeding, sitting astride a branch, like a child on a see-saw, with his enormous black-socked legs dangling. With his hands, he was reaching above his head, plucking selected young leaves and stuffing them nonchalantly in his mouth. The other two sat close by. They proved to be a pair. As they were a little smaller, I assumed they must be a young couple. If they were, where was the old male's mate? Quietly, we investigated and at last I detected her, hidden in a tree some distance away. To have approached her would have alarmed the others, so we stayed where we were, contentedly filming.

We watched this family day after day for over a week and, slowly, we came to know their daily routine. Michel had been absolutely correct. They were indeed creatures of habit. They slept each night in the same tree. Soon after dawn they would depart, clambering leisurely through the branches towards the place where we had first found them. There they ate. They sang at almost exactly the same time each day – about five o'clock, soon after the sun rose, and in mid morning between ten and eleven. Towards midday, they moved off across the stream and we lost contact with them. But in the afternoon, at about four o'clock, they sang again from the opposite side of the valley and by taking a different track through the forest we were able to find them again, eating their evening meal. As evening approached, they left once more to return to their sleeping tree.

We came to recognize the family individually. The old male was of a phlegmatic disposition and somewhat sedate. He often sat on a branch with his back against the main trunk and his long legs outstretched in a comically human-like position. Although he could leap great distances when he was alarmed, he usually clambered from one branch to another. He never, however, used his arms in the way apes do – to swing from one bough to another – and as a trapeze artist he could not compare with, say, a gibbon.

The two youngsters were an extremely affectionate couple and spent hours each day caressing and licking one another. The position they chose in which to practise their endearments, squatting on a thin horizontal bough, seemed very perilous. They reminded me of a pair of skilful circus acrobats nonchalantly pretending to enact episodes of their daily lives on a high wire. But the indris had no need of balancing poles or safety nets. Their feet were so large that with their middle and big toes they could completely encircle the branch on which they sat with a grip so firm and steady that there was no need to cling on to anything with their hands. They were, however, rather skittish and nervous. Any sudden noise, whether made by us or by some other forest creature, alarmed them. A couple of black parrots flying overhead squawking raucously would make them crane their heads up anxiously. Once as they sat facing one another, the male gently licking the fur of the female's neck, a large blue coua, the Madagascan cuckoo, came hopping up one of the lianas, grunting its loud gruff staccato call. The female immediately abandoned her relaxed posture and sat upright, twisting her head to try and identify the creature that produced this alarming noise. The male looked down too, less alarmed, and then made a tentative effort to resume his affectionate lick-ings. But the female remained tense and nervous, so the male reached up to a branch by his head and neatly swung himself round so that he sat behind his mate. Then he placed one of his long legs on either side of her, as though to reassure her. She bent back her long neck and rewarded him with a lick on the chin.

The fourth member of the family group, the old female, we seldom saw. She seemed to settle only in the thickest foliage. Perhaps she had good cause for her reticence. It was only after several days of concentrating our attention on her that we discovered the reason. Clinging to her back, she had a small

An indri mother and young

black-faced baby with hairy puckish ears and bright eyes. He was barely a foot long. Sometimes he rode on her back, sometimes he clambered round to suckle from his mother's nipples. She behaved with endearing tenderness towards him, licking him gently from time to time.

Our detailed knowledge of the family's daily routine made our task of filming them much easier. We had photographed them feeding, dozing and caressing one another, but one shot we lacked. We had never secured any good pictures of the indris leaping, for when they did finally move off, they always jumped away from us. If we were to get the film we wanted, then we should have to devise some new method of approach. We knew their lunchtime tree and we knew where they sang in the late afternoon. To get from one place to the other, we realized that they would have to cross a wide road leading from the fish ponds. At only one place was it narrow enough for the indris to leap comfortably from one side to the other. A simple calculation was enough to show that they must make the crossing between three and four o'clock in the afternoon. Accordingly at half-past two, Geoff and I set up our cameras a little west of the trees we judged they would use, so that the sun was behind our backs. We waited.

Prompt at half-past three, the old male appeared in the take-off tree. The young couple joined him a few minutes later, and finally the mother and her baby emerged from the forest behind to sit on one of the branches overhanging the road. As soon as they were all assembled, the old male clambered leisurely to the most outstretched branch. Geoff began filming. The male poised himself, then leaped, a single soaring jump right across the road to the tree on the other side. One by one, the rest of his family followed him and disappeared. Geoff switched off his cameras, beaming. Our film of the private life of the indris was at last as complete as we could have hoped to make it.

Were the creatures we had filmed and watched with such pleasure for so many days really the origin of the legend of the dog-headed man? They were undeniably dog-headed and, particularly when they clambered through the branches, they seemed very human-like, the length of their legs in proportion to their torsos being very close to that of a man. Further, the legends seem to have stemmed from the Arabs. Their dhows have been trading for centuries between the north-east coast of Africa across the Mozambique Channel, calling at the Comoro Islands as a halfway stage. They might well have brought the stories of the indri back to Africa with them. In addition, the arrow-reflecting coat of the cynocephalus quoted by Aldrovandus, and the stories of the indri catching missiles and throwing them back at its attacker, were suggestively similar. Of course there can be no positive proof of a connection between such a wide-spread legend and this particular animal, but I would like to think that the connection existed nonetheless. Of one thing, however, I was certain. Of all the strange creatures we had filmed in Madagascar, this was the rarest, the least known scientifically and the most endearing.

When we returned to Tananarive, we found all the animals which we had collected during our journeys in other parts of the island awaiting us in the cages and enclosures of the Institute's handsome little Zoo. There was much now that we had to do, for within a week a small charter plane was due to fly us and our collection back to Nairobi where we could tranship on to a freighter aircraft bound for London. Travelling cages for the animals had to be constructed, certificates for their health, and permits for their export had to be drafted, stamped and countersigned, and we had to make our farewells to all those people who had helped and advised us. M Paulian himself had been called to a scientific congress in Europe, but he had left the last of his kindnesses to be revealed to us in his absence. Well aware of our disappointment in not being permitted to catch any lemur, apart from the little *Microcebus*, to take back to London, he had given instructions that we were to be presented with two ring-tails and a female ruffed lemur from the Institute's own collections.

The ruffed lemur was by far the most handsome of all the animals in the Zoo and vied with the sifakas and the indris as being the most beautiful of all lemurs. Its dense, silky fur was patched in white and a lustrous jet black, the colours being distributed in a manner reminiscent of a giant panda. There were three of these magnificent creatures in a single cage. One of them, which came from a restricted locality in the eastern forests, had patches which were not black but a splendid orange brown. No one knows for certain the function of such conspicuous patterns. For the skunk, heavily armed with its disgusting squirt glands, it seems very likely that they serve as a conspicuous signal to warn other animals to get out of its way. But this cannot be the function of the gentle, vegetarian, ruffed lemur's patterning. It is significant, however, that the animal is largely nocturnal and several creatures of the night, such as the badger, are distinctively marked with black and white, perhaps to aid in seeing and recognizing one another as they prowl through the darkness.

The ruffed lemurs were all enchantingly tame and every day that we went to the Zoo, we made a special visit to their enclosure to feed them on stick insects and bananas and to tickle their stomachs as they lay on their backs on the ground squirming with delight. The gift of one of them thrilled us greatly and provided us with the most spectacular member of our collection.

The second of M Paulian's presents, the ring-tails, are perhaps the lemurs that are the most widely known and most frequently seen in zoos all over the world, for they flourish and breed readily in captivity. Their short fur is a most elegant dove-grey toning to pure white on their undersides and faces, and they have long swishing tails ringed with black. Their scientific name is *Lemur catta* − cat lemur − and many writers have said that it is a most inappropriate one. The animals, however, are the size of cats and have somewhat cat-like faces. Even more aptly, as I came to discover when I kept our pair for a month or so at my home in London, they have the voices of cats. Not only do they miaow but when I gave mine some particularly delectable titbit such as a prune, or when I fondled them at the back of their ears, they would express their pleasure with the most feline of purrs; they seldom did so for any length of time, nor did they perform with any great frequency, but there could be no doubting it. I do not know if any other animal outside the cat family is able to purr, but certainly to hear the cat lemurs doing so totally justified their name to me.

They were the easiest of animals to feed, for they seemed to accept gleefully a wide variety of the most unlikely foods and were prepared to sample almost anything vaguely vegetable that we chose to give them. In the end, and in the belief that many animals do not relish an unvaried monotony of diet, I presented them each morning with dishes containing several types of vegetable food. Fresh grass, raisins, baked potatoes, lettuce, carrots, chicory, grapes and bananas were all accepted eagerly, though their particular fancy varied from day to day. One morning they would rummage around their food tins to find the raisins, ignoring everything else until they had eaten the last; the next day they would carefully sort out all the lettuce before sampling anything else. As pets they were fascinating and endearing – lively, full of ingenuity and curiosity, dazzling acrobats and filled with a passion for licking themselves, one another, and me, whenever I gave them a chance.

The elder of them, however, was already growing his adult canine teeth, sharp as scimitars, and I played with him only with considerable caution, making sure that I never attempted to restrain him and caressing him only when he showed he was in the mood to accept such endearments by licking me. They were very selective in their affections and whereas I could handle both of them, I did not dare allow strangers to take liberties with them. If they disliked someone, they would show their feelings by suddenly flashing their arms through the wide mesh of their cage, grabbing the unwelcome visitor's sleeve and giving it a sharp tug. Then they would race around their enclosure, as though exulting at having caught him unawares. These assaults were by no means easily laughed off, for the ring-tail's claws are long and needle-sharp and on several occasions they succeeded in drawing little beads of blood, even through the fabric of a shirt.

The collection we took back to England was not a large one. Nevertheless, the London Zoo regarded many of the animals as rarities for, although they were common in their original home, so few Malagasy creatures had reached Great Britain that it was the first time that several of them had ever been seen alive in the Zoo. The spiny tenrecs and the mouse lemurs settled down so well that they produced babies season after season. The ruffed lemur was sent as a mate a lone male from the Paris Zoo. To everyone's delight, she eventually produced twins and so started a line whose descendants, twenty years later, still lived in Regent's Park.

Ring-tailed lemurs at the London Zoo

BOOK THREE

Quest Under Capricorn

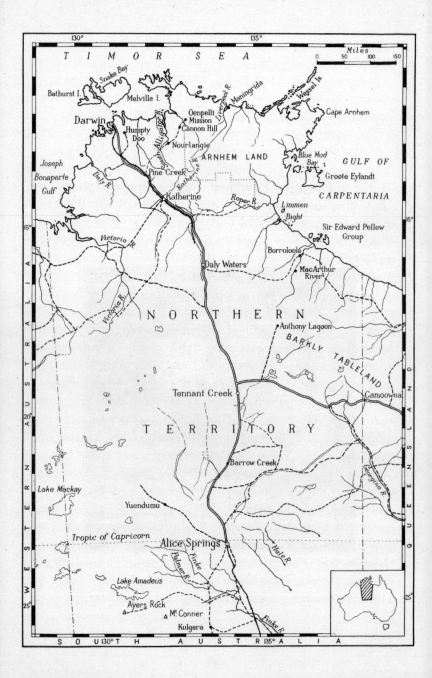

18

East from Darwin

The statistics are daunting. The Northern Territory of Australia extends for a thousand miles from north to south and for nearly six hundred miles from east to west – an area of over half a million square miles. In this immense rectangular segment of a continent lived a mere twenty thousand white Australians and sixteen thousand Aboriginal people. It is as though the British Isles were increased in size six times and populated only by the inhabitants of one small town – say, Dover or Pontypool; as though the mayor of Maidenhead were responsible for an area extending from his town hall to Berlin in one direction and Tangier in the other, and his townspeople were scattered in a dozen or so small settlements in between. Or, to put it another way, the density of population is the same as if the people of Ashby-de-la-Zouch or Dartmouth were spread out to inhabit the whole of Britain from Land's End to John o' Groats.

The Tropic of Capricorn runs across the Territory close to its southern boundary. Its northern coast is closer to the Equator than is Fiji or Jamaica, Aden or Madras. Here in the north, the country is clothed by jungles that during the monsoon are dripping wet and, over great areas, water-logged and impassable. Down in the southwest begins one of the most ferociously arid deserts in the world and one that is still not completely explored. The administrative capital of this huge land is Darwin.

No one else on the aeroplane taking us to Australia was going to stay in Darwin. The place for them was just an irritating interruption in the middle of the arbitrary period which the airline had labelled as a time in which to sleep. When we all stumbled out, it was, in Darwin's terms, four o'clock in the morning and in our terms it was no identifiable time at all, since wristwatches had been swivelling throughout the preceding thirty-six hours. Bleary-eyed, we submitted to the strange cate-chism of the Customs, which at this time in the deserted airport seemed even more nonsensical than normal. Had we any insects with us in any stage of development? Why were we coming to Australia? Were we importing any firearms or horse rugs? Had we a list of the numbers of all the lenses of our cameras? Most of our fellow passengers, having filled in the forms, moved on to the part of the airport known internationally and hideously as the Transit Lounge. For them Darwin was merely the back door to a continent whose great cities were still two thousand miles distant. For us, it was the biggest town we were to see in the whole of the time that we were to spend in Australia – on this trip at least.

With me, once more, was Charles Lagus. We had been together in Darwin five years earlier, on our way to film birds of paradise in New Guinea. This time, our purpose was rather different. Although we hoped we should be filming birds and many other animals in the Territory, our objective was a wider one. We wanted to bring back a series of films that would give a rounded picture of the Territory – its people, its landscape, as well as its animals. For the first time, on a journey like this, we had an additional companion. Bob Saunders had come with us as sound recordist. This was his first journey outside Europe. He looked round at the depressing empty airport.

'Right,' he said with an enthusiasm that seemed almost inde-cent at this low ebb in our affairs. 'How do we start?'

Darwin, perched on the northern rim of Australia, is a lonely town. It has proffered many excuses for its existence since it was named in 1836 – a port for pearlers, a clearing house for bullion during the gold rushes of the eighties and nineties, a terminal for oil tankers, a link between the end of the Overland Telegraph that reached here in 1872 and the submarine cables that took messages on to London – but none has been convincing enough to sustain a town of any size.

Its population has come from all over the world. Chinese families, whose forebears came here to work the gold mines, now ran several of the stores. Newly immigrated Italians and Viennese had travelled up from Sydney to start restaurants and serve schnitzels and ravioli which were revelations to bushmen brought up on damper and wallaby stew. In the Post Office, you meet Cockneys and New Zealanders, a man from Birmingham and another from Brisbane. Only a minority seem involved in the ferocious wilderness that begins at the end of the main street. You may occasionally hear a man in a pub talking about gold strikes or a lonely uranium mine. A few Aboriginals in vividly coloured sweatshirts lounge outside the cinemas sucking soft drinks through straws. And occasionally a tall cattleman in a cowboy hat and spurs strides down the street among the dapper bank clerks.

We met the most flamboyant of these pioneers of the outback in the bar of Darwin's smartest hotel. He was a florid-faced man, dressed in an extravagant bushwhacker manner with a red hand-kerchief knotted at the neck of his check shirt, tight threadbare breeches and riding boots. Doug Muir, the owner of the local air charter firm, whom we already knew, introduced the three of us.

'This is Alan Stewart,' he said, 'and if you blokes are wanting to see wildlife in the bush, this is the chap to set you right.'

We shook hands, feeling very hot and unhealthily pallid in comparison to our two deeply suntanned companions. I explained that we hoped, among other things, to film animals.

'You'd be set like a jelly down at my place,' said Alan. 'Ducks, geese, 'roos, barramundi fish the length of your arm, crocs, everything you want.'

He drained his glass of beer and smacked his lips. 'That one went down without touching the sides,' he remarked appreciatively.

Doug took the hint. 'It's my shout,' he said. 'You blokes can ease in another charge, I reckon.' He gathered up the empty glasses and went over to the bar.

'Mind you,' continued Alan, 'you'd have to watch out for buffalo while you are taking your snaps. They can be a bit cranky. You ask Doug about his dad.'

Doug returned with five more beers. 'Yeah,' he said, 'the old bloke was just fossicking around in the scrub and this big bull buffalo shot out from nowhere, whanged him down and started giving him a going over. He's tough, the old man, and he caught hold of the buff's horns and started twisting its neck. Eventually the buff reckoned it had had enough and left. But the old man was in a poor way. Four broken ribs and some nasty bruises here and there. Had to bring him in to hospital to get him fixed up. That was three weeks ago and he only came out today.'

'These buffalo sound rather bad-tempered,' I said in what I hoped sounded a nonchalant tone. 'What does one do to avoid trouble?'

'Shoot 'em,' said Alan draining his glass. 'I suppose you blokes carry guns.'

'Well, no,' I admitted, feeling more than ever the effete Englishman. 'And as a matter of fact, I doubt if I'd be able to hit a charging buffalo even if I had got one.'

'Then don't carry one,' said Alan severely. 'There are too many blokes going around with guns who couldn't hit a bull's backside with a basketful of wheat at two yards.'

'But what do we do if a buffalo turns nasty then?' persisted Bob.

'Shin up a tree,' said Doug. 'Quick time.'

'There was a girl who was knocked over by a buff, and as it

knelt on her, she just stroked its nose and said "There, there". She got away with no more than bruises. You might try that,' said Alan helpfully.

'Course, if you are in a car, it's not so bad,' said Doug. 'One chap last year met a buff head-on in the road. He drove at a fair lick for two miles in reverse before the buff slowed down and decided that it wasn't interested.'

'Still, I suppose they're pretty scarce, these buffalo,' said Charles, endeavouring to look on the bright side.

'Scarce!' said Alan in an indignant tone. 'There's mobs of them couple of hundred strong around my place. I told you, it's the best country for wildlife in the whole of the Territory.'

These buffalo were not the shaggy hump-backed creatures that once swarmed on the plains of North America, but the very different cow-like beasts of Asia, water buffalo. A big bull may weigh up to three-quarters of a ton and be armed with horns curving back from his brow over his shoulders that measure ten feet from tip to tip. In their native country they behave with misleading docility. Uncomplainingly they drag enormous carts and submit to the ferocious beatings of their drivers. They wallow in canals and allow small boys to clamber over them and scrub their hides. Yet even there, they have their moments of ferocity and the unfamiliar smell of a European can be sufficient to irritate them so much that they will suddenly run amok, overturning their carts and charging anyone who comes near them.

Over a century ago, they were imported into Australia from Timor to provide the newly founded military settlements at Raffles Bay and Port Essington on the north coast with meat and milk, and serve as draught animals. But in 1849, the garrisons were abandoned and the buffalo turned loose. The country suited them and since then they have flourished. For the most part they are now left to wander across the plains unharmed – except around places such as Nourlangie, Alan's camp.

Originally, Nourlangie was a timber concession, but when the trees had been worked out, Alan took over the lease, built some huts as additional accommodation and called the place a safari camp. The buffalo became transformed into big game, and were listed with crocodiles, kangaroos and wildfowl as an attraction for sportsmen from the cities of the south who were anxious to savour the inexplicable thrill of slaughter.

However, it seemed that Alan's campaign to flood the Territory with big game hunters was not flourishing. Nourlangie was almost deserted. If we went there, we should have huts to live in, the service of a bush radio, and a private airstrip. It seemed a good place to use as a base. There were obviously plenty of buffalo there and doubtless many of the other creatures that we were hoping to film. We decided to accept Alan's invitation. He himself was flying back that afternoon. We would follow by road, with all our gear, as soon as we could hire ourselves a Land Rover.

The Stuart Highway

There was only one way out of Darwin by land – the Stuart Highway. The road was affectionately known as 'the bitumen', a name which in itself gave an indication of its unique character, for apart from a branch leading eastwards into Queensland, it was the only surfaced road in the entire Territory and, being so, the only one negotiable during the rainy season.

The bitumen was built between 1940 and 1943 to bring military supplies up to Darwin, when the Japanese invasion of New Guinea put the town into the front line. Twenty yards wide and nearly a thousand miles long, it ran almost due south through eucalyptus scrub and across rocky desert to Alice Springs. There it was succeeded by a stony potholed track that continued for another thousand miles to Adelaide.

Soon we had left behind the last of Darwin's ramshackle suburbs and had started the long drive to Pine Creek, where we would spend the night before turning east, off the bitumen, for Nourlangie. The road cut through eucalyptus scrub, often blackened over great areas by bush fires. Termite hills, buttressed and pinnacled, stood ten feet high in the dry yellow grass like megaliths. Occasionally a wallaby, sitting back perkily on its tail, peered at us through the sparse gum trees before it bounced away. These creatures are a dangerous hazard on the bitumen. At night they sit on the road, perhaps relishing the heat which the tarmac still retains after its daytime roasting, and cars travelling at seventy or eighty miles an hour through the darkness often crash into them. Sometimes the cars are badly damaged and knocked off their course into the bush. Nearly always, the wallabies are killed. The bodies of the previous night's casualties lay on the roadside, already so bloated by corruption that the hides were inflated like wineskins, the legs sticking awkwardly into the air.

We drove for over a hundred miles without passing any settlement of more than half a dozen houses and at last reached Pine Creek. Even here there were barely more than a dozen buildings. The biggest was splendidly labelled 'Residential Hotel' in illuminated lettering. We drew up thankfully and went in. It was

Saturday night and the bar was full of men in their shirt-sleeves bawling in one another's ears. The barman directed us through a glass door etched with the word 'Foyer' and we found ourselves in a wasteland of chromium tubular steel tables adorned, in this country of wattle, orchids and bougainvillaea, with white plastic tulips. A statuesque lady emerged from the kitchen beyond to welcome us.

A magnetic termite hill

She produced a meal, and sat down with us to talk. As we ate, the shouts of the men in the bar grew louder.

'Do you keep a chucker-out here?' I asked conversationally.

'Do it myself,' said our hostess, folding her muscular arms. 'My oath, I do.'

I was fully prepared to believe it.

'Things are quiet these days, though,' she continued. 'This isn't the back of beyond any more – though people down south still seem to think we're a rough mob here. Do you know,' she added in outraged tones, 'when my daughter got married here a few months ago, some writer from a newspaper rang up from Sydney and asked how many of the wedding guests arrived on camels!'

We shook our heads sympathetically. From the bar beyond came a sustained crash of breaking glass followed by angry shouts. 'Excuse me,' she said meaningfully and strode out.

The next morning we set out early to cover the remaining eighty miles to Nourlangie. The country was much the same as that we had seen on our way to Pine Creek, but now we had turned off the bitumen and the unsurfaced road soon dwindled to a winding track. On the bitumen we had at least seen other cars occasionally, there had been road signs, and although it was a lonely road, there was plenty of evidence of the hand of man. Here, apart from the track itself, the country was unmarked. There were no buildings, no telegraph poles, nothing. The land seemed completely empty. Once, when we stopped to let the engine cool, we heard to our astonishment the sound of hooves. A tall horseman emerged from the scrub. He was bare-chested and bare-footed. A can of beer hung from his saddle.

'If you see a couple o' blokes with a mob 'er cattle, tell 'em that the Goodparla jeep is buggered,' he said. Then, without waiting for a reply to this enigmatic request, he pulled round his horse's head and trotted away. He was the only human being we saw between Pine Creek and Nourlangie.

We reached Alan's camp in time for lunch. As we sat in the mess hut, quenching our thirst, the only other guest staying there appeared at the door. He had just emerged from a shower and was clad only in his underpants and a long shapeless vest that barely covered his enormous slack stomach. He was a butcher who had come up from Melbourne for a few days' sport. The sun had scorched an angry scarlet triangle at his neck. His forearms were peeling. He was not my conception of an intrepid white hunter.

'G'day,' we said, slipping into the vernacular. 'Yer right?'

'Ball o' muscle,' he replied with gusto, giving the side of his chest such a clout with his fist that the whole of his body rippled like a blancmange. 'If I felt any better, I couldn't stand it.'

We discovered that the cause of his exuberance was that only a few hours before he had put a bullet through the brain of a large bull buffalo as it stood looking at him in the scrub.

'Yeah,' he said enthusiastically, and with surprising perception, 'it's been a great trip – a real busman's holiday.' And he laughed.

Although the butcher, on the strength of having spent four days driving through the bush with an Aboriginal guide beside him to point out the buffalo, was prepared and indeed anxious to tell us all about the habits of the beasts – where we should find them and how close we could approach them – we felt that we could get more reliable information from an old buffalo hunter named Yorky Billy.

Yorky lived a mile away from Nourlangie with his wife, five children and a string of horses. His home was simply a large patched tarpaulin stretched over poles. From its guy ropes hung strips of meat drying in the sun. In front of it smouldered a small log fire. Yorky was in his seventies. His hair was grey and his legs bowed by a lifetime spent in the saddle. His skin was as dark as an Aboriginal's but his features were European. Few people could know the country and its animals better than he, for he was born here.

'My father came out here to prospect for gold,' he said. 'They called him Yorky Mick, because he came from Yorkshire.'

'Yorkshire?' I said, surprised.

'It's part of the British Empire,' Yorky explained patiently. 'A territory north of London somewhere. My old man used to grow spuds and onions up there. But I don't reckon it can be much of a place. Covered in snow most of the time. My father reckoned this is much better country.'

He stroked his walrus moustache.

'Didn't find his gold though.'

Yorky Billy

Like his father, Yorky married an Aboriginal. She was a young girl, with the thinnest legs I had ever seen. While we talked she stayed shyly with the children in the tent.

'She's my second wife,' Yorky said. 'I found my first one just wanderin' about in the bush. She's dead now. This one was given to me by tribal promise. Her parents promised her to me before she was born. That's a promise you don't break. Course, it's a bit of a toss-up. Might not have been a girl for one thing. Then I had to wait a bit of time before I could marry her. But she's a good wife to me.'

Yorky had camped by Nourlangie with his horses in order

to hire them out to any of the big game hunters who might want them. Most, however, preferred to do their shooting from a jeep and Yorky was on hard times. The old days had been better, when he worked as a buffalo shooter on the plains.

'Used to get twenty pounds for the hide of a big bull but there's no price for them now,' he said. 'So I make a few pounds where I can. Get a quid a tail for dingo. Crocs' skins still fetch a fair price when you can get 'em. And I still keep an eye open for the gold my old man never found.'

'Are these buffalo really dangerous?' I asked.

'My word they are. You get an old bull that's had a bullet in his backside sometime and he'll come for you all right. And then there are others that are just naturally a bit frisky. They'll come for you too. I've often had to jump up a tree in a hurry.'

'How do we avoid trouble?'

'Don't go nearer to them than fifty yards. You can tell the bad 'uns, because they've got cranky expressions on their faces.'

I explained that we were not sufficiently familiar with buffaloes' expressions to distinguish a sour look from a friendly one – especially at a distance of fifty yards.

'Well, if he comes for you and you haven't got a gun, and there's no tree to shin up,' he said, 'there's only one thing to do. Wait till he gets within a few yards of you and then fall flat on the ground. He'll just jump over you and gallop on.'

19

Geese and Goannas

The South Alligator River rises a hundred miles south of Nourlangie in a wilderness of empty hills. As it winds its way northwards, it is joined by smaller streams that come tumbling down the fretted western edge of the great rock plateaux of Arnhem Land. Strengthened, the river slides on towards the coast, sometimes, in the dry season, sinking from sight beneath spits of hot white sand, sometimes swelling into stretches of deep amber water, haunted by cockatoos and crocodiles. And then, as it nears its final destination in the Timor Sea, it loses its way. It spills over the wide flats near Nourlangie and lingers, entangled by reeds and clutched by the arching roots of mangroves, in a maze of shimmering swamps.

It was late in the evening when we went down to these marshes for the first time. To reach them we had to drive across wide plains of blue earth, bare but for isolated tussocks of coarse grass. Only a month or so previously all this land had itself been submerged. But the sun, beating on the waters from a cloudless sky, had transformed the shallow tepid lagoons first into bogs and then into acres of mud. To these quagmires herds of buffalo had come, plodding hock high, to wallow in the softness. But they had not been able to enjoy the squelching bog for long. As the last drops of moisture evaporated, the sun, with the swiftness and ferocity of a fire in a potter's kiln, had baked the mud stone-hard. Now as we drove across the plains, once so viscous that they had sucked at the buffaloes' legs, the rigid curling edges of the deep hoof-marks shook the wheels of our truck as violently as if we had been driving across a field of granite boulders.

We jolted slowly across the flats towards a belt of trees that marked the beginning of a permanent lagoon. A hundred yards short of them we stopped and, as the rattle of our engine died away, we heard, rising from beyond the trees, a throbbing chorus that filled the air like the sound of a gigantic swarm of bees. There was no mistaking it. It was the contented murmur of honks and grunts made by an immense flock of wildfowl.

Cautiously we walked towards the trees and picked our way through them, stepping with the greatest care lest the snap of a twig breaking underfoot should signal our presence. We reached the far edge of the thicket and peered through a chink in the veil of leaves that screened us from the swamp.

No matter how often you have seen great gatherings of waterfowl, moments such as these are unfailingly thrilling. The lagoon was vast. It stretched from within a few yards of where we crouched for at least a mile ahead. Away to the left, the sun was already setting behind a small bush-covered island, tingeing the opal-grey expanse of water with pink. And everywhere there were birds; strings of ibis flying across the red-flecked sky; black duck, pygmy geese, whistling duck, teal and shelduck, each keeping to their separate flotillas; pied herons standing in tightly packed ranks on the shores; pratincoles, small brown wading birds, pattering about in the shallows excitedly flicking their tails from side to side as they searched for insects; and most abundant of all, dominating the lagoon as their voices filled the air, magpie geese.

It was the geese which held our attention. Most of the other birds in front of us are found elsewhere in Australia, and there were few species that we had not seen before. But nowhere in the world, except in tropical Australia and New Guinea, can you see magpie geese in any number, and nowhere do they congregate in larger flocks than in the swamps around Nourlangie.

They were strange-looking creatures, somewhat gawky

compared with other species of geese. Their legs were unusually long, their bodies rather heavy. On top of their heads they had a curious conical hump, like a clown's cap. In colour, they were black with a broad cummerbund of white encircling their breasts and back. Most of them were dabbling in the water, plunging down their long necks to search for the bulbs of water plants. Some had already finished feeding and were standing motionless. How many there were I could not begin to judge, but in the South Alligator swamps alone there were said to be about a hundred thousand – so many that some people in the Territory had come to regard them as a pest.

Hunting magpie geese

Some years before, an attempt had been made to grow rice at Humpty Doo, forty miles south of Darwin. Enormous areas of land were cleared and planted with rice seedlings. Wild rice has always been one of the favourite foods of the magpie goose and when the birds discovered this new and munificent addition to their feeding grounds, they descended on the fields in huge flocks. The farmers tried to scare them away with bright lights, rattles, scarecrows and hooters. But nothing was really effective. Poisoned bait was put down for them, but although many were killed, the size of the flocks was scarcely affected, for birds were continually arriving from all over the Territory. Eventually, the military were called in. Squads of machine gunners, in watches, maintained a regular fusillade over the sprouting crop. But the acreage involved was too big; the geese merely flew away from the guns and settled down again out of range. Finally the whole project was abandoned. The geese had won.

But if this was a victory for the birds, it had been preceded by a whole series of defeats. Once magpie geese lived all over Australia. They were spectacular prizes for sportsmen and were heavily hunted, many of the swamps on which they depended for food in the dry season were drained, and by the middle of this century they had been exterminated as a breeding species over most of the continent. Today they still disperse widely over Australia during the rainy season, but as the billabongs and marshes disappear with the coming of the dry, they retreat again up here to the northern coast, which is now their last refuge.

We crouched among the mangroves for some time watching the birds, but to tackle any serious filming we needed a hide and to build it we should have to reveal ourselves. I stepped through the leaves on to the muddy shore. There was a thunder of wings and the whole flock peeled off the surface, circled and flew to a distant part of the swamp, leaving the water in front of us empty but for the ripples of their wake.

I now saw a finger of dry land, jutting out from the shore, that would provide an ideal site for an observation post. From it we could get a wide view of the swamp; behind it the bush was sufficiently thick to allow us to approach unseen; and at its farthest tip grew a paperbark tree with a branch that dangled close to the ground, forming a framework which we could easily clothe with extra leafy twigs and convert into a screen.

We built the hide that night. The next morning, before dawn, we sat down inside it and began watching and filming the geese.

Hides are seldom comfortable places and this one, although it was ideally placed, was more uncomfortable than most. The ground on which it was built, although superficially quite hard, soon softened beneath the weight of our feet, so that we and the camera tripod slowly sank deeper and deeper into mud. The leaves that hid us so effectively from the birds also served to screen us from the few cooling breezes that occasionally played over the lagoon, and the interior of the hide became as airless and stifling as a Turkish bath. In the mornings and evenings, mosquitoes droned in from the swamps and harried us unmercifully, submitting us to a torture that was the more maddening because we dared not wave our hands about or smack ourselves too vigorously, for fear of scaring the birds. But the geese made up for everything.

They grazed so close to us that we could see clearly the bright pink skin at the base of their bill and the vivid yellow of their legs. Many of them, we noticed, had spent so much time here that their white breasts were stained a scruffy chestnut by the mud in which they dabbled. Now too, we could clearly see that their feet were only half-webbed – one of the characteristics that sets them apart from all other wildfowl.

Within the hide, we moved with exaggerated slowness and talked in whispers. Our behaviour was not unlike that of people in a holy place and, as the posture of the body often induces the appropriate emotion, so we felt a reverence for the scene in front of us. We were acolytes to whom a vision was being revealed; we were gazing upon another world. It was like this before human beings appeared on earth. Here, none of their logics or preferences, moralities or rules, had any place. This world was governed only by elemental things – by the heat of the sun, the evaporation of the water, the burgeoning of the reeds and the unknowable urges of the geese.

And then, after two or three hours, a gust of wind caught the whirr of the camera and swung it across the swamp. A goose that had strayed to within a few feet of us, craned its neck in fright and flew. Within seconds the alarm had spread and soon all the geese were taking off, their contented honking replaced by the sound of their frantic wing flaps. We sat infuriated, for we had missed an important film shot. But even more saddening, the spell was broken. We had intruded, and the balance and harmony of the world on which we had been eavesdropping was shattered.

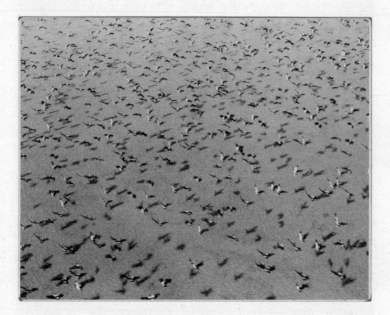

Magpie geese taking flight from the lagoon

This lagoon was the headquarters of the geese. Here the water was just the right depth, and the spike rush, their favourite food, grew thickest. Other parts of the swamps belonged to other species. On one placid billabong, a fleet of pelicans regularly held their manoeuvres. All pelicans seem to be dominated by a compulsion to perform every action in unison. These always sailed in formation, on parallel courses with their grotesque heads tucked gravely on their chests at identical angles. When they fished, they dipped their baggy bills into the water simultaneously, with the precision of a well-drilled line of chorus girls. Unfortunately, their particular stretch of water had very little bush on its banks and it was almost impossible to approach them without being seen. As soon as they became aware of us, they temporarily abandoned their naval discipline, frantically thrashed their way across the water and pulled themselves up into the air. Once in flight, however, their instinct to do everything together returned. They formed up into an echelon, and flapped slowly away, the wing strokes of the entire group perfectly synchronized. Sometimes, they would glide – and all of them stopped flapping at the same moment. If they changed direction, each one of them would do so simultaneously. No one understands how the individual birds manage to perform this feat. Presumably they must have some form of communication, the mechanism of which is totally unknown to us.

Elsewhere, when we were lucky, we found brolgas – Australian cranes. Chastely clad in grey, with small scarlet caps, they walked in a stately manner along the shore, two by two, as though engaged in a deep and serious conversation. All members of the crane family have a predilection for dancing, but none, from all accounts, do so on such a scale as the brolgas. Usually they perform in pairs, but on occasion whole flocks of them dance together in a sort of quadrille, lowering and stretching their necks and clacking their bills. It is even said that if one bird forgets its steps, the others, outraged, peck it angrily and bring it back into line. But the few brolgas we found never danced for us. We were too early in the season. Instead, they flapped their wings as we approached and hurtled away into the centre of the swamp where we could not follow, there to resume their grave conversations.

Egrets were almost as common as the geese. They blanketed some parts of the swamp in such numbers that their flocks resembled vast snowdrifts and, when something disturbed them, they rose into the air like a cloud of swirling white smoke.

Filming birds around Nourlangie was, from a technical point of view, relatively simple. By building hides, by cruising slowly across the flats in the car with the cameras at the ready on our knees, by stalking slowly and quietly through the pandanus thickets, we soon had shots of pygmy geese, three species of ibis, four different kinds of duck, four species of egrets, herons, darters, stilts, eagles and many other birds, as well as long sequences of the magpie geese.

Recording them also posed few problems and Bob steadily accumulated on tape the voices of every species we filmed. Often it was easier for him to work alone, away from the noise of the camera, and as long as there was a group of the same kind of bird both on the film and the recording, the sound and picture would match one another and there would be no difficulty later in putting the two together.

But if we were filming a single creature, then in order to capture its individual calls and the precise rustles made by its every movement, filming and recording would have to be done simultaneously. This was a much more difficult technical problem. Charles would have to muffle the noise of the camera by shrouding it with a padded canvas cover called a soft blimp. This was so bulky and cumbersome that it made the use of a tripod essential and entangled the lenses in so many layers of foam rubber and padding that adjusting focus and aperture became a major operation. Bob's job would be equally compli-cated. He would have to set up his microphone in such a position that it couldn't be seen by the camera, and had not only to run a cable between it and the recorder, but also to lay another, linking the recorder with the camera so that the tape received a pulse from the camera's motor which would enable us later to synchronize exactly the sound and the picture. All this would have to be done before the animal concerned took fright and disappeared.

The first opportunity to try this technique came one evening after we had spent several hours trying to film the pelicans without success. While Bob and Charles were dejectedly dismantling the equipment and stowing it away in its boxes, I strolled into a nearby spinney of gum trees. I had gone about two hundred yards when suddenly I became aware that what I had taken from a distance to be a log was in fact a surprisingly large lizard. It was a goanna, a creature we were very anxious to film. He lay broadside on to me, his head held erect, as motionless as a statue. He was about four feet long, dull grey with tinges of yellow on his throat, and he stared at me with an unflinching piercing gaze, like a sergeant major infuriated

The goanna

into speechlessness. I backed away quietly. After I had retreated several yards, I quickened my pace. Then I turned and ran.

I arrived back at the car just as Bob and Charles were snapping the last clasps on the equipment boxes.

'Goanna,' I yelled. 'Synch shooting. Quick.'

Then I dashed back to the lizard. He had not moved. I leaned against a tree, panting, and waited for Charles and Bob to arrive. The goanna and I stared at one another for what seemed like hours before Charles eventually appeared, staggering under the load of the reassembled tripod, camera and blimp. Leaving him to watch over the lizard, I ran back to Bob to see if I could help him. He was sitting in the back of the car carefully sorting through a box of microphone leads. 'Funny,' he murmured ruminatively, 'I'm almost sure I had a synch lead somewhere.'

I waited, gritting my teeth with impatience, while Bob, with maddening slowness, assembled his gear. There was nothing I could do, so I ran back yet again to rejoin Charles. The goanna still lay in exactly the same position as I had first seen him.

At last Bob arrived. 'Well,' he said brightly, 'got it sorted out in the end.' He set up the microphone, carefully laid out the leads, and linked the recorder to the camera. 'Sound ready,' he announced.

With that, the lizard moved for the first time since we had appeared. It ran. With astonishing speed, it tore through a patch of fallen leaves and disappeared down a hole in a tangle of roots at the bottom of a tree. There was no possibility of digging it out.

We walked back to the car in silence. None of us said anything as we packed away the gear once more, and we were back in Nourlangie before any of us trusted himself to speak.

The creature we had failed to film was, in scientific parlance, a Gould's monitor. There are species of monitor to be found throughout the tropics. Australia has twelve, including the smallest of all, a charming miniature a mere eight or ten inches long which lives in the west of the continent. Gould's monitor is by no means the largest. Two other kinds, the prentie and the lace monitor, which are found in the central deserts, grow to over six feet long. In Indonesia, a thousand miles away to the west, lives the biggest monitor of all, the Komodo Dragon. It attains the length of ten feet and qualifies as the largest lizard in the world today. But Australia once possessed a creature which exceeded even that, for fossil remains have been found of a monitor called Megalania, which grew to the astounding length of twenty feet.

The name 'goanna', which is applied to all Australian monitors, is a little misleading. It is a corruption of the word 'iguana' which, properly speaking, should be applied only to the handsome lizards of South America that have scaly crests running down their spines. Monitors are quite different. Of all lizards, they are the ones most closely related to the snakes. They have long deeply forked tongues which they flick out continually just as a snake does. Their tongues, in fact, are even more spectacular than a snake's, for they are much longer. Both creatures use their tongues for the same purpose – as a sensing device to carry back samples of air which are savoured in a pair of pits at the back of the palate.

One characteristic of some snakes which monitors, fortunately, do not share, is venom. With the exception of the Komodo species, none of these lizards is poisonous. They feed on carrion and small, easily caught creatures such as frogs or nestling birds. But this does not mean that they do not have to be treated with a certain amount of caution. They have long claws with which they can inflict nasty wounds. Furthermore, if you interfere with them, they get very angry, hiss at you in a very frightening manner and then lash their tails with considerable force. I certainly did not relish the thought of being clouted by one.

All the same, our failure to film the monitor by Pelican Lagoon rankled. All three of us were determined to try again. We devised a special placing of the boxes in the back of the car, so that they would be available at a moment's notice, and not submerged beneath mounds of other equipment. Bob reorganized his gear so that he could assemble it within seconds of taking it from its case. Next time, we were confident, we should be able to flash into action with the speed and efficiency of a gun crew at the Royal Tournament.

It seemed too much to hope that we should find the goanna again, but we went down to Pelican Lagoon just in case he was still there.

He was. This time he was sitting in the middle of an open flat that bordered the lagoon. We stopped some distance short of him. Within seconds, Bob had the microphone and recorder connected up. Charles flung the blimp over the camera. We walked cautiously towards the lizard over what had appeared to be solid earth but proved to be a huge drift of powdery dust that puffed into clouds at every footstep. The goanna waited patiently for us. When we were ten yards away, Charles set down the camera on its tripod and focused.

'Right,' he whispered.

'Right,' whispered Bob.

'Shoot,' I said.

The camera whirred for a few seconds and then stopped. Charles ripped off the blimp and opened the camera. The film had jammed in the gate, filling the inside with a tightly squashed concertina of celluloid. Working as swiftly as he could, Charles tore out the film and took a new roll out of his pocket. I edged my way a little closer to the goanna to try and get the microphone into a better position. The goanna hissed, and suddenly charged me. Startled, I stepped back to avoid him, tripped on one of the tripod legs and knocked the camera over. It fell open-side down into the thick dust. The goanna swung round and continued running down to the lagoon, splashed into the water and swam away. Charles picked up the camera and blew a huge cloud of dust from its inside.

'I don't suppose it will take more than a couple of hours to clean this lot out,' he said bitterly. 'And – who knows – it might still work.'

Attempting to record the splashes of the goanna

In the morning we set out for our third attempt, the Melbourne butcher, whom we had met on our arrival, decided he would like to come with us. We felt very much on our mettle. To fail yet again, and in his presence, would be unbearably humiliating and I had a sneaking hope that maybe we should not find the goanna this time and so escape without our professional skill being put to the test.

But the goanna was there, slumbering in the sun within a yard or so of the water's edge. This was the worst position of all from our point of view, for if he wished he could disappear into the water within seconds.

We stopped the car twenty yards away and held a whispered consultation. The butcher, who had been sitting in the back admiring the view, suddenly leaned over our shoulders. 'There she is,' he bellowed. 'She's a beaut.'

By now we had perfected our routine. We each completed

our jobs swiftly and within half a minute all was ready. Cautioning the butcher to stay in the car, we walked slowly down towards the goanna, pausing at each step in order not to frighten the animal into the water before we were close enough to get a good shot.

'Get a move on, mate,' the butcher yelled. 'She's not going to hurt you.'

Charles set down the camera once again and focused. Bob, squatting by the recorder, handed me a pole with a microphone slung on the end and I gingerly lowered it towards the goanna. This roused him. He lifted his head, slid out a good twelve inches of purple forked tongue, inflated his yellow throat and hissed obligingly into the microphone. It was perfect.

'Shall I stir her up with a bullet?' called the butcher helpfully. 'Don't yer want a little drama in your movie?'

The goanna heaved itself up on to its feet, took three threatening steps towards me, and then, as though to oblige the butcher, lashed its tail ferociously. Charles was able to keep it in focus the whole time. Bob, wearing his earphones, was smiling happily at the recorder. The goanna turned round and strolled arrogantly along the water's edge. Then, as if to display to us all its talents in one sequence, it waded into the lagoon and, with graceful sideways undulations of its body, swam away.

We continued filming it until finally it dived and disappeared. We walked back to the car, preening ourselves.

'Piece o' cake,' said the butcher.

'Yes,' I said. 'Nothing to it, really.'

20

Painted Caves and Buffaloes

No man need starve in the country around Nourlangie. The sparse dusty bush, the rocky ridges roasting in the sun, may seem barren and inhospitable, but for those who know the land, there is food in abundance. The squat burrawong tree, a type of cycad palm, conceals in its crown of feathery leaves a cone of nuts; the stems of the pink lotus flowers that star the surface of the lagoons lead down to succulent bulbs buried in the mud at the bottom; even the mangroves and pandanus, in season, produce fruits that are edible, if you know how to cook them. For meat, a man can hunt among the thickets of gum trees for the herds of wallabies; he can catch the huge barramundi fish that cruise lazily in the clear waters of the creeks; or he can draw from the most bountiful larder of all, the huge flocks of waterfowl. Yet the country was empty. A few Aboriginals worked at Nourlangie camp, the men as hunting guides, the women helping in the kitchen and doing the washing. But we saw no Aboriginals living in the bush.

It was not always so. Only fifty years before, this land was the home of the Kakadu people. They were nomads, roaming through the bush in family groups, occasionally assembling in larger numbers to perform their complex ceremonials, but seldom staying in one place for long. At the turn of the century, Paddy Cahill, one of the Territory's great white pioneers, settled at Oenpelli, sixty miles from Nourlangie on the far bank of the East Alligator River. He came to hunt buffalo commercially for their hides, but soon he had vegetable gardens, plantations of cotton and a herd of dairy cattle. The Kakadu found employment there, shooting the buffalo and tending the crops. With their pay, they bought knives and sugar, tea and tobacco. Life at Oenpelli was comparatively easy for them. Family by family, the tribe ceased to wander and stayed close to the station. In 1925, Oenpelli was taken over by the Church Missionary Society. The new owners did their best to speed the process that Cahill had started and encouraged all the Aboriginal people from the surrounding country to come and live permanently on the station, so that their children could have continuous schooling and the sick and the aged be given medical care.

Anchored to the mission by their desire for a more modern life, the life of the Kakadu changed radically. Many forgot the old skills and traditions that had been essential for their nomadic existence. They lost their tribal identity among the other people that came to the mission. Today, the Kakadu, as a tribe, no longer exists and their ancient hunting grounds around the South Alligator are deserted.

Although they tilled no fields nor built any permanent houses the Kakadu, nonetheless, left their mark on the land, for they, like most of the northern tribes, were artists and their paintings still decorate the cliffs and shelters where they once camped. The hills around Oenpelli are famous for the wealth and beauty of their paintings, but Alan Stewart knew of rock galleries close at hand and rich with drawings, which had only recently been discovered by Europeans and which few outsiders had ever seen.

To reach them, we drove for a mile or so along the track that leads to Oenpelli and then branched off it southwards, bumping and crashing through the bush towards a rock mountain that towered six hundred feet above the scrub like a great stone fortress. We drove around its base for half an hour, weaving our way between the trees, sometimes having to knock over smaller saplings with our bumper in order to clear a path. At its south-western end, the foot of the mountain was cluttered with gigantic boulders, the size of houses. Some lay several yards from the cliff, others leaned against it to form caves. The main rock wall rose up above us in a series of towers and battlements, split here and there by deep cracks.

Paintings on Nourlangie Rock

Alan stopped the car at a place where the cliff leaned outwards to form a shallow open shelter. The rock was grey, streaked with brown and black where water had trickled down the face, but the interior wall of the shelter was dramatically different. From ground level to a height of eight or ten feet it glowed with designs in white, yellow and rust red.

It took some time for our eyes to make sense out of the tangle of lines and shapes. Then we realized that in the centre, dominating the shelter, stood a line of almost life-size human figures, painted in white and neatly outlined with red ochre. They appeared to be wearing headdresses, or else their hair had been arranged in an elaborate coiffure, for their tiny white featureless faces were surrounded by large discs of red, patterned by a few radiating lines in yellow. Most had bangles or bindings on their wrists and upper arms. They were female, for large stylized breasts swelled sideways across their armpits. The lower parts of their thin attenuated bodies were rubbed and faded, but we could just distinguish that the feet of some of them had been painted, not with their soles horizontal as though standing on the ground, but hanging downwards so that the figures seemed to be floating in the air, like saints around the walls of a Byzantine church.

Female figures, Nourlangie Rock

Among them pranced a different being. It was portrayed in movement, its knees slightly bent. It lacked breasts, yet it was without male genitals. Its arms, instead of hanging by its side like those of the female figures, were crossed in front of its torso and it was without a headdress, its face being simply a large white oval. Its thighs were crisscrossed with white lines, as though adorned for a corroboree, and we could see that the legs of some of the female figures, though faded, were similarly decorated.

Above these images swam a huge barramundi fish. This was painted in extraordinary detail. Its creator had shown not merely the external appearance of the fish as he saw it, but the reality of the creature as he knew it to be, for over the white silhouette of the fish's body, he had drawn in red its gullet, its stomach and its gut. It was an X-ray picture.

Above the female figures, we found a naïve drawing of an ancient-looking pistol. Elsewhere we discovered pictures of muskets and sabres, sailing ships, and steamers with twin funnels pouring smoke. Had the artists painted these things for some ritual reason; or had they done so merely to amuse themselves and to show their companions the latest wonders that they had seen, maybe on one of their walkabouts to the coast fifty miles away?

The most vivid of all the images, however, were, for me, not the bizarre portraits of spirits, nor the naturalistic sketches of animals, but two simple handprints which partly underlay the pistol. One of the men who had come here had dipped his right hand in red ochre and pressed his palm on the rock. Another had done similarly alongside and had left, in addition, the imprint of his wrist and forearm. These two human hands, reaching upwards from among the weird supernatural beings that they may well have designed, poignantly evoked the presence of these artists, who had come here, with motives we could only guess at, to execute their mysterious drawings.

We scrambled among the rocks, exploring the caves with torches, climbing up the cliffs to look at small groups of paintings in high corners. We found pictures of goannas and crocodiles, turtles and kangaroos, and a huge graceful dolphin. Some had been painted in sections of the cliff that, even allowing for the agility of the Aboriginals, seemed almost impossible to reach. Maybe a ledge had fallen away since the drawings were made, which would be some evidence of their antiquity. Or perhaps the artists attached so much importance to their work

Kangaroo painting

and to the positioning of their paintings, that they had gone to the trouble of building a ladder or a scaffold.

While I was searching for more, I peered down a narrow rock cleft. There, wedged between the rock walls, staring back at me from empty eye sockets, lay a bleached human skull. Leg bones and ribs were scattered beneath it. Nearby, propped against the cliff face by the fork of a long branch, I found a bundle of faded canvas. It contained a few polished pebbles, a rectangular piece of wood cross-hatched with ochre lines, a woven tassel so rotted by age that it fell to pieces in my hand, and a small battered tobacco tin, its lid printed with a florid Victorian trademark of a firm that doubtless had long since gone out of business. This must have been the dead man's swag, his most cherished possessions that, after his funeral rites were completed, had been left here, close to his bones. The tassel was a pubic cover, the only clothing that Kakadu men ever wore. No doubt the tin was a rare and highly valued treasure. The pebbles and the painted piece of wood were extremely sacred ceremonial objects, the most important and intimate of an Aboriginal's belongings which only a few privileged people would have been allowed to see while their owner was alive. I wrapped them up again in the tattered canvas and put them back as I had found them.

Of all the animals around Nourlangie, we expected the buffalo to be the easiest to film. We were wrong. There were plenty of them and they were easy to find. Often we spotted them in the distance half-hidden in the bush and, had we been hunting, it would not have been difficult to shoot them with a rifle. But when we tried to get closer to photograph them, they soon smelt or heard us and cantered away deeper into the bush. By using our longest telephoto lens, we managed to get shots of them wallowing in the centre of the marshes, half a mile from the shore, tended by their faithful flocks of egrets. But photographically, these were poor pictures, for the heat reflected from the surface of the swamp made the air above tremble so much that the image of the buffaloes wavered like a reflection in the rippled surface of water. To get the intimate shots we wanted, uncluttered by intervening branches and bushes, we should have to be really close to the animals; and neither the buffalo – nor we – showed much desire to reach such a situation.

By this time, we had been joined by a team of three zoologists from Canberra, who were making a survey of the animals in selected parts of Arnhem Land. One of them, Harry Frith, had carried out pioneer research on the magpie geese here at Nourlangie several years before. He knew the area well and understood buffalo. 'Let's drive out in the car,' he suggested. 'When we find a group of buffs, you and Charles can hop out with the camera and hide yourselves. Then Bob and I will drive on, circle the herd and approach it from the other side. We'll chase the buffs towards you and, provided you don't do anything silly, you'll get all the shots you want.' It seemed a good idea.

Five miles from the camp, we found the largest herd that we had seen so far. It was difficult to estimate its numbers, for the animals were a considerable distance from us, and we could distinguish nothing more than a group of brown shapes moving slowly between the trees. We guessed that there were probably a hundred or so. To the left of us lay a bog; to the right the ground rose in a rocky ridge. In the middle of the corridor of flat land that stretched between, stood a dead gum tree with a hollow trunk. Harry drew up alongside it. Charles and I quickly slipped out of the door on the far side from the herd and hid ourselves behind the tree. Within seconds the car drove on. The buffalo could not possibly have seen us emerge. The wind was blowing from them to us, so that it was very unlikely that they could catch our scent. Everything was working perfectly.

The hollow trunk was sufficiently spacious to accommodate one of us and, furthermore, there was a small hole near the ground from which we could observe the country ahead. I peered through this spyhole, while Charles squatted outside with the camera. We could hear the car, rattling away somewhere to our right. So far, I could detect no sign of disturbance among the distant buffalo. As the noise of the car faded, the bush around us returned to life. A small lizard crept out from beneath a piece of bark and resumed its hunt for flies. A flock of brightly coloured finches swept across and settled, twittering on a nearby bush, oblivious of us. We sat stock still.

In the distance we heard the faint blare of the car's horn. Harry and Bob must have succeeded in reaching the far side of the herd and were already beginning to drive them towards us. I crouched inside the tree watching the buffalo. Charles checked the camera. Everything was ready. Through the spyhole, I saw the leaders of the herd walking slowly directly towards us, plainly heading down the corridor just as we had hoped they would. As yet they were not seriously alarmed by the car and were cautiously taking avoiding action. When they discovered that the car was right on their heels and actually pursuing them, no doubt the whole herd would break into a gallop and come straight towards us. Protected by the tree, we should be as safe as if we were standing on a traffic island in a busy city street during the rush hour and the pictures we should get would be most exciting – close-ups of hooves in the swirling dust, rolling eyes, frothing muzzles, and a forest of savage horns sweeping by within a few feet of the lens. Charles braced himself against the tree. Closer they came. The leaders were now trotting, their heads held nervously in the air. Away to the left, a small flock of white cockatoos came flying towards us. They could not have noticed us, for they settled on one of the branches of our tree, directly above our heads. Now we could hear the drumming of the buffaloes' hooves and the roar and hoots of the car behind them. The leaders of the herd were a mere fifty yards away and were coming straight for us at a canter. Charles dared not peer round the tree, for to reveal himself at this moment might ruin everything. Leaning against the trunk, he put the camera to his eye. Suddenly, one of the cockatoos on the branch above peered down and saw us. It craned its neck, as though unable to believe its eyes, and then it let out a piercing shriek. Its companions looked down too and added their strident voices to its outraged squawkings. Through my observation hole, I saw the leading buffaloes hesitate momentarily in their stride and then swing round to the left in alarm. Those immediately behind them followed and the whole herd splashed into the marsh and disappeared among the pandanus. We had not been able to take a single shot of them. It was the first of many times that our presence was betrayed and our photographic plans ruined by cockatoos, the most inquisitive, keen-eyed and loud-mouthed sentinels in the bush.

Yorky Billy felt sure that we would never succeed in getting the film we wanted of buffalo anywhere close to the camp. 'They're too scarey round here,' he said. 'Too many blokes been takin' pot shots at 'em.' He recommended the plains around Cannon Hill, just a few miles short of Oenpelli to the east. 'Big mobs of buff up there and you can get a good look at 'em coz it's nice open country.'

Cannon Hill had another attraction as it and a nearby outcrop called Obiri were said to have some of the most beautiful cave paintings in the whole of Australia.

Cannon Hill was seventy miles away, and to film both the paintings and the buffalo would doubtless take us several days. We decided to carry enough stores to last us for a week, in case we got into difficulties. The limiting factor, however, would not be food but water. Alan Stewart lent us two empty eight-gallon drums that had once held methylated spirits. We washed them out and filled them with water, and slung two more canvas water bags from the front of the car. It was all we had room for. Provided we did not have to use too much of it in the car's radiator or waste it on washing ourselves, it should last the three of us for some time.

The track to Oenpelli was largely the creation of the lorry drivers who every few weeks during the dry season drove out to the mission with stores. Often it split into three and we soon learned that it was foolish to drive straight on, and much safer to take one of the side branches, for they implied that ahead lay a patch of badly rutted mud, a tree that had fallen across the road, or some other obstacle that the lorry drivers had simply bypassed by bulldozing for themselves yet another twist in the track.

We forded several creeks that at this time of the year were no more than trickles linking a chain of brown pools. Soon, we had passed the white fortress of Nourlangie Rock away to our right. The track wound ahead of us, for mile after mile, and behind us we trailed a swirling plume of dust. At last, after three hours, the bush suddenly came to an end and we emerged on to the edge of a wide open plain.

This, like the flats bordering the Nourlangie swamps, had, a few months before, been covered by a shallow lagoon. Now it was a continuous carpet of deep iron-hard pock marks and ruts, made by the trampling of buffalo. On the far horizon shimmered a long stretch of silver blue water, with bushes mirrored in its surface. Had we been travellers racked by thirst, the sight would certainly have sent us out across the scorching plains to refill our water bottles at this providential lagoon. But it did not exist – it was a mirage. The still air, undisturbed by any wind, had formed an extremely hot layer close to the ground which was acting as a mirror, reflecting the blue cloudless sky above and, by refraction, twisting the images of trees far on the other side of the plains so that, to our eyes, they appeared to be bordering the illusory lake.

Away to the right of the mirage, the far side of the plain was bordered by a line of cliffs, like Nourlangie Rock, but free of vegetation at their base. A long stone finger projected horizontally from the face of one of them, like a gun from the side of a man o' war. This, we judged, must obviously be Cannon Hill, in which case Obiri must be one of the smaller outcrops farther down to the right. In the middle of the plains, however, we saw something that was more immediately exciting – a swarm of black dots clustered around a brownish patch on the plains, which we judged from its colour to be a lingering patch of mud. I looked at them through binoculars. They were buffalo.

Here, at last, was our chance of getting, in safety, the close-up shots that we wanted so badly. With luck, we should be able to drive towards the herd and film without even getting out of the car – and we had already discovered that the beasts often ignored a car and only took fright at the sight of a walking human figure. Charles took out the camera.

Slowly we rattled across the corrugated plain. We were still nearly a mile away, and the herd was taking no notice of us. Here and there, as we drove towards them, we came to a long curving depression marking the bed of a stream that had mean-dered across the plain until it was sucked dry by the sun. We crossed two of these without any trouble. When we were only half a mile away from the buffalo, we came to a third. We dipped down into it and accelerated to pull ourselves up the other side. The engine roared, but the car stopped moving. The rear wheels had broken through the hard crust and were spinning in soft blue mud.

The buffalo were still ignoring us. To free the car would certainly involve a great deal of digging and pushing. Probably we should also have to unload all the baggage as well, in order to lighten the load. The buffalo could certainly see us, and all this activity might well alarm them sufficiently to make them prudently stroll away into the bush out of sight. We should have missed a marvellous opportunity. On the other hand, we were not yet close enough to get good shots of them. It seemed unwise to walk up to them carrying a heavy tripod and camera, for if they charged we should have to choose between abandoning the camera to be trampled and tossed by their horns, or trying to run back to the car and being so encumbered that we were caught ourselves.

There was, however, a compromise. I could walk towards the herd and see how close I could get before they seemed to resent my presence. If they charged before I was within camera range of them, then, unimpeded by the gear, I could race back and seek safety in the car, which, although it was stuck and immovable, was at least something to dodge behind. But if, as I hoped, I could get sufficiently close without disturbing them, then Charles could join me with the camera.

'Don't forget what Yorky said,' advised Bob with relish. 'If they come for you, just fall flat on your face.'

I was within a hundred and fifty yards of them before they even raised their heads. Slowly I advanced. All of them were now staring at me, but none seemed in the least aggressive. I remembered Charles's anxiety to avoid heat shimmer, and stepped a little closer. When I was sixty yards away, a particularly large bull took several paces towards me, swung his head up and down and shook his horns. I stood still and tried to remember, without looking back and taking my eyes off the bull, how far away I was from the car. The calculation of how fast I could run and how long it would take the buffalo to overtake me seemed a very complicated sum. I began to lose confidence. Yorky's method of escape began to seem less attractive than ever.

The big bull took a few more menacing steps towards me and shook his horns again. The beasts were certainly not going to allow us to film from this position. I had come too close. Before I took ignominiously – and probably unsuccessfully – to flight, it seemed better to try and forestall a charge by bluffing. I jumped into the air, waved my arms and shouted. The bull reared back, swung round and cantered away. Suddenly I felt brave and ran after it to consolidate my victory, yelling loudly. The whole herd galloped away in a cloud of dust.

I stopped running and turned round to return and apologize to Charles for having ruined our chances of filming. To my astonishment, he wasn't at the car at all, but standing midway between me and it. He had been following some twenty yards behind me and had filmed the entire proceedings.

Freeing the Land Rover took us nearly two hours. The wheels had sunk so deeply that the back axle was resting on the ground and the springs were buried. We crawled beneath the car, and, lying on our stomachs, clawed the mud away with our hands. In order to give the wheels something on which to grip we returned half a mile to the bush on the edge of the plain, felled some saplings, dragged them back to the car and thrust them beneath the tyres. Bob started the engine. Charles and I levered desperately with poles beneath the back axle. The wheels spun, there was an unpleasant smell of hot rubber, and then the wheels gripped on the branches. Valiantly the truck hauled herself out of her self-made pit. We were free.

We drove straight to Obiri, for here Alan had said were some extremely impressive paintings. He had not exaggerated. The rock was stratified horizontally, and on the western side one massive horizontal leaf projected some thirty feet into the air to form a great ceiling some fifty feet above the ground.

The wall at the back of this natural open hall was covered by a magnificent frieze of red barramundi fish. Each of these monsters was four or five feet long, with its head tilted downwards. Like the ones we had seen at Nourlangie, they were painted in the X-ray style, but their detail was even more elaborate. The backbone, the fin rays of the tail, the lobes of the liver, the bands of muscle along the back, the gullet and the gut – all were shown. Among these noble fish were snake-necked turtles, kangaroos, goannas, emus and geometrical patterns. The designs stretched for fifty feet in a band six feet high, and had been painted so thickly and so many times that the heads and tails of previous paintings protruded from beneath the later ones. Excitedly we explored the cave, calling out to one another as we found a new variation, a different kind of animal or a particularly magnificent example.

It was too late to start filming, for within an hour it would be dark and we had not yet made camp. Although there was no water here, we decided to spend the night by the cave.

It was an idyllic and impressive campsite – the huge rock behind us, the plains stretching away on one side and the bush on the other. Apart from its lack of water, it had only one disadvantage. It was plagued by flies. They settled everywhere in black crawling swarms – on our foreheads, our hands, our lips and our eyes. Although they were quite harmless, the sensation of their feet on our skin was almost as irritating as if they had been stinging us. That night I cooked an omelette, and as we sat round the fire eating, the flies alighted on our plates and clung to the food so persistently that merely waving a hand would not dislodge them. The only way to avoid swallowing a dozen or so with every mouthful was to blow hard and continuously on each morsel of food until it was close to our lips and then to thrust it quickly into our mouths before any more of the hateful insects could settle on it again.

We assembled our low safari beds, erected the tent of mosquito netting above each of them and with considerable relief crawled beneath, safe at last from the attentions of the flies. I read for some time by the light of a torch. As I lay there, I could see nothing of the outside world, for the light of my torch illuminated the mosquito netting and made it seem solid. I felt as though I was lying in a small white room. Then I snapped off the light and immediately the white walls disappeared and I looked up into infinity and the glory of the Milky Way. Ahead of me, Obiri Rock loomed against the bespangled sky. Even now, it was very hot and I lay naked on my sleeping bag.

I awoke some time after midnight. The darkness was full of noises. Occasionally there was a shrill scream. I guessed it was some bird but I could not recognize the call. A scuffling came from where we had left the stores. Some small creature – maybe a rat – was investigating our larder. Further away, there was an even louder rustling in a patch of pandanus, followed by a heavy thump.

'I say?' It was Bob. 'What's that noise down there?'

'Fruit bats, I expect,' I whispered back reassuringly. I wasn't quite sure why I whispered.

'Bit loud for fruit bats, isn't it?'

There was another sustained rustle, followed by a thud.

'How does a fruit bat make a thumping noise?'

'That's the fruit falling. Go back to sleep.'

But Bob's questions had raised doubts in my mind. If it wasn't a fruit bat among the pandanus fifteen yards from where we were sleeping, what was it?' I realized that I wouldn't be able to go to sleep until I knew. I clambered out of the mosquito net, and naked, with a torch in my hand, picked my way barefoot towards the pandanus. As I arrived, there was an explosion of sound and a huge shape erupted from the thicket and crashed away into the darkness. It was a buffalo.

The next morning we drove along the line of cliff, looking for paintings. There were so many outcrops of rocks, such a complex of tumbled boulders, that it was difficult at first to know where to search. But slowly we began to recognize the sort of site favoured by the Aboriginals for their work – an overhang, a rock corner shielded from the rain, a cave, a particularly unusual rock formation like an arch or a monolith – such places were always worth investigating and usually we found that they had been decorated. The surest indications of all were circular pits on the top of slabs or flat boulders. These were the places where the artists had prepared their paints, grinding the mineral ochres into powder with a pebble. The very existence of these pits, which must have taken many years to produce in the hard quartzite, was evidence that these sites were not selected as a passing fancy, but had such a significance to the artists that they had visited them year after year to renew the designs or add fresh ones.

As we explored, we sometimes caught sight of little black rock wallabies, miniature kangaroos the size of terriers, that scampered away from us, often leaping up sheer rock faces with the most astonishing agility.

Although we wandered a long way from our camp at Obiri we found the most interesting and aesthetically satisfying of all the paintings in a small rock shelter opposite the main cave. It represented a line of hunters. Each figure was armed with one or more spears. Some, in addition, carried spear-throwers, fans of goose feathers, baskets hung from their shoulders or a string bag slung from their necks. There was nothing stereotyped in the way in which they were shown; each differed from every other in posture and in the weapons and accoutrements that he carried. They were painted in a style quite different from the great X-ray barramundi. The huntsmen's bodies were not shown in full detail, but merely indicated by single lines scratched in white through the reddened surface of the rock. Whereas the fish had been placed apparently haphazardly, one overlapping the other, these figures formed a balanced rectangular composition; and while the fish and the other animals had been static and monumental, these were full of life – running with springing strides. Together they formed a hunting scene full of excitement and vitality.

No one knows which tribe made these drawings. The Aboriginals who live in this country today are emphatic that neither they nor their fathers did so. They explain the drawings by saying that they were executed by a spirit people, the *mimi* – and that these are their self-portraits. The *mimi*, as can be seen from their pictures, have bodies as thin as reeds and so frail that they cannot venture out in a high wind, for fear of being buckled and bent. They hunt and eat, cook on fires and hold corroborees just like Aboriginals. Their home is among the rocky cliffs, but no one ever sees them, for they are very shy and have an acute sense of hearing. When they detect a human being approaching, they simply blow upon the surface of the rock, which splits open at their command and allows them to slip inside while the rocks close behind them.

Spirit figures painted in a rock shelter near Nourlangie

They are said to be harmless happy spirits, but drawn across this hunting scene were the images of two malevolent witches, the *namarakain* women. These, like the *mimi*, had stick-like bodies, but they were painted in red and had triangular faces. They, the Aboriginals say, steal men's livers, roast them and eat them. Between their hands, they held a loop of string, a magical device with which they can miraculously transport themselves over great distances during the night.

We filmed many of these paintings, illuminating them with small battery lamps. The great barramundi frieze was far too large to be artificially lit, but it was painted on the western side of Obiri and for a short period of ten minutes each evening, the almost horizontal rays of the setting sun struck the inside wall of the cave and flooded it with light. This was the time to film it. As sections of the wall were confusingly thick with paintings, we decided that I should walk along the length of the

Our camp beside Obiri rock

panel, pointing out the different images and describing them in words. This, once more, would require synchronous recording.

We prepared to tackle this sequence on our last evening in camp. Bob tested his equipment and Charles set up his camera well in advance. We rehearsed the movements that I should make as I walked along the rock face. It was absolutely vital that we made no mistake, for we could not delay our return to Nourlangie any longer; we had almost exhausted our water supply and if we failed to complete the shot satisfactorily that evening, we should have to leave without any film at all of the spectacular barramundi. With everything ready, we waited as the sun sank lower and lower and its light slowly crept up the inside wall of the cave, the redness of its rays enhancing the rich colours of the ochre fish.

At last, the moment came when the entire height of the frieze was illuminated. We now had ten minutes in which to take the shot. We started and almost immediately Bob called out in exasperation. The recorder, inexplicably, was producing a loud electronic howl which was ruining the recording. Rapidly he dismantled it and spread it out in pieces on top of a boulder. No connections seemed to be broken and Bob could find no obvious fault. He assembled it again, without putting it back in its case, and when he did so, he noticed that, having been standing in the sun, it was quite hot. Maybe this was the fault, for some of the transistors which then were only just coming into general use were known not to work above a certain temperature. Bob put the machine in the shade of a boulder and fanned it with his hat. Slowly the screaming noise died in his earphones. We completed the shot with Bob still fanning frantically as Charles filmed. A minute or so after we stopped the camera, the sun dipped behind the bush and the cave was in twilight.

No one knows how old the paintings of Arnhem Land are. There are signs that some of them, at least, are of considerable antiquity. We had found a few that were varnished with a thin transparent layer of a stalagmite-like deposit, formed by water

Charles Lagus filming paintings in a rock shelter

trickling down the surface of the rock. The pistols we had seen at Nourlangie were of a type that could not have been seen in the country for many years. The fact that the local tribes deny that they produced the *mimi* drawings suggests that these were made by people who lived here some considerable time ago and have since moved away or disappeared. Some at any rate must be over a century and a half old, for Matthew Flinders reported finding drawings of turtles and fish at Chasm Island in the Gulf of Carpentaria during his great voyage of exploration in 1803. The paintings are well able to survive for a long time, for the iron oxides which give colour to the ochres do not fade, and their sheltered position protects them from the worst of the wind and the rain.

There is little doubt, therefore, that painting in this fashion has long been one of the traditional skills of the Aboriginals. It is equally certain that some have been executed comparatively recently and it is this, as much as their antiquity, which makes them both fascinating and important, for in many ways they are similar to the first pictures ever made by human beings – the magnificent frescoes painted during the Stone Age twenty thousand years ago in the caves of Europe.

In subject matter, the European ones appear to be rather different for they show wild oxen, bison, deer, mammoth and rhinoceros. But these creatures resemble the barramundi, turtle and kangaroo in one important respect – both groups are animals that were hunted for food. In Spanish caves, there are drawings of stick men, astonishingly similar to the *mimi*. In both France and Spain there are handprints. In Lascaux, the finest of the French caves, as well as elsewhere, there are enigmatic geometrical designs just as there are in Australia. In both areas, the paintings are often superimposed haphazardly on top of one another.

The European and Australian paintings are also similar in technique. Both are executed in mineral ochres; they are placed in the same kind of situation – in rock caves and shelters. In France, spear-throwers and decorated ritual objects have been discovered in association with the paintings, and we ourselves had found similar things at Nourlangie and Obiri.

Much has been written about the prehistoric caves and many speculations made about why Stone Age man produced his remarkable art, but no one can ever know for certain. But we can still discover why the Aboriginals paint, for they still do so today. Cave painting has largely stopped, but the painting of similar designs on bark continues. If we could see these painters at work, we might learn from them something of the reason why they paint and so, by analogy, get an insight into the motives that impelled mankind, before the dawn of history, to inscribe images in paint on rock and create the first works of art.

21

The Artists of Arnhem Land

To find Aboriginal people who still produce designs comparable with those emblazoned on the rocks around Nourlangie and Cannon Hill, we had to go into Arnhem Land, the vast slab of territory that lay on the far side of the East Alligator River. Bounded to the south by the Roper River and to the north and east by the sea, it is as big as the whole of Scotland. No road crossed it. A mere handful of explorers had traversed it. The only parts of it to have been mapped in any detail on the ground were the immediate surroundings of the half-dozen mission and government stations strung out along its coast. It is the wildest, least-explored tract of country in the whole of northern Australia.

No large-scale attempt to settle the country has ever been made and while, in the temperate south of the continent, great cities grew and the rolling grasslands were cleared of Aboriginals to make way for cattle and sheep, Arnhem Land and its people were largely left alone. As a result, it is here that the Aboriginals have survived in greater numbers than anywhere else in Australia, here that they have had the least compulsion or opportunity to change their ways and conform to the conditions of life dictated by the white man. In 1931, after the conscience of Australians had at last been roused by the tragic history of the first inhabitants of their continent, the whole of Arnhem Land was declared an Aboriginal reserve. Traders and prospectors could only travel in its valleys, crocodile shooters could only sail up its rivers, if they had special permits – and these were not freely given.

We had applied for such a permit when we had been in

Darwin and had received one to visit Maningrida. Of all the settlements, this offered us the best chance of finding painting fulfilling its original tribal function. It was the most recently established, having been opened officially by the Government Welfare Department a mere two years before, and the Aboriginals were therefore still little affected by European ways. Furthermore, it was the only settlement without a missionary. If painting had any ritual function, then the presence of a man or woman dedicated to weaning the Aboriginals away from their tribal religions must inevitably distort the nature of their art.

No one had yet reached Maningrida by land. A small ship took in supplies every few weeks by sea, but the most convenient way of getting there was by air. Accordingly, we chartered a small single-engined plane to come from Darwin and fly us over. As we took off from Nourlangie, the pilot swung the little craft round and flew low over the swamps so that we could have a last look at the country in which we had been filming for the past few weeks. As we approached, the dots that speckled the glinting coffee-coloured lagoons spread black and white wings and seemed suddenly to double in numbers as they detached themselves from their racing black shadows. We banked again to leave the geese in peace, and headed east over Arnhem Land.

Now it was easy to see why this brutal, sun-ravaged country had repelled settlers for so long. Naked plateaux of sandstone, deeply dissected by ravines and scored by long straight faults, stretched endlessly ahead. As we droned over them, I amused myself by trying to devise a route along which one might drive a team of pack horses or even a truck. Each time I traced with my eye an obvious eastward-heading valley where the going seemed tolerably straightforward, it ended suddenly in a savage scarp or twisted away at right-angles to the direction I had wanted to pursue. It was like a child's printed puzzle which invites you to trace with a pencil a path through a maze and reach the treasure in the centre – except that here there was no route without obstacles and no visible sign of any treasure. As so often in the puzzles, the least difficult way for an earthbound traveller to reach Maningrida was obviously the longest – to travel around the coast in a boat.

The pilot leaned over his shoulder and yelled at me.

'If the engine went crook now, what d'ye reckon we'd do?'

I looked at the landscape, appalled at the thought.

'Crash?'

'Head for that little patch over there,' he shouted, pointing ahead to a minute open rectangle of land, relatively free of bush but encircled by crags. 'We've got enough height to make it even without an engine and I reckon it's just about big enough for me to put her down – though how the hell they'd get in to fetch us I don't know. Always try to remember places like that on overland trips. Comforting.'

We droned on. The landscape below was now unrelieved rock. I tapped him on the shoulder.

'What would you do if she packed up now?'

He looked contemplatively on either side.

'Pray,' he shouted.

After just over an hour of flying, we sighted the coast. The pilot pointed to a river that coiled tortuously into an estuary. On its far bank, dwarfed by the surrounding wilderness, we saw a pathetically small cluster of toy-like buildings. This was Maningrida.

Five years before, when the ships of the Welfare Department ran their keels into the sand at the mouth of the Liverpool River, there was nothing in front of them but mangrove. Since then, building machinery and bags of cement, tractors and supplies of food had been ferried every few weeks round the coast from Darwin, three hundred sea miles away. Gangs of carpenters and bricklayers had come to work in monastic isolation. Already they had completed a school, a hospital, communal kitchens, storehouses and accommodation for the staff. Gardens, a parade ground, and a football field had been cleared and the Australian flag flew from a tall mast.

The people for whose benefit all this work was being done were encamped on the outskirts of the station. Some had erected simple shelters of bark along the edge of the long curving beach. These were the Gunavidji, a tribe of people who seldom strayed far from the sea. The men knew how to make dugout sailing canoes and used them to fish for turtles and barramundi, the women searched daily along the edge of the reefs at low tide for shellfish and crabs. On the other side of the station, among the thick straggling eucalyptus scrub, lived a different tribe, the Burada. Unlike the Gunavidji, they knew little of the sea and normally lived inland, gathering roots and hunting for bandicoots and wallaby in the rocky hot scrub.

Some of these people wore old European clothes, but many of the men were naked except for loincloths – a simple square of material passed between the legs, the corners knotted at each hip. In complexion, they were a shiny ebony black of an intensity unequalled by any other people I had seen. Their limbs were so thinly fleshed that they seemed undernourished, but in fact this lankiness is typical of some Aboriginal peoples. Their hair was not frizzy like some of the other people in New Guinea and the western Pacific, but silky and often curling and wavy.

That afternoon, Mick Ivory, the superintendent, showed us round. He was emphatic that Maningrida was far from being a charitable institution, although clearly it cost the government a great deal to run it. If an Aboriginal joined the settlement, he must work – and there was work here of a sufficient variety to suit everyone – cutting up logs of cypress pine at the sawmill; mixing cement for the gangs of European contractors who were still putting up new buildings; tending the gardens where pawpaw and bananas, tomatoes, cabbages and melons grew under arching sprays of water; clearing and planting land with new grass that, Ivory hoped, would soon be thick enough to support a herd of cattle. Girls could help in the hospital, women in the kitchens; old men could chop sticks for firewood. In return, every man and his family were given regular meals and pay.

With the money, he could buy tea and tobacco, flour and knives at the station canteen. His children could attend school and soon, as building work proceeded, there would be small wooden houses for many. There was medical care for everyone. Two European nursing sisters ran the hospital under the supervision of a doctor who flew in from Darwin once a fortnight and could be summoned at a few hours' notice to deal with emergencies. Difficult cases he could take back with him in the plane to Darwin hospital.

Many of the Aboriginals here had known something of the white man's ways before the settlement was founded – they had worked on board pearling luggers, had visited Darwin or had spent some time at one of the missions elsewhere along the coast. But some had drifted in from the surrounding country and had decided to stay. Every now and then a new family of myalls, wild Aboriginals who had never lived on any settlement of any sort, came and camped close to the station. From the security of the bush, they watched broodingly the strange things that their countrymen were doing on the station. Mick Ivory would send men out to try and encourage them to join the station. Sometimes the invitation was met with abusive jeers and the myalls left. But sometimes they accepted and came in. For a fortnight they would be given free food with everyone else – no small temptation when game was scarce – but after this period they must start work or leave.

'But it seldom comes to that,' Mick said. 'After all, turning them away achieves nothing. If they stay, we can usually persuade them to work all right. The trouble is that a lot of them don't want to live on the station under any circumstances and are only too ready to go back into the bush.'

Soon after we arrived, Mick took us down to the Burada encampment. He led us to a shelter of branches reinforced with a few pieces of bark and cloth that stood some way apart from the others on the fringe of the scrub. In its shade sat an elderly man, naked but for a grubby loincloth, his knees on the ground and his legs crossed in front of him in a position impossible for anyone to achieve who has not squatted in this way throughout his life. His chest and upper arms were marked with long scars of the wounds he had accepted during the initiations of his youth. He grinned as we arrived, showing his white teeth, ground down to near the gums by a lifetime of eating gritty foods.

'G'day, boss.'

'G'day, Magani. These men,' Ivory pointed to us, 'want to see blackfella painting. I tell 'em you're the best painter in Maningrida. That's right?'

Magani nodded. 'That's right, boss,' he said, acknowledging the remark not as a compliment nor as a personal opinion but merely as an accepted and indisputable fact.

'Will you show 'em how you paint?'

Magani looked at us with his black eyes for some seconds.

'Orright.'

Magani

We did not stay long with Magani on that first visit and indeed, although we called at his shelter every morning and afternoon for the next few days to sit and smoke and talk, we left our cameras behind. He was engaged in painting a series of kangaroos on a thin rectangle of bark, but there was no urgency to complete it apparently, and he was always ready to talk as he worked.

He spoke in pidgin, but it was difficult at first to understand him, for the rhythms of his speech, his pronunciation of individual words and the idiosyncratic stressing of syllables were bafflingly unfamiliar. As our ears became accustomed to his talk, I endeavoured to speak in the same way, sometimes falling back on the pidgin that I had learned in New Guinea. The two versions differed considerably and I suspect that, in my efforts to make myself understood, I confused Magani more than if I had spoken straightforward simple English. But, perhaps irrationally, it seemed discourteous not to make some attempt to modify my own speech to match the manner in which he found it easiest to talk himself. Primitive and inadequate though our conversations were, I soon realized that Magani had a considerable sense of humour.

One afternoon, Bob, Charles and I were sitting in his shelter watching him paint. Two other men had joined us and were squatting at the back of his shelter. Suddenly, one of them shrieked and leapt to his feet. 'Shernake, shernake!' he yelled, and stabbed his finger at a small emerald-green snake that was sliding from beneath a pile of bark fragments on to the earth floor. We all jumped up except Magani. While everybody else hurled sticks at the reptile, he sat immobile, his brush loaded with ochre and poised above the bark. At last the snake was killed and thrown out of the shelter. Magani moved for the first time since the commotion had started. He turned to me, smiled beatifically and pronounced, with an impeccable Australian accent, and the timing of a born comedian, two short words of appalling obscenity.

'Magani,' I said in mock horror, "im bad words.'

'Oh, sorry.' He rolled his eyes upwards and pointed to the sky. 'Sorry,' he repeated in a louder voice as though apologizing to the heavens. Then he looked back at me. 'No. 'E orright,' he said brightly with exaggerated relief. 'Today no Sunday,' and he shrieked with laughter.

'Magani, where you learn those bad words?' I asked.

'Fannie Bay.' Fannie Bay is the prison in Darwin.

'What for you go Fannie Bay?'

'Long time back – one fella – 'im bad bloke – me killim.'

'Where you killim?'

Magani leaned over and jabbed his fingers under my ribs.

'Jus' there,' he explained in a matter of fact tone. "E bad bloke. Me gotta killim.'

Magani had a particular companion, Jarabili, who helped him with his paintings and who spent a great deal of time in Magani's shelter. Jarabili was a younger, taller man with a lantern jaw and blazing eyes. He was a sombre character, with none of Magani's relish for jokes. Everything we said to him was always taken very seriously and pondered upon. Once, I asked him the name of an animal in his own language. This interest he construed as being an indication that I had ambitions to speak Burada fluently and for a long time afterwards he came to look for me every evening and insisted that we sat down together while he dictated a lengthy vocabulary. Then he would make me put away my notes and would test me on the list he had given me the previous evening. I was a poor pupil, but Jarabili was both persistent and patient, and though I never learnt enough to carry on the simplest conversation I was able, every now and then, to inject a Burada word into my pidgin and this was enough to bring a rare smile to Jarabili's face.

The shelter where we all spent so much time was not the only one that Magani owned. It was merely the one in which he did his paintings. His wife and children lived in another, closer to the station, but Magani only went there to sleep and to have his meals. He also had another, away in the bush, where he kept his dogs. One of his favourite bitches, he told us, had just produced pups. 'No bring 'um here,' he said. 'Maybe Mik-ibori 'e shoot um.' The station had recently been infested with half-starved dogs and Mick Ivory had been forced to take strong measures. Magani seemed to have a haunting suspicion that we might take the same attitude and, even though he was proud of the pups, he was obviously unwilling to show them to us. We did not press the matter. Sometimes, when we came to look for him, he was neither at the studio shelter nor with his family. On one of these occasions, we found Jarabili. He looked uncomfortable when we asked where Magani was. "E gone bush – makim business.' 'Business' was the word he used for all matters associated with religion. We did not press that inquiry either.

None of the Burada people had any great number of material belongings. The nomadic existence that they had led until recently had not allowed them to develop the obsession to possess things that so bedevils many of the rest of us. A dilly bag, an elongated woven pouch decorated with long tassels, hung at the back of Magani's painting shelter. He also owned a few spears and a wommera or spear-thrower, a long slat of wood shaped into a handle at one end and fitted with a spike at the other. The spike slots into a notch on the end of a spear and the wommera virtually doubles the length of a man's arm, thus increasing the leverage on the spear and greatly augmenting the power with which he can hurl it. Magani also possessed a pipe, a slender piece of hollow wood with a small metal cup at one end for the tobacco, a type known as a Macassar pipe, for it had been introduced to the Aboriginals centuries before by the Indonesian traders. The stem of this pipe was always kept bandaged with a strip of frayed dirty cloth. Why this was so, we were not to discover for some time.

Jarabili owned a didgerido – the branch of a tree, hollowed out by termites, which he had smoothed to form a simple trumpet. Sometimes he played this for us, making a throbbing bass drone into which he was able to introduce rasping crescendos with considerable rhythmic variation. To produce a note at all was difficult enough, but Jarabili was able to sustain the sound for many minutes on end, managing to continue blowing by contracting his cheeks while taking in a breath through his nose to refill his lungs, just as an expert bassoon player is able to do.

At last we felt that Magani and Jarabili knew us sufficiently well for us to ask if we might begin filming. Magani agreed to begin a new painting specially for us, so that we could follow every stage of its production. The bark on which he painted came only from one kind of eucalyptus, the stringybark. We set off together to collect a piece which Magani promised would be a 'proper big one' so that he could produce a really splendid painting. We borrowed an axe from one of his neighbours and together we all went off to the bush.

Once we reached the bush, stringybark trees were abundant. But Magani was hypercritical. Nine out of ten he rejected at a glance. Occasionally he took a tentative chop at a trunk with the axe, but the bark, he said, was too thin, or else it did not separate freely from the wood beneath. The bark of some was cracked, others had too many knot holes. Many had already been stripped of their bark for making shelters or paintings. At last, when I was beginning to fear that we should never find a suitable tree and that Magani in his anxiety to make a superb painting for us had set himself too high a standard, he found a tree that seemed to satisfy all his requirements. With the axe, he ringed the trunk about three feet from the ground. He propped a fallen branch against the tree, climbed up it and, gripping the branch with his toes in order to keep his balance, dexterously cut another ring, five feet above the lower one. Then he cut out a vertical strip joining the two rings and slowly peeled away an immense sheet, leaving the trunk of the tree naked white and running with sap.

Magani stripping bark for a painting

Back at camp, he carefully trimmed off the outer fibrous layers of the bark. With these shavings he lit a fire on which he threw the curling sheet, inner side downwards. The heat was not sufficient to burn the bark, but enough to turn some of its sap into steam and make the whole piece pliable. After a few minutes he put it down on the ground and weighted it with boulders so that it would harden absolutely flat. This was to be his canvas.

He used four pigments and showed us where he found each. In the dry rocky bed of a stream he collected pebbles of limonite, a hydrated iron oxide. Their quality he assessed by scratching them on a boulder. Some left yellow marks, some red, and these kinds he kept. From a pit, dug among the mangroves by the shore, he obtained a white kaolin. Black he produced by grinding up charcoal. These were the four basic colours in his palette. But in addition to the red limonite pebbles, he had another ochre which was a richer deeper red. This was not of local

354

origin, but came from somewhere to the south and was traded from the people in whose tribal territory it occurred. Accordingly it was very precious and Mangani kept it in his dilly bag, carefully wrapped in a packet of paper bark.

One further material was necessary – the fleshy stem of the Dendrobium orchid, which grew on the high branches of the gum trees. Magani said he was too old to collect this for himself and Jarabili was the one who clambered up the trees to gather it. The juice from it would serve as a fixative to prevent the paint from flaking.

Magani testing the quality of a pebble of ochre

The sheet of bark had now dried and painting could begin. Magani put it flat on the ground and sat cross-legged in front of it. By his side he placed a cockle shell and several cigarette tins, all full of water. He ground a red pebble on a small piece of sandstone, tipped the ochre into the cockle shell and daubed the resulting paint over the bark with his fingers, to make a solid red ground for his design. Each figure he roughly outlined with the orchid stem, having chewed its end to make it juicy. For the detailed painting, he used three different brushes – a twig with a chewed splayed end which produced broad lines, another with a burred end which he used for stippling, and a third with a trailing fibre attached to the tip with which, by drawing it skilfully and steadily across the bark, he made thin delicate lines.

Starting the painting

Slowly and carefully, he painted kangaroos and men, fish and turtles. The designs were stylized and simple. In none did he try to represent the exact appearance of an animal. That was unnecessary, for everyone knew what a kangaroo or a man looked like. A spectator was expected to use his own imagination to clothe the images with an appearance of reality. His aim was simply that the nature of the images should be clear and he ensured that this was so by selecting and emphasizing the particular characteristic that proclaimed identity. Even we, with our untutored eyes, were usually able to recognize the designs. The symbols were precise. His lizards were not simply lizard-like creatures but geckos or goannas and quite distinct from crocodiles; his fish were recognizably barramundi or sting ray or shark. Some designs, however, were so stylized that no inexperienced person could divine their meaning. Circles with a hump on them separated by cross-hatching represented a fresh-water lagoon, for the first was the symbol for the lily bulb and the second the pattern for water. When the image of a long stick was added – representing a woman's digging stick – the scene became one of people out foraging for bulbs in a billabong.

Many of his compositions were very detailed, a mosaic of figures enmeshed by the geometrical symbols of sea and sand, clouds and rain. There was no perspective. The tightly organized

Magani and Jarabili at work

composition could be viewed several ways up and in those that contained human figures, it was unusual to find one in which all stood the same way.

But simple and elementary though his pictures were, they were endlessly interesting. His restricted palette dictated a subtle harmony of colour and the stark economy of the symbols gave them dignity and power. To our eyes, the pictures had a peculiar beauty.

Every man we asked agreed readily that he was a painter. People seemed surprised that we should consider the possibility that a man might *not* be an artist. On the other hand, if they gained pleasure from painting, it was from the activity, not from contemplation, for few seemed to derive much enjoyment from looking at other people's work. When the word got round that we were interested in paintings, many brought their barks to us. But few could compare with Magani's. No one painted with such skill, imagination or application as he did.

Magani and the half-finished painting

I asked Magani why he painted. He was mystified by the question. His first answer was simply that we had asked him to do so. But he painted before we came to Maningrida. Why? Because Mik-ibori gave him money for the barks and with that he could buy tobacco at the store. For some time this was the only answer I could extract from him. But it could not be the only one, for Magani and his people, as we knew from the rock paintings and from the records of the early explorers, had been painting long before any white people came here to buy the paintings. 'We always bin makim,' was Magani's only reply.

When he had finished the big bark painting, which we had photographed at every stage, we sat down together and I asked him to identify the images, one by one. Down the centre of the bark were two long shapes with small stubby arms projecting from the sides or the end. Internally, they were subdivided into rectangular sections and cross-hatched in white, yellow and red.

'Honey sugar-bag,' Magani said. Wild honey filling the hollow trunk of a tree. The arms were branches, which, being irrelevant to the main conception were therefore greatly reduced in size. On one side of these were three small cameos – 'This fella – gotim axe, dilly bag – cut honey sugar-bag.' 'This man – takim spear – killim dingo dog.' 'Two woman – one man – makim fire – lie down, go sleep.' Above these lay a goanna, a gecko and a third lizard with red flaps projecting from its neck. 'Gottim big ear'oles,' Magani pointed out. It was a frilled lizard, a magnificent creature we had seen around Nourlangie with a great sheet of skin wrapped round its neck which it can erect like an Elizabethan ruff.

On the other side of the wild honey tree, I saw a symbol which mystified me. It was a long rectangle, cross-hatched in the centre section and broadly striped in red, yellow and white at either end. The figure of a man leaned over one end, his face touching the rectangle. Beneath him were drawn two other figures, one dancing and the other apparently striking two sticks together, as singers often do to give themselves a rhythmic accompaniment. I pointed to the rectangle.

'What this one?'

Magani, so far, had been answering loudly and without hesitation. Now he leaned over and whispered into my ear a name I didn't recognize.

'Why you talk so soft?' I whispered back.

'If we talk loud – young boy, woman might be hearin' me talk his name.'

'Why must they not hear?'

''Im secret. 'Im belong business. God made 'im.'

I had little idea what he was talking about. Obviously it was connected with ritual and a subject not to be discussed before uninitiated boys or women. But whether it was a physical object or a spirit, or both, I did not know.

'Where this?'

''Long bush.'

'Magani, I no woman, I no young boy. 'Im orright me see 'im.'

Magani looked at me hard and scratched his nose.

'Orright,' he said.

It was this one image on the bark that was to reveal to us the most powerful compulsion that motivated Magani's art, the greatest single force that made him spend his days painting.

22

The Roaring Serpent

Magani strode purposefully through the bush. He walked erect, leaning back slightly from his hips, his arms dangling, his bare feet treading unfeelingly on twigs and thorns. Close by the Burada encampment, the scrub was criss-crossed by paths, but as we went further, they thinned out and soon we were in part of the bush that was evidently largely unfrequented. After half a mile, we arrived at a large shelter of branches. In front of it sat Jarabili. He was doing nothing. Just sitting, cross-legged, looking into space. As we came close to him, he started visibly and turned his smouldering eyes on us. Magani spoke to him rapidly in Burada and the two of them went into the shelter. They brought out a sacred object, covered with paintings, which was to be used in a ceremonial ritual.

Discovering the nature of the ceremony and the myth connected with it was a long and slow process. Every day we talked about it and I wrote down what Magani told me. I recognized the myth as one which occurs in various forms all over this part of Australia. Many versions of it have been recorded, but, as I listened to Magani, I tried to forget all I had read of other people's accounts and listen only to his. I endeavoured not to ask leading questions, nor to force the story into a neat plot; not to require happenings to have causes nor to connect events into the logical sequence of action and consequence demanded by our own fictions. Our own myths, in their original form, are seldom obviously logical. When we first learn them, we accept them unquestioningly as a series of facts, one succeeding another.

The story that a snake persuaded an ancestral woman to eat an apple and thereby deprived a man of the gift of immortality and doomed him to die is just as divorced from logic as Magani's story.

I knew, too, that though I could note down the happenings that Magani related, I could only dimly comprehend the meaning that the story had for him. How could I, to whom the creation myths of my own culture seemed no more than curious allegories, understand Magani's attitude to a story which to him was the literal explanation of the origin of his own people and of the very land that he lived in, a story whose facts were so saturated with meaning and awe that the very name of some of the protagonists could not be breathed in the presence of a woman who had no right to the knowledge.

His story, as we eventually deciphered it, was this.

In the Dreamtime, when the earth was flat and featureless, when animals were almost human and people almost gods, two women came up from the Wawilak country to the south. Their names were Misilgoé and Boaleré and as they came they gave names to the animals and plants that they saw, that hitherto had been nameless. Misilgoé was expecting a child and when they came to a waterhole called Mirramina, near the Goyder River away to the east of Maningrida, she felt the babe stirring within her. So they camped by the waterhole and while Misilgoé rested, Boaleré gathered food. She collected yams and lily bulbs, and caught goannas and bandicoots.

Unknown to the sisters, the waterhole was the home of a great serpent, who lay asleep at the bottom, beneath the black waters. Soon Misilgoé's child was born. It was a boy and they named him Djanggalang. When Boaleré went to cook the creatures she had killed, they suddenly came to life and jumped into the waterhole. Then the sisters suspected the truth. 'This must be because there is a snake beneath the waters,' they said. 'We will wait until the sun goes down and then maybe we can catch them again.'

But meanwhile, Misilgoé's blood shed during the birth of Djanggalang trickled into the well and defiled it. The serpent tasted it and now he knew that the sisters were at the waterhole. Misilgoé gathered paperbark and made a cradle for the babe. Then she built a shelter in which they could all spend the night. But the serpent, angered by the tainting of the water, came out of the well bringing with him the goannas that had taken refuge there. He hissed and with his breath blew clouds into the sky. The world became very dark. Misilgoé was sleeping now, but Boaleré took rhythm sticks and struck them together, singing and dancing to placate the serpent. Exhausted by her dance, she joined her sister in the shelter. She set up the rhythm sticks in the ground and worshipped them. Then she went to sleep.

Now the serpent came out of the waterhole. He bit Djanggalang the baby in the hip and swallowed him. Then he ate the two sisters. He arched into the sky. His body was a rainbow, his tongue lightning and his voice thunder. From the clouds, he called to other serpents elsewhere in the country and told them of all that had happened at the waterhole. The other snakes derided him and called him foolish. It was wrong, they said, to have eaten these women and their son. Chastened, the serpent returned to the waterhole. There he spat out the women and the child, still alive, and sank once more back into his well.

This was only one episode in a long saga which chronicled the doings of the two Wawilak sisters and the Wongar men who came up to look for them after the serpent had spat them out. In the course of the myth, all the animals of the world were created and named, the rites of circumcision and scarifaction ordained, the rhythms of the dances and the patterns of the celebratory rites established. The structure of Burada society – the totems, clans and moieties – were also determined, for each man was related to the protagonists in the story and thus was able to ascertain his status with regard to other men.

It was a story as long as the Ring of the Nibelung, as meaningful as the Book of Genesis. Women could never know it in detail, and a man only became aware of it gradually throughout his life. Before his birth, his spirit left the totemic waterhole, where his ancestral spirits had first appeared, and went into the womb of his mother. When he was eight or nine years old, he was circumcised and introduced to some of the less sacred parts of the story. As he grew up, more and more of it was revealed to him, more of the sacred symbols were displayed to him until at last, as an old man like Magani, he knew the whole meaning of life. At his death, his spirit was freed from his body and returned to the totem place from which it came.

Magani and Jarabili were preparing for the performance of one small episode of the myth, in order that the young men who had reached the appropriate age could see the sacred symbols and learn the chants and dances, so reaching another stage in their understanding of the universe. They practised the chants every day.

Jarabili and his son

Once, at the end of his chant, Jarabili was deeply moved. He sat with the rhythm sticks motionless in his hands, stony-faced while tears trickled down his cheeks. "Im remind me of my daddy,' he said in explanation.

———

While Magani and Jarabili prepared, many other rituals were being held covertly in odd corners of the bush, for the two tribes, Burada and Gunavidji, were each divided into several clans which were again subdivided into totemic groups and each of these communities was responsible for its own rituals. Furthermore, each man owned objects that were sacred, which he cherished and communed with in solitude and which only his close relations, belonging to the same totem, were permitted to see. To walk through the bush thus became a matter of discretion and delicacy if one was not to intrude on some stranger's privacy.

Sometimes we recruited a young man to carry our camera gear and on the first occasion that we did so, I spotted, sitting in an acacia tree, a lory, a beautiful parrot-like bird with a red head and breast. It flew off and I followed it excitedly, calling to the boy with the gear to follow me. I pushed through some bushes, and crept slowly ahead, my eyes riveted to the bird. I turned round and saw that the boy was standing rooted to the ground. The bird took flight again and as I went after it I called once more to the boy in harsher tones. Only then did I notice an old man sitting on a log some twenty yards away. Across his knees, he held a sacred object. The boy had stopped some distance behind me, but he had come close enough to see the old man. While we stood there, the old man removed the object from his knees, pushed it beneath the log and covered it with a piece of bark. Then he walked over to us and spoke to the boy. Between them they agreed on a fine that the boy would have to pay – two tins of tobacco. Obviously I had to pay the fine. Doubtless they realized that I would do so and increased the amount accordingly. Nonetheless there was no question that such infringements of ritual privacy had always to be expiated in some way, and in fully tribal conditions similar crimes would only be settled by much more severe penalties.

———

Finally, it was time for the ceremony. Magani held his sacred object and said: 'Tomorrow time, makim dance.' We now discovered the parts that the two men were to play in the ceremonial. Jarabili belonged to the goanna clan and he would enact the part of his totemic ancestor. Magani, on the other hand, had a different, though closely associated, totem or 'dreaming' as he termed it. To show us what it was, he took us back to the studio shelter. He brought out his pipe and, making sure no women or children were about, carefully unfastened the wrapping. Along the stem were engraved a line of triangles, alternate ones being neatly cross-hatched – the symbols of rain clouds. 'This my dreaming.'

The next day was a Saturday. Soon after noon, men began to drift to the shelter. Among them I recognized the man who was in charge of the settlement garden, another who mixed concrete for the constructors. Some were old men whom I had not seen before. Several arrived wearing trousers, but they removed them and put on loincloths. Jarabili and another man cleared a wide space in front of the shelter of bushes and saplings. One man lay down on his back and another produced ochres and began drawing a goanna on his companion's chest. Soon there were several couples painting one another. They used exactly the same technique as Magani had employed in making his bark paintings. The outline of the design was first roughly smeared with the juicy end of an orchid stem and the painting in white, red and yellow was executed with just the same type of twig brushes. While they were being decorated, the men lay with their eyes closed, motionless and impassive, almost as though they were entranced. Though the designs were similar, the placing of them varied. Some had their heads pointing upwards on the chest, others downwards. Jarabili's goanna was even bigger than most. Its tongue reached to his hip, its tail stretched over his shoulder. But they were all drawn in exactly the same style – viewed from the top, legs splayed, cross-hatched on the body, heart and gut represented just as we had seen them on Magani's barks. All the men had a broad white stripe daubed across their foreheads and another, in red, below the eyes and across the bridge of the nose. Each man carried a dilly bag.

When Magani appeared, he was more spectacularly decorated than anyone, as we might have expected, knowing his impish flamboyant character. Around his forehead he had bound a long rope of woven lory feathers and he had broader, more brilliant red and white face stripes. He did not, however, bear a goanna on his chest, for that was not his totem.

It was not until the late afternoon that all had been painted. Those who had been decorated first had been sitting in the shade of the surrounding bush. Now they all assembled in the shelter. A group of young men were escorted to the ground. They stood to one side, their eyes averted. It was for them that the ceremony was being held. They were about to witness a holy mystery that hitherto had been an awesome secret. I was to witness this holy mystery too – but as much as I would like to describe what transpired, it is not my secret to tell.

We had gone to Maningrida to try and gain a fuller understanding of why Aboriginal people paint. Magani had shown us clearly that, for him, the most important purpose of painting was to serve in ritual. The designs he employed had been created by his ancestors to meet the needs of ceremonial. Thereby, they had become consecrated and imbued with such significance that no woman could properly appreciate them and even men could only understand their full import by passing through a series of rituals that took a lifetime to complete. The act of painting, in itself, had become an act of worship, a means of attaining communion with the spirits that had once shaped the world and still rule it. By contemplation of the designs, young men became aware of the nature of their origins and of the pattern of the universe.

This link between pictures and the supernatural makes it possible for painting to influence the course of nature in other ways. Anthropologists have found that drawings are sometimes used in sorcery. If a man wants to bring sickness or death to another, he may invoke an evil spirit by secretly painting its image on a piece of bark or on a rock; if someone wishes his wife to bear a child, he may draw a picture of her heavily pregnant. Sometimes, too, men paint to ensure the existence and increase of the animals on which they depend for food. An old man, who has the totemic secrets of the kangaroo in his charge, may be responsible for renewing an ochre kangaroo that for generations has marked the cave where the first ancestral kangaroo appeared during the Creation; for if the image fades from the rock, then kangaroos in the surrounding desert may decrease and disappear.

Nonetheless, Magani had also demonstrated that paintings were not always sacred. The goanna designs painted in the cere- mony were the same in every detail as the one he had painted on the barks that he produced to show us. These had no overt religious significance and could even be viewed by women and children. Out of context, unconsecrated by ritual, they were no longer charged with power. How could this secular variety of art have arisen and what part did it play in people's lives? One authority has pointed out that, in Northern Australia, there is a long wet season during which families must have spent days and weeks confined to their shelters by torrential rains. Maybe as they sat there, with the rain drenching the gum trees, turning the plains where they had hunted into sodden quagmires, they painted on the rock and the bark that shielded them, simply to pass the time or to practise the designs that on other, secret occasions, must be used for sacred purposes. Perhaps, then, to amuse themselves and one another, they invented new images that served no significance except to illustrate their talk – and drew pictures like the ships and pistols that we had seen at Nourlangie.

But the mainspring of Aboriginal painting was certainly religious. Even the simplest shapes had sacred connotations that the uninitiated could not possibly divine. If we had been archaeologists and had found Magani's Macassar pipe, we might well have thought that the lines of striated triangles engraved along its stem were no more than idle decoration, geometrical patterns scratched by the pipe's owner merely to ornament one of his personal possessions. We could not have known that the lines were the symbol of a man's personal totem so secret that they had to be shrouded by a bandage from the eyes of women and children.

What light could all this shed on the motives that made man, before the dawn of history, produce in the caves of Europe the first flowering of art that the world has seen? These ancient pictures, particularly those in the magnificent galleries of Lascaux, are certainly greatly superior aesthetically to any pictures produced by the Aboriginals. Nevertheless, as we had seen at Nourlangie, the Aboriginal pictures, in the manner they were placed on the rock, in subject matter and technique, closely resemble the prehistoric ones. Can any valid comparison be drawn between the two people who made them?

The Aboriginal seems to have migrated to Australia by way of Asia and the islands of Indonesia, which then were not so widely separated by sea as they are today. Certainly, he has not always lived in Australia, but arrived in the continent between forty to fifty thousand years ago. The rocks of the Sahara and the caves of Southern Spain still bear friezes of running stick-like figures made by a vanished race that are astonishingly similar to the *mi-mi* of Arnhem Land. Perhaps if the Aboriginal originated in Europe, these are clues marking the trail of their centuries-long journey across half the globe.

Of one thing there can be little doubt – the Stone Age men of Europe and the early Aboriginals of Australia once shared a similar level of technological achievement. Both were wandering hunters, the one pursuing kangaroos and turtles, the other wild bulls and mammoths. Neither had yet learnt the secrets of domesticating animals or cultivating crops that would enable them to lead a settled existence in one place. Maybe this similarity in their modes of life gave rise to similar religious beliefs and accounts for the resemblance between the paintings that the two peoples produced. But this is speculation.

Even so, the elaborate and complicated web of meaning that surrounds the Aboriginals' painting is enough to suggest that no single, simple explanation is likely to account entirely for the prehistoric pictures. One, certainly, is that the men of Lascaux painted as part of their hunting magic, that by depicting a bull with arrows in its side, a wounded bison with its bowels trailing, they hoped to increase their chances of a successful hunt. But might not totemism and a more subtle philosophic meaning also underlie these splendid frescoes?

Aboriginal boy with young wallaby

The parallels must not be drawn too closely, for whatever the origins of Aboriginal peoples, they themselves are no longer prehistoric. No society remains static, with all the details of its culture eternally fossilized. The life of the Aboriginals has continued to evolve, stimulated by new ideas and beliefs arising from within their own communities, and even though they have been hidden away for so long from the mainstream of human traffic, they have been influenced by other peoples – Indonesians from the west, Melanesians from New Guinea in the north.

Now Europeans are adding their influence. How Magani and his fellow painters will react to the increasing flood of new materials that will inevitably reach Arnhem Land has yet to be seen. Will they have the talent or the discipline to grapple with the enormous variety of colours that will soon be theirs for a few pence? Or will the traditions that taught them to manipulate the four colours of their ancient palette prove too inflexible to deal with such a sudden and enormous addition to their materials? It is possible that they can absorb them but more likely that the ancient painting will be swept away and replaced by something totally different both in style and in purpose.

Whatever happens, the inevitable decay of their ritual life, eroded by the work of the Christian missions, coupled with the new techniques that come to their hands, will radically change the whole nature of their art. When that happens, the bark paintings that we watched being made with such care and reverence in Maningrida, will have become as antique as the frescoes of prehistory.

23

The Hermits of Borroloola

We flew back from Maningrida to Darwin. Our work in the north was almost ended. Next, we planned to go south to Alice Springs and see something of the very different desert country of central Australia. Before we left Darwin, we had to buy more stores, get our car overhauled and say goodbye to the many friends that we had made.

It was so hot in Darwin that a walk down the length of the main street was enough to make our shirts cling to our backs with perspiration. We wanted a drink. Darwinians are apt to boast that they drink more beer per head of the population than any other citizens in the world, so, as might be expected of a town with such a formidable record, there is no difficulty in finding a bar. You can drink beer in the formal lounge of one of the smarter hotels, sitting in an easy chair among plastic flowers and waiters with black ties and cummerbunds, but really serious thirst quenching is more properly carried out in bars. Here the atmosphere is much more business-like. The one we chose was tiled and chromium-plated throughout and devoid of any frills or decorations that did not directly further the primary purpose of the place. The whole of one wall was occupied by one vast refrigerator with glass doors. From it, a brassy and energetic barmaid was dispensing chilled beer with extreme speed. The glasses in which she served it were also frozen, to ensure that the beer was not a degree warmer than absolutely necessary by the time it reached the eager lips of her customers. Freezing glasses, to the fastidious Australian beer drinker here, is as essential a ritual as warming the teapot in England.

In the bar, we met Doug Lockwood. Doug was an author and journalist. It is difficult to imagine that there has been anyone with a wider knowledge of the Territory than he – and impossible to believe that anyone could be more generous with information, or more hospitable. We talked of some of the characters in the Territory and the conversation turned to no-hopers.

A no-hoper is a man who has forsworn the comforts of civilization, shunned society and gone to live in solitude, and the empty immensities of Northern Australia enable aspiring no-hopers to achieve their aims with a greater ease and success than anywhere else in the world. But such men are not by any means restricted to the Northern Territory. Charles and I had met one some five years earlier in Queensland.

We were then on our way to New Guinea and had left Cairns to sail up the Great Barrier Reef. About a hundred miles north of the town, the engine of our launch stopped with a crash that shook the entire craft. A connecting rod had broken, shattering the piston head and bending the main shaft. By clearing out the debris, we were able to get the engine turning again, but the best speed we could make was a mere two knots. While we were still wiping the oil from our hands, the radio warned us of an approaching hurricane. If we were caught in a storm while we were still crippled, we should be in serious trouble. Making the best speed we could, we limped towards the coast to seek safety. The most suitable haven seemed to be a dot on the map marked Portland Roads. It was as remote and isolated as any place on that desolate coast, but during the war the Americans had built a jetty there in order to bring supplies to a military airfield they had constructed in the scrub a few miles inland. As far as we knew it was now abandoned but the jetty, at least, would give us a degree of shelter if a hurricane did come our way.

With agonizing slowness we wallowed westwards. At last a

smear of hills appeared above the horizon. As we came nearer, we saw to our surprise a tiny figure seated on the end of the jetty. He was fishing with his back towards us. As we came alongside, I stood in the bows and yelled out to him to catch our line. He didn't move. I hailed him again and again; but still he showed no sign of hearing me. Eventually, our bows scraped against the piles of the jetty. I jumped out and clambered my way up the timbers. It was a painful process for they were encrusted with barnacles and oysters. Charles threw me a line and we made fast. Together we went over to the man who had remained stolidly fishing throughout. I found it hard to believe that anyone in as lonely a spot as this would not be keen to see a new face or to talk to another human being. He was a little shrivelled man, naked but for a pair of torn shorts and a frayed straw hat.

'G'day,' I said.

'G'day,' he replied.

The conversation lapsed. For some vague reason I felt it encumbent upon me to keep it going. I explained who we were, where we had come from and why we had arrived there. The old man listened impassively, blinking up at me through a pair of steel-rimmed spectacles. When I finally came to an end, he pulled in his line, stiffly got to his feet, looked at me meditatively and said, 'The name's Mac.'

With that he turned and slowly walked away down the long jetty, his bare calloused feet slapping on the hot sun-bleached planks.

We were stranded at Portland Roads for several days. Mac, we discovered, had actually got a job. He received a small salary from some official authority to be permanently on hand on the jetty in order to catch the lines of any craft that might put in. We must have been his only customers for months.

The Americans' airstrip inland had to be kept clear of bush in order to serve as an emergency landing ground, and Mac had also the additional responsibility of taking up heavy drums of aviation spirit landed at the jetty every six months or so to a dump on the airstrip. To do so, he used a lorry. This was an astonishing machine. Mac had run it for years on top-grade aviation spirit. The engine, he said, was well-nigh perfect. In fact, its only fault was the radiator which had a tendency to leak. He explained, with an aggrieved air, that he had applied all reasonable remedies; he had plastered it front and back with cement and poured repeated billyfuls of porridge into it, but still it continued to drip. This, he reckoned, was wilful obstinacy. On the other hand, he admitted that the vehicle was now getting a little old. The mudguards had been replaced with flattened kerosene cans, the timbers at the back – what few of them remained – were secured with pieces of string. Even more serious, the main frame of the vehicle was cracked and the front half seemed only very tenuously connected to the rear. Riding in the cabin was, therefore, a somewhat unnerving experience, for when the front wheels hit a bump your knees were pushed into your chest and when they went into a dip the floorboards seemed suddenly to drop away from beneath your feet.

Having sent a radio message to Cairns asking for a launch to be sent up with spare parts, we had nothing to do except wait and we occupied ourselves by chipping oysters from the piles of the jetty. Raw or fried, they were the most delicious I had ever tasted.

Mac lived on the hill above the shore in a shelter of rusting corrugated iron that was almost submerged by a huge tip of empty beer cans and broken bottles. When he wasn't sitting on the jetty with a fishing line in his hand, he spent most of his time outside this shack – just sitting. One evening, I went up and joined him. In a burst of unusual loquacity, he told me what had first brought him here. He had come to search for gold. Many other men had been prospecting in the same area both before and since. A few of them had made good strikes. But not Mac.

'Found a few colours,' he said in a matter-of-fact tone, 'but never enough to make it payable.'

He rolled himself a cigarette, one-handed. 'I didn't bother goin' on lookin' after a couple of years at it. There's still plenty up there, if you're interested,' he added. 'But as far as I am concerned, it can stay. I'm right.'

'How long have you been here, now?' I asked.

'Thirty-five year,' he replied.

'Well, Mac,' I said jocularly, 'I reckon I know why you stayed. Those oysters on the jetty are the finest in the world, I reckon.'

Mac lit his cigarette. The paper flamed and he puffed hard until the tobacco was properly alight.

'That's good,' he said. 'I'm partial to a nice oyster. Often wondered what they would be like.'

He leaned against the wall of his hut.

'I've been meaning to get round to pickin' off a few. Jus' never seem to have the time.'

Doug Lockwood laughed at the story and ordered another round of beer. 'Yes,' he said, 'Mac would be a dinkum no-hoper. But you can find lots of blokes around the Territory who are just the same. If you wanted to see three together, then the place to go is Borroloola. It's a ghost town. Just a few crumbling shacks and, among the ruins, these three blokes.'

'Sounds interesting,' I said, 'where is it?'

'You just drive straight down the bitumen, and when you get to Daly Waters, turn left. From then on it's a straight run.'

So the next morning before dawn we drove through the dark cool streets of Darwin and headed south. That day was uneventful. The road stretched monotonously ahead, a strip of bitumen twenty yards wide and a thousand miles long. There was little traffic and even settlements were as much as fifty miles apart. Well before nightfall, we arrived at Daly Waters.

The next day, we started on the second lap and turned left at a signpost which said, simply 'Borroloola 240 miles'.

We bowled along the even road at a steady fifty miles an hour.

The track was so straight that, for twenty or thirty miles on end, there was no need to move the steering wheel more than a few inches. Desiccated dusty bushes, intermingled with low termite hills, grew thinly on the arid gravelly ground. The unwavering straightness of the road, the uniformity of the vegetation, were tiringly monotonous, and when we were not driving, we dozed. And when we opened our eyes again, the view was so similar that we might never have moved.

A hundred miles, a hundred and ten miles, a hundred and twenty miles. We rattled on. Every hour and a half, we stopped, changed drivers, allowed the engine to cool, topped up the water, oil and petrol. Our progress, if dull, was at least satisfactory.

Then we hit the dust. In the Territory, it is always called 'bull dust'. No one is sure why, but most people were able to suggest a coarse origin. Whatever its derivation, the word has now become enshrined in official literature and to call it simply dust would be slightingly inadequate. I do not believe that there is any other dust in the world quite like it. It is so odd that scientists have awarded it a special geological identity. In Alice Springs, we were told, people bottle it and sell it for good money to tourists who take it back south to substantiate their stories of the rigours of travel in the Territory. In consistency it is so fine that it has the sticky quality of talc. It lay across the road in great drifts that completely concealed pot-holes and boulders big enough to break an axle if a car hit them at speed. Sometimes we plunged into a patch so deep that it broke right over the car like a wave of water over a launched lifeboat. Sometimes it took on an eerie personality of its own, like an ectoplasmic monster in a horror film, for when we slackened speed, the clouds in our wake overtook us, creeping alongside our window in a threatening dirty white wall. We would then accelerate quickly, with the sensation that we were being pursued.

We kept a close watch on the mileometer. Our speed had now dropped to nearly half. With maddening slowness, it clicked up past 220, past 230. When it reached 240, we were still driving across a flat expanse of empty plain. According to the signpost at Daly Waters, we should have arrived at Borroloola. Yet here there was no sign of human habitation. Maybe our mileometer was wrong; maybe the signpost was wrong. Maybe, bemused by the straightness of the road, we had not noticed a turning off to Borroloola and we were now driving down a track which continued for another three hundred empty miles into Queensland. And then, when the mileometer read 248, we saw a signpost lying in the grass by the side of the road. Its finger, pointing vertically to the sky, proclaimed 'Borroloola Store 3 miles Petrol and Oil'.

Once, we judged, it must have directed the traveller down a vague turning on the opposite side. Heartened, we drove down it and within ten minutes we saw ahead a derelict building of corrugated iron beneath a mango tree. Beyond, a line of verdant trees marked the course of a river, the MacArthur. We had arrived.

We camped that night on the bank of the MacArthur. It was a perfect site. We pitched our tents on a wide sandy flat in the shade of a grove of casuarina trees. On the other side of the wide rippling river stood the remains of a few Aboriginal shelters. As the sun went down we built a large log fire. I spread out my sleeping bag beside it and read by the light of its leaping flames. From the dark river, came the flatulent honks of crocodiles and the slap of leaping fish. Now it was deliciously cool and I was grateful for the cover of my sleeping bag. The stars shone through the feathery leaves of the casuarinas with a crystalline brilliance. After the breath-robbing heat, the dust and the din of the drive, the place seemed paradisial. It was easy to understand why men had chosen this place to found a town.

The next morning, we looked round the remains of the settlement. Only three buildings still stood – each widely separated from the others. The old police station was now the residence of a government officer whose responsibility it was to look after the welfare of the Aboriginal people who camped in the bush on the other side of the river. A mile beyond it, across a ravine which in the wet season is the bed of a torrent running into the MacArthur, stood the small store to which the fallen signpost had directed us. There you could buy petrol and oil, beer, tinned fruit, bully beef, papier-mâché cowboy hats and boiled sweets. Its customers were Aboriginals, the occasional traveller on his way from or to Queensland, or horsemen from the cattle stations who, when out on a wide-ranging muster of their stock, might find themselves within a few hours' ride of Borroloola and reckoned it would be worth while calling in to have a beer and talk to another human being.

The third building, and the biggest of the three, was the derelict hotel, near our camp by the river. Its half-stripped corrugated-iron roof clanged and creaked ominously in the slightest wind. Its verandas were buckled and sagging. All around it, like flotsam accumulated around a breakwater, lay drifts of rubbish – broken rum bottles, jagged rusting beer cans, oil drums, half the chassis of a car, its steering wheel entwined with withered creepers, and strange wheels and levers of cast iron that must have formed part of some machine whose function we could not even guess at.

Inside, the floorboards crumbled beneath our feet – they were no more than paper-thin shells, their heart wood having been eaten by termites. A mildewed mirror hung askew on the wooden wall, an iron bedstead rusted crookedly in a corner. Among a pile of rubbish, I found a book. Its title *The Imitation of Christ* by Thomas à Kempis. Who could have brought such an erudite mystical work all the way out here? I turned over its title-page. Inside the termites had eaten nearly all the holy man's words, apparently relishing the taste of ink, for they had left the surrounding margins intact. Close by, curling and so brittle that pieces broke off in my hand, I found a map. It was dated 1888 and boldly titled, 'The Town of Borroloola'.

The old hotel at Borroloola

Towards the end of the last century, cattlemen, having established stations the size of English counties in Queensland, were moving west around the southern shores of the Gulf and into the still unexplored emptiness of the Northern Territory. Although the MacArthur River is tidal and brackish, its waters are sweet enough to be drinkable and here the stockmen watered the herds a thousand or more strong with which they hoped they would be able to populate their unseen cattle runs. Here too they could collect stores, for the river was easily navigable up to this point and, although the voyage from Darwin was a thousand miles long and might take six months to complete, it was cheaper and quicker to bring them in here than to haul them overland from Alice Springs. So the banks of the MacArthur became a regular camping place where men and beasts could rest and recoup before launching off once more into the dusty aridity of the Territory.

When gold was discovered away west in the Kimberleys, prospectors started overlanding from all parts of Australia in their haste to make a fortune. Many followed the cattle trails from Queensland and into the Territory by way of Borroloola. Those were tough times. Fights broke out between Aboriginal tribes and the white men who marched across their tribal grounds. The solitary prospector was in constant danger. To add to his difficulties, the country in the dry season was so arid that a man could easily die of thirst. Many did. The wiser ones proceeded cautiously from one known waterhole to another. One famous character in Borroloola was more successful than most for he had married an Aboriginal woman. With her as his guide, he was able to travel in areas where no European could go on his own, for she, a nomad who had spent her life wandering through this country, knew exactly which fold in the rocks held water the longest, just where to dig with your hands to make a hole into which underground water would seep as a brown, scummy fluid. Together the two of them explored the Territory inland from Borroloola. Each night they built a fire and when his wife lay down to sleep by the side of it, the old bushman rolled his blankets into the shape of a body and put it down as a dummy on the other side of the fire. Then he climbed a tree and spent the night sleeping in the crotch with his rifle in his lap. Only too often in the morning a gash in his blankets showed where it had been silently speared during the night.

By then, Borroloola had grown to the size of a small frontier settlement and seemed destined to blossom into a full-blown town. The map that we had found in the hotel showed the positions of hypothetical thoroughfares and squares, each labelled with a splendid-sounding name – Leichardt Street, Burt Street, MacArthur Terrace. The main road, Riddock Terrace, extended into a blank on the chart and ended with an arrow labelled 'To Palmerston'. Maybe this was a somewhat macabre joke on the part of the surveyors, or perhaps a device to encourage property speculators in the south to buy plots, for Palmerston was the contemporary name for Darwin which was separated from the infant township by five hundred and forty miles of trackless desert.

Nonetheless, Borroloola had the makings of a town. A police corporal, with his own gaol, was stationed there to try and bring some semblance of law to the wild horde of cattlemen and desperate prospectors who congregated on the banks of the MacArthur. He was a man with literary tastes and he sent a request down to Melbourne for a library. Astonishingly, a thousand books were despatched almost immediately. They were six months on the road before they reached their destination. Further consignments increased it to three thousand volumes. Horse teams and wagons waited by the government wharf on the river, ready to take the cargoes of stores discharged by the supply ships and haul them out into the Territory and up into the fertile Barkly Tablelands where cattle stations were now established.

About 1913, the first car left the main north–south highway in the centre of the Territory and drove out to Borroloola. Its tyres were protected by wrappings of buffalo hide and it followed a track which in the past had taken the best part of a year to cover in a horse-drawn buggy. Gold, coal, copper and silver-lead were discovered in the surrounding hills. In addition to the police station there were by then two hotels, five stores and a permanent population of fifty white folk. Borroloola seemed at last to be about to fulfil the hopes of the surveyors who so many years before had pegged out the lines of streets in the desert.

But in Australia, towns seem to be much more frail than they are elsewhere. In crowded Europe, a settlement seldom dies. Once it is established, it usually acquires a momentum of its own, even after the initial stimulus for its foundation has lost its validity, and it continues to create new activities and careers for its inhabitants. But human settlement in the Territory has flickered only fitfully over the vast empty spaces. It dies out here and springs up elsewhere, and only in a few places does it burn continuously. And when it gutters and dies, people just move out, leaving the empty buildings behind them. There is no over-spill of unhoused people anxious to take them over. No one bothers to knock down the rotting shacks for the sake of tidiness or for the benefit of a land-hungry population. No one even sees the deserted site. The homes are left to moulder, lost and forgotten.

As time went by, more and more artesian wells were bored inland and Borroloola lost its importance as a watering place. The Kimberley gold rush petered out. The big migrations of cattle and men from Queensland came to an end. New roads in the Territory made it easier for the stores to reach the cattle stations overland.

One by one the wagons rotted where they stood until nothing was left of them but the iron tyres of their wheels. Termites ate the entire library except for the one surviving volume we had found in the hotel. Few cars followed the pioneering motorist of 1913 and several of those that did roared and coughed their way to Borroloola and got no further, for although the mechanical ingenuity of the Australian bushman is great, there are some breakages inflicted by the ferocious terrain that can only be put right by replacement – and there were no spare parts in Borroloola. Up in the hot hills, the last of the full-time pros-pectors, sitting alone on his claim, shot himself. Slowly, Borroloola dwindled and died.

But to some, the three men we had come to see, the husk of the dead town was more attractive than it would ever have been if it had grown and flourished. To them, this was the best place on earth.

Jack Mulholland had been the last keeper of Borroloola's hotel. We found him sitting on the threshold of a small, dilapidated outbuilding that had once served as the post office. It was a position that he occupied with the permanence of a statue on its pedestal. Whenever we visited him, Mull was there in exactly the same attitude. If we drove by at dusk, we could see his dim outline framed against the permanently open door. If we arrived soon after dawn, Mull would be seated at his post. I was almost tempted to creep up in the middle of the night with a torch to see if he slept in this position as well. So accustomed did we become to seeing him there, that when, one afternoon towards the end of our stay, I arrived and found the doorway empty, I feared that something calamitous had happened. It was as though Nelson was missing from the top of his column. Alarmed, I looked inside the door. There lay Mull, outstretched on the floor in the midst of a litter of blankets, old car batteries, and tattered magazines. Apprehensively, I took a step inside. His chest heaved and, to my relief, he emitted a reverberating snore.

Jack Mulholland

Mull was a short, stocky Irishman in his late fifties. Although he had spent much of his life in Australia, his voice still retained a twang of brogue. He spoke slowly and softly. His eyes were permanently narrowed against the ferocity of the sun. His hair was still ungreyed and thick. He first came up this way, he told us, because he had heard that the 'Loo was a good place. He hadn't seen this part of the country so he decided to look it over. He found it to be all that its reputation had promised.

'So I just stayed,' he said, 'and put in four or five months' reading at the library. Then the owners of the hotel wanted someone to run it for them. I took over and I've been here ever since.'

He looked contemplatively at the huge crumbling building.

'Wasn't a very demanding job,' he added modestly. 'It suited me.'

'How many guests might you have at any one time?'

'Oh, never more than one at a time,' said Mull, shocked at the thought. 'Come to think of it, I can't remember more than three guests in all the time I've been here.'

'No wonder it closed,' I said.

'Yes,' said Mull, rubbing his unshaven chin reflectively and squinting up at the withered fronds of a palm tree that the wind was brushing against the roof. 'It wasn't really a tremendously vigorous financial concern.'

We were sitting on the steps at his shack. Around us stretched a sea of tin cans and broken rum bottles.

'Been doing a bit of drinking?' I asked.

'No,' said Mull stoically. 'Don't get a chance, really. Most of those bottles would be twenty years old.'

'Ever thought of tidying the place up?'

Mull looked at me severely.

'Tidiness,' he said, 'is a disease of the mind.'

Although Mull had very few material needs, he still had to buy flour, tobacco and ammunition from the store. I asked him how he managed for money.

'Shootin' crocodiles for their hides; huntin' for dingo, but they're pretty scarce round here these days; and of course I do a bit of radio repair work.'

This last seemed as unlikely an occupation as could have been devised for someone living in such a remote and unpopulated spot as this. We discovered, however, that Mull had a considerable reputation throughout this part of the country for being able to coax antiquated radios to life. He effected most of his repairs by a process of continuous cannibalism. A cattleman, riding through Borroloola, would dump a busted radio on Mull and ask him if he could fix it. In his own good time, Mull would identify the fault. Soldered joints and connections in this climate only too often came adrift and sometimes the repair was easy enough. But more often, a valve was burnt out, or a part needed complete replacement. Mull would then wait for maybe six months or so until another set came in for repair. Then he would remove the part from the second that he needed for the first. The cumulative demands made on each set meant that eventually some unfortunate man would be told that his radio, lying in the back of Mull's shanty stripped of its valves and condensers, was totally irreparable and then the process would start all over again. 'I right 'em or wreck 'em,' he said.

Mull, indeed, was a bush mechanic of a stature amounting to near genius. Beside his shack stood a 1928 Pontiac car – according, at least, to the badge on its bonnet. Very few of the original parts still remained, and the machine was more of an anthology of extracts from vehicles that had arrived and stayed to rot in Borroloola over the last fifty years. Its mammoth wooden-spoked rear wheels were of a quite different vintage from those on the front. All its tyres were flat and a large termite hill lay in the middle of the engine on top of a rectangular cylinder block of primitive simplicity and elegance. Superficially there was little to distinguish the machine from the other wrecks that lay nearby in the grass and it was difficult to imagine that it had been going within the last ten years. I nearly offended Mull by putting this thought into words and asking when he last used it. Fortunately I checked myself in time and rephrased my question.

'How often do you take her out?' I asked.

'I can start her any time you like,' he replied defensively. 'And she'll go places your Land-bloody-Rover won't.'

Mull and his ancient car

To prove his point, he offered to take her out on a spin the next day. The preparations necessary for this were considerable, but Mull had been so hurt by my imputation that he was stung into activity. First a water pump had to be fitted. He discovered one in an old hulk that lay in the courtyard and spent the afternoon filing grooves and notches in it so that it fitted his machine. The next morning all was ready. The Pontiac had been constructed long before the advent of electric starters, and the handle that was originally provided had long since been lost. But Mull had his own magnificently logical methods. First he jacked up the rear wheels until they were well clear of the ground. Then he put the engine into gear and started turning the back wheels by seizing hold of the spokes and heaving them round. It was an arduous job and Mull poured sweat. After five minutes, there was a tremendous roar and the engine shook into life. Mull dashed to the front, put the shuddering engine into neutral, and jacked down the back axle. With dignity he walked to the front, clambered into the seat and then proudly drove out to do a lap of honour round the hotel.

On one occasion, we learned later, Mull had taken an extended trip into the bush, the stimulus being provided by the impending arrival of a police officer in Borroloola. It wasn't that he had anything to hide or be afraid of, but he saw no sense in becoming entangled with the law unnecessarily. For three weeks, no one saw him. Then one day the distant, unmistakable roar of the car heralded his return across the flat plain. When he was within half a mile of home, the engine stopped. Mull could either have repaired it there and then, or have covered the remaining distance on foot, so that after so long an absence he could sleep once more under his own roof. He did neither. He clambered out, lit a fire, put on a billy for tea, spread out his swag and went to sleep in the shade beneath the car. He stayed there for three days, pondering on what might have gone amiss with the engine. Finally, he looked inside the bonnet and cleaned the plugs. The engine started immediately and, unruffled, he completed the journey home.

I asked Mull what he did on these trips out in the bush.

'Oh, prospectin' mostly,' he said.

'Have you ever found anything?'

'Well, got a bit 'er gold, opal, silver-lead. But never payable.'

'Isn't that a bit disappointing?'

'Not at all,' he replied with unaccustomed vehemence. 'It 'ud break a man's heart if he did discover anything. What else would there be to live for? Money's no good to you anyway.'

'It can make life comfortable and easy,' I suggested.

'What are you goin' to do with it then,' said Mull. 'Buy yerself a few luxury yachts, drink it, spend it on beautiful women. I see no sense in that. No, no. If I've learnt one thing in my life, it is that the measure of a man's riches are the fewness of his wants. I'm happy enough.'

'Well,' I said, 'there can't be many people who could live with as few comforts as you have and still say that they are happy.'

'Ah,' said Mull compassionately, 'then they've a screw loose somewhere. Definitely a screw loose.'

Mull's nearest neighbour was Borroloola's oldest inhabitant, Roger Jose. He had arrived here in 1916 and had only left it for short periods of time on three or four occasions since. He was a noble-looking man with a long grey beard of patriarchal proportions, curling silver hair and deeply scorched wrinkled skin. The clothes he wore were bizarre – a strange peaked hat, in shape like a French legionnaire's kepi but made to his own design from pandanus fibres. The arms of his shirts he had deliberately cut off at the shoulder, and he had trimmed his trousers just below the knee. If he had walked on to the stage in a production of *Treasure Island* as Ben Gunn, the audience might well have thought that the costume designer and make-up men had indulged their imagination a little too freely.

No one knew how old he was, and Roger himself was not a reliable guide, for he had been saying that he was sixty-nine for at least the last six years.

His house was as odd as his dress – a circular construction of corrugated iron, windowless and with a single small door in the side. Originally, it had been a five thousand gallon water tank holding the hotel's supply of rainwater. Roger had dismantled it and re-erected it a mile away, partly to escape the danger of falling sheets of corrugated iron flung from the roof of the disintegrating hotel by high winds that sometimes sweep the plain, and partly because, when Mull took up residence, he reckoned the hotel was becoming a little overcrowded.

Roger was the last custodian of the library. Before the books were entirely consumed by the termites, he had read nearly all of them and, in doing so, had acquired a passion not only for learning but for words. Words, indeed, obsessed him. He savoured them like succulent sweets. He rolled them off his tongue with relish. He pondered their precise meanings and derivations.

When I asked what food he ate, he replied, 'Well, I would fain crave my master's oxen, but I can't get 'em. Thus I am compelled to pursue the elusive marsupial.'

Roger Jose outside his hut

Occasionally, Tas Festing, the Welfare Officer who toured the area, visited Roger, and Roger would welcome the opportunity to share some of the more delectable words that he had dredged up from his memory since Tas's last visit. The conversation would usually start with Roger remarking absently, 'I was reading something the other day . . .' As far as Roger was concerned, 'The other day' might well have meant ten or fifteen years ago for his eyesight had prevented him from reading anything for a long time past. Then Roger would innocently put a question, hoping that Tas might either be stumped for an answer or give a wrong one, so that Roger could triumphantly correct him. This began to irritate Tas and one day he took the initiative.

'Roger,' he asked, 'have you ever, in the course of your reading, come across a *leotard*?'

Roger squinted suspiciously at Tas.

'Think I saw a skin of one once,' he said, tentatively.

'Couldn't have,' said Tas. 'Leotards don't have skins.'

Silence.

'Well what is a leotard?' challenged Roger.

Roger beside his water-tank home

But Tas wouldn't tell him. Three days later, Roger made the journey over to Tas's camp. The unsuspected gap in his knowledge had worried him so much that he had been unable to sleep. He had to know the answer. Only then did Tas tell him that a leotard was a ballet dancer's practice costume.

'Felt a real quarter-wit,' said Roger when he told us about it. 'Should have known that one.'

But Roger had gleaned more than mere words from all his reading. He had a taste for poetry and was fond of quoting Gray's 'Elegy', Shakespeare, Omar Khayyám, and the Bible. He recognized, too, that he was an abnormal character.

'But I'm not sub-normal,' he added quickly. 'Don't run away with that idea. I used to live in towns once with other people and got on perfectly all right. But that was before I got this superiority complex – before I decided that I could find no company better than my own. I came out to the wilderness looking for peace. This here is as far as I can go. In a sense, I suppose, I'm at bay.'

'Don't you ever find the loneliness overpowering?' I asked.

'How can I be lonely,' he replied softly, 'with God.' His voice quavered and he stopped. Then he brightened. 'And Old Omar and the Immortal Bill.'

Two miles beyond Roger's tank, across the dry creek bed and beyond the store, lived the most determined recluse of Borroloola – Jack, the Mad Fiddler. He sat alone in his cabin, week after week, playing his violin. We were warned that it was not advisable to visit him without an invitation to do so. Jack, on occasion, had been known to greet unexpected arrivals with a shotgun and angrily warn them off his property.

One morning, however, when we drove up to the hotel to pay a call on Mull, we saw an unfamiliar lorry standing by the old post office. On the running board sat a small bird-like man with spectacles and matchstick thin legs.

Mull introduced us to him. Jack looked at us suspiciously, said a grudging g'day, got to his feet and opened the door of his truck. For a moment I thought he was going to leave immediately. However, he merely reached inside and brought out a small screw-topped jar full of water. He unscrewed the lid, took a few sips, carefully replaced the top and set it down on the bonnet of the truck.

Mull and he were deep in conversation about the nature of free will. This may sound as though these men, in their loneliness, were exclusively concerned with questions of philosophy. I do not think that this was so. It was simply that in these circumstances it is almost impossible to make small talk. There is no raw material to base it on. Jack spoke quickly and nervously, with a hint of an Edwardian upper-class accent beneath his Australian phraseology. He spoke of 'gels' and 'motoring'. I remembered hearing that he was the titled son of an English aristocratic family.

'These fellers,' Mull said to Jack, pointing to us, 'have been asking me why I came out here. Why do you reckon you came, Jack?'

Jack looked at us aggressively. 'I was sent out of England for England's good,' he said flatly.

There was an embarrassed pause.

'They tell me you play the violin,' I said, anxious to change the subject.

'Yes. I've been at it for seven years now.'

'What sort of thing do you play?'

'Scales mostly,' he replied.

'What about tunes?'

'Wait on,' Jack replied mildly. 'The violin is a very tricky instrument you know. Fritz Kreisler and fellers like that had a fair start on me, because they were learning when they were knee-high to a grasshopper. I've taken it up rather late in life.' He took a sip from his jar of water.

'Still,' he said, 'I'm thinkin' of having a crack at Handel's Largo next year. But I'm in no hurry.'

It was Jack's ambition to play eighteenth-century music. There was nothing much, before or since, that was worth anything in his estimation.

'And anyway,' he added, 'this modern stuff costs quids for a few sheets. You can get Bach and Beethoven by the bale for a few bob.'

'Well,' he said, 'I can't waste all my time jabbering to you blokes. I'd better be going.' He climbed into his car.

'I was wondering whether we could come and visit you some time, Jack.'

'I don't think you'd better,' he said. 'You can never tell what mood I'm in.'

He swung the starting handle. The engine rattled asthmatically and he clambered inside. He engaged the gears with a screech. Then he leaned out of the window. 'If you don't bring any of them cameras and recording machines, I suppose it might be all right. See yer.'

He let out the clutch and drove away.

We took up his invitation the next day. We found his cabin on the edge of a beautiful crescent-shaped billabong, haunted by pelicans, egrets, ducks and cockatoos. When we drove up, Jack was busy inside his cabin and for some time he did not speak or acknowledge our shouted g'days but stayed hidden inside. It was as though he were screwing himself up for an ordeal. When he finally emerged, he was attentive and polite, offering us boxes to sit on. No sooner had we seated ourselves, however, than he disappeared again inside the house. Through the open glassless windows I saw him standing motionless holding his violin in his hands, staring at it. After fully two minutes, he replaced it tenderly in its case and slowly closed the lid. When he came out again I asked him if we might inspect his instrument.

'I'd rather not,' he said quietly.

We had done as we were bidden and not brought either cameras or recording machines with us. After we had talked together for some time, I raised the subject of his violin again.

'Why,' I said, jocularly, 'the world should know that they've got a budding violinist in the Northern Territory. Who knows, you may be a star in the making.'

Jack leaned forward and answered with passion. 'I've had all I want of fame. I was appearing in theatres in the north of England forty years ago with actors who are now famous all over the world. I want nothing of that sort of thing.'

For a moment I feared I had offended him. He got to his feet and picked up an enamel mug that lay on the improvised table of stringybark, drying. He started to polish it vigorously with a cloth.

'People call us hatters, you know,' he said bitterly. 'Well, they're right. You think old Mull and Roger are happy, don't you? That's what they've been telling you, isn't it? Well, they're not telling the truth. They're hatters, just the same as I am. They're miserable blokes most of the time, just like me. But a man comes out here for a bit for one reason or another, he stays on and before he knows what has happened, he's got to a stage where he can't change his way of life, even if he wanted to.'

He hung the mug on a nail, alongside an enamel plate which, with a hole punched in its rim, was hanging from another nail.

'Time you fellers were going,' he said and he disappeared once more inside his cabin.

24

The Centre

Halfway through our stay in Borroloola, I drove across to the store to buy some food. 'Is there one of you pommies by the name o' Lagos, or somethin' like that?' inquired the woman behind the counter, "cos the bloke runnin' the jabber session on Darwin radio is sendin' messages to 'im all over the Territory. My set's on the blink an' I didn't get the details, but it's urgent.'

It took us nearly a day to trace the message. When we succeeded, it was bad news. One of Charles's family was very seriously ill and he had to return to London immediately. We chartered a plane using Tas Festing's radio. It arrived the next day. Leaving our car and baggage with Tas, we all returned to Darwin. In a mere two and a half hours, we flew across country that had taken us two days of hard, rough driving to cover overland. That night Bob and I said goodbye to Charles as he climbed aboard a jet aircraft. Within twenty-four hours of flying time, he would be in London. It seemed extraordinary, as well as merciful, that even so remote a place as Borroloola which, in Roger Jose's eyes and in ours, was one of the loneliest places in the world, could, by the combined use of radio and aircraft, be linked so rapidly with a city on the other side of the globe.

I found a cable awaiting me in Darwin. Another cameraman, Eugene Carr, was already on his way from London to take Charles's place. The two unknowingly passed one another, somewhere in the air over India, and Gene landed in Darwin the following night. The next morning, we rushed him round the town to get him a driving licence and a pair of shorts. In the afternoon we hustled him on to the charter plane. That evening we were back in Borroloola.

Gene hardly knew what had happened to him. One day he had been filming a politician in London; four days later, he was in Borroloola filming Jack Mulholland. He did not say which of the two seemed to be talking better sense.

We had one more subject to tackle if we were to present even the sketchiest picture of life in the Northern Territory – the way that human beings once lived in some numbers in the empty desert country that lies in the south of the Territory across the heart of Australia. Perhaps we might meet some of the few Aboriginal people who can still make all the tools and weapons they need from the rocks around them, who can read the desert sands like a book and find food where strangers would starve.

So soon after Gene arrived, we left Borroloola and drove back along the bull-dust blighted track to Daly Waters. From there the bitumen led south, for mile after mile as straight as a ruled line, across a blank immensity of sand, stone and withered scrub. Only occasionally did a rocky outcrop or a stretch of drifting sand deflect it. The few cars that travelled along it moved at speed. There was nothing in the surrounding wilderness to tempt their drivers to linger. Their only anxiety was to cover as quickly as possible the brutal thousand-mile hiatus in civilization that separated Alice Springs from Darwin. Once or twice we passed a land train, a line of gigantic trailers, each the size of a large furniture van, stretching for fifty yards and drawn by an immense diesel lorry, the size of a military tank transporter, with twenty-two gears and the speed of a saloon car. Once it was moving fast, its driver, high up in the monumental cab, could not possibly stop it within a quarter of a mile or even manage a swerve. All other traffic made it their business to get out of its path. These mammoth vehicles were the links between the railhead at Alice Springs and the strange stunted little railway that straggled down from Darwin for a hundred and forty-six miles before giving up in the bush, over eight hundred miles short of the Alice.

A male bowerbird at his bower

Even the emptiest desert must have its meeting place where its inhabitants, scattered for much of the year, can assemble to exchange news, to see old friends, to have a party. Central Australia has the Alice. Long before the first European explorers rode in, Aboriginals had come padding barefoot through the red ranges, carrying long spears and boomerangs, to camp by the deep waterhole among the rocks and drink. For longer than anyone knows, the place was theirs. Then, in the late nineteenth century, the Overland Telegraph was built and when the poles came marching across the horizon from the south and continued beyond into the thirsty wasteland north, the Telegraph men built a wooden repeater station here and made the settlement one of their main bases and a dump for their supplies. Soon a railway followed the poles, and the Alice grew accordingly. Stringy, stubble-chinned men from the cattle stations farther north overlanded their herds along the stock trails down to the town and, when they had loaded their beasts on to the railway wagons and sent them rattling away down south, they stayed on to relax and celebrate; and the Alice soon had bars and a race track to encourage them to dally. Later, when small frail aeroplanes began to buzz daringly over the desert, the Rev. John Flynn, of the Australian Inland Mission, selected the town as the centre for what was to become the Flying Doctor Service.

And now the tourists come. For them the Alice is the embodiment of the Outback, the magical country that every Australian city dweller knows vaguely to be his birthright, where pioneers are tough lean men on horseback and the land is still wild and empty. The Alice caters for them too. We found a brand-new shining hotel standing brashly several storeys high in a town dominated by bungalows. Among the shops selling saddles and stock whips were others with sheaves of spears standing in the corner, shell necklaces made by Aboriginal girls on coastal missions a thousand miles north, and miniature boomerangs, gaudily painted with the bearded face of an Aboriginal.

West of Alice Springs begins a desert so harsh that it cruelly repulsed many of the travellers who first tried to enter it, scorching their skins, torturing them with thirst, crippling their horses, deceiving them with its mirages and sending them back, half-blinded and close to starvation. We had come to its edge to look for desert Aboriginals, people who understood the nature of its rocks, its plants and its animals so well that they could survive in a wasteland where others would quickly die. Many of the tribes who inhabited this desolate land fifty years ago have now abandoned their old territories and come to terms with the white men, to live on cattle stations and in towns. Some have disappeared altogether. But one tribe, the Walbiri, stubbornly resisted attempts to change them and clung to their ancestral land, arid and hostile though it is.

A few of them, in order to get the white man's goods that they most coveted – axes and knives and blankets – came out to work for the prospectors and cattlemen during the last century. But they seldom became dependent on their temporary employers and when they had earned enough to buy what they wanted, or if they were treated in a manner they disliked, they retreated into the desert, much of which was still virtually unexplored by the whites. In 1910, two miners did wander deep into their country. The Aboriginals attacked them with spears and one of the white men was killed. The incident confirmed the Walbiri's reputation for being truculent and dangerous.

So the situation continued until 1924. In that year, a drought began that was to be the worst in the history of the Territory. Waterholes that even in the most severe seasons had retained a green scummy pool of tepid water, now dried up completely. Kangaroos, possums, bandicoots and the other animals on which the tribe depended for food disappeared. After two years even the Walbiri could endure it no longer. Many died in the desert. Others, starving, came out to seek help from the white men settled on their frontiers. And still the drought continued. After four years, a band of tribesmen, desperate for food, came across an old prospector, sitting beside a soak in the desert. They murdered him and stole his stores. To take revenge, a policeman rode out in search of Walbiri and shot seventeen. Few, if any, of his victims could have taken part in the original murder. That was not the point. The blacks must be taught a lesson.

When the five-year drought ended, some of the tribe remained labouring at the mines or working as stockmen for the pastoralists, but most, remembering the brutality of the white man's reprisals, went back into their wilderness.

The government then established settlements for them, first at Haast's Bluff in the south of their country and later, in 1946, at Yuendumu, 170 miles north-west of Alice Springs. Even though both stations have now been running for many years, the Walbiri who live there have remained among the least changed of all the people who once inhabited the desert. It was to Yuendumu that we went.

The focus of life on the settlement was a tall clanking windmill that pumped up water from a hundred feet below ground and spilled it into a great tank. This was the strongest of the shackles that kept the nomads tied to the station and they had built their untidy shelters of bark, branches and corrugated iron in the scrub nearby. There were some four hundred of them. They looked tough, proud people. Many of the men, particularly the older ones, bore frightening scars on their bodies. Those that puckered their thighs had been self-inflicted. They were mourning scars that a bereaved man slashes with a knife to show the depth and intensity of his sorrow. But others, on the shoulders and the back, had been received in battle. One of the Walbiri methods of fighting is simple and appallingly stoical. The two enemies sit cross-legged in front of one another. One leans over and stabs a knife into the back of his unresisting opponent. Then it is his turn to submit. Again and again they stab one another until one admits defeat or more likely collapses from loss of blood.

In physique, these people were more heavily built than the Arnhem Landers we had seen. They had barrel chests and strong well-muscled legs. It is difficult for men to appear noble when dressed in rags and clustering around a lorry to receive a daily handout of flour and sugar. But these people were not submissive or servile. When we talked to a man, he looked us straight in the eyes. He had his standards and we had ours. The two of us inhabited different worlds and here, where they met, he was at a disadvantage. But we knew – and he knew – that stripped of the material wealth bequeathed to us by our own society, and abandoned alone in the desert, he was the better man.

It was not easy to make friends immediately. A time for eyeing one another was necessary. We must neither appear to presume to have authority, as though we were trading on the colour of our skins, nor must we seek easy popularity by handing round gifts indiscriminately. The Walbiri would take them, but would doubtless consider us foolish and profligate. The first man we came to know at all well was Charlie Djagamara, one of the elders. He was constantly to be found somewhere in the camp, for he was too old to learn the skills of stockwork which occupied many of the younger men. But he was not so aged that, like several of the patriarchs of the tribe, he could do little but squat in the shade of his shelter and wait for the daily distribution of food. He habitually wore a curious wig-like hat made from coarse grass, thickly bound with strings of twisted human hair. Both his thighs were deeply criss-crossed with mourning scars and his chest was marked with the long weals produced by initiation cuts. He seldom wore any clothing other than a rag around his loins. It is scarcely surprising that a people living in a waterless desert should have no tradition or taste for washing, and it would be dishonest not to admit that when Charlie clambered into the truck alongside us, he brought with him a strong rancid smell.

We explained that we were anxious to see how he and his people had managed to live in the desert 'in time belong before, all same custom belong Walbiri' and Charlie put himself out to show us.

Unfortunately, I found it very difficult to understand much of what he said, for his pidgin was not as good as that of younger men and as a result we often had to follow him without knowing exactly what he had decided to reveal to us.

When he went out into the bush, he usually took with him two or three boomerangs and a wommera. The wommera, functionally, was the same as the ones we had seen at Maningrida, with a peg at one end which slotted into a notch in the butt of a spear, thus becoming an artificial extension of a man's arm and enabling him to throw the spear with greater leverage and force. But in shape, this wommera was rather different. Whereas the Maningrida ones had been simple slender strips of wood an inch or so wide, the Walbiri version was broader and had curling edges that formed an elegantly shaped elongated dish, two feet long, in which a man could carry things.

We had not seen boomerangs before, for the Arnhem Land people did not make them – they would be useless in the relatively thick bush of the north. Charlie's were not returning boomerangs. That type was only made by the tribes of the east and west. They were sometimes used in hunting – a man might send one spinning through the air above a flock of ducks to frighten them down into nets – but mostly they were playthings. Charlie's, on the other hand, were weapons, long heavy pieces of hardwood, beautifully balanced with a short bend in the end. A Walbiri warrior throws them straight at an animal or an enemy. He does not expect them to come back. He expects them to wound and kill.

Charlie referred to these objects as 'boomerangs' and 'wommeras' for our benefit. The names were not Walbiri ones and Charlie had learned them from the white men. These words, like 'corroboree' and 'myall' and other names that the European uses for Aboriginal customs and objects had first been picked up by the colonists of Botany Bay and other settlements in the south from the local tribes. They have survived as part of the English language. The Aboriginals who created them are now extinct.

Charlie led us out to a ridge and went straight to an outcrop of boulders, gesturing to them and grinning at us, to explain that these particular rocks were in some way special and valuable. To us they seemed very similar to the other boulders that lay everywhere in this stony wilderness. With three deft blows of a pebble, he knocked off a series of flakes from a boulder. Picking one up, he held it in his hand and demonstrated that it was a very serviceable knife blade. But that was not all. Charlie got to his feet and beckoned. We followed. He marched determinedly down past the stock fence, beyond a second water bore that had been sunk for the cattle, and into a small valley. There he gathered a

Charlie knocking a series of flakes from a boulder

pile of prickly dry spinifex grass and began thrashing it with a stick. Clearing away the grass, he carefully collected the dust that had fallen from it and piled it on to a piece of bark.

Next, he found a dry cracked log. By sawing the sharp edge of his hardwood wommera across one of the cracks, he produced smoke and a pile of hot black powder in the crack. Quickly, he tipped the powder on to a handful of grass and blew on it. It smouldered and then burst into crackling flames. In less than two minutes, he had produced a fire. He built it up with logs until he had a fierce blaze and into the middle of it he threw half a dozen stones. When they were really hot, he took one out of the fire with a pair of sticks, screwing up his face against the heat, and dropped it into the middle of the grass powder. There was a sizzle, a little smoke, and the dust, which was composed mainly of tiny beads of resin that had exuded and solidified on the stems of the spinifex, melted into a soft plastic substance. Two or three more hot stones completed the process. Carefully picking up the putty-like mass and throwing it from hand to hand, he moulded it around the stone flake so that it gripped it firmly. Then he put it by the fire again so that once more it became soft and malleable and he could perfect its shaping. He had made, from rocks and grass, an excellent sharp knife, quite strong and sharp enough to skin and butcher an animal – or to inflict a dreadful wound in a fight.

Another day, he led us to a different part of the desert. After walking purposefully ahead for some time, he suddenly slackened his pace and began to examine the ground carefully. At last he discovered what he had been seeking – ants. Charlie went to great pains to indicate a minute yellowish spot on their tiny bodies. It was this, he made clear, which made them different from all others. Pushing his way through the bushes, he followed the scurrying insects along their meandering trail until they disappeared down a hole. There he dug, clearing away the red earth with his boomerang until, three feet down, he exposed the galleries of their nest. Reaching down, he delicately brought out handful after handful of translucent amber objects, the size and shape of small marbles. He handed me one. It was alive – an ant, with six tiny legs wriggling at one end of a vastly bloated abdomen. Holding one by the head between his fingers, he put it into his mouth and gestured for me to do the same. As the soft sac-like abdomen split between my teeth, I tasted sweet warm honey. I grinned. Charlie smacked his lips and roared with laughter.

These were honey-pot ants. The workers labour in the bush, collecting honeydew exuded by the desert plants during the brief rainy season, and, instead of storing it in combs, as bees do, they feed it to newly emerged workers in the nest until they become so distended that they cannot move. These then remain clinging to the roof of their gallery, holding their honey, like living jars, until the other members of the colony, in the dry season when food is not to be found elsewhere, make them surrender it again.

Collecting honey-pot ants

Charlie could not show us every technique of wresting a living from the desert. There were some jobs that would have been undignified for him to tackle, which were only done by women. We understood this and asked him, therefore, if he could guide us to the place where the women collected the roots and seeds. But this was difficult. Just as the bush around Maningrida had been subdivided by invisible frontiers into territories belonging to different people, so there were similar geographical divisions around Yuendumu. One large area adjoining the encampment was strictly women's country. Any man going there, particularly if he was alone, would be suspected of having ulterior motives and might well be inviting a fight from a suspicious husband. After some hesitation, Charlie conceded that nobody would be scandalized if he and we went together, accompanied by one of his three wives and a younger girl. We drove out in the truck, but when we reached the place where the women wanted to stop, Charlie had second thoughts and decided that it might after all be more proper if he stayed in the truck and we went no further than a few yards from it. The women began to clear away the earth at the base of a low acacia bush with their long digging sticks, poles of heavy wood pointed at each end. With these they excavated the roots and cracked them open. From inside many of them, they extracted fat white squirming witchetty grubs, the larvae of a wood-boring beetle. The women ate them alive, there and then.

Charlie claimed that he was too old these days to go hunting. Instead, he said, it would be better if we went with some of the younger men. There was no shortage of volunteers when we let it be known that we would take a party of hunters out into the desert in our car, for this meant that whoever came could visit distant country which was little hunted and where the game therefore were less scarce. Before we left, the four men who were to come with us held a short conference to decide which part of the country we should visit. They selected a place over fifteen miles away. Not only were they confident that animals would be abundant there, but nearby was a small waterhole, and also a tree which, they estimated, would now be in flower.

It was exactly as they had predicted. We came to a low hill of bare granite and, in a fold in its flank, we found water. Having drunk, they went over to the tree which was covered in yellow flowers and pulled off handfuls of fleshy-petalled blossoms and ate them, relishing the taste of the nectar. Then, refreshed, they left with their boomerangs in one hand and their spears and wommera over their shoulders. We let them go alone, for to have accompanied them would have been to reduce seriously their chances of success. A kangaroo hunt depends on stealth and an ability to freeze completely motionless for as long as the kangaroo being stalked is looking in your direction. We knew only too well that we would prove awkward and noisy hunters, so we stayed on the granite hump and watched them through binoculars.

They scattered and one by one searched the ground for tracks. All people who live by hunting have powers of observation and deduction which seem, to city dwellers, little short of the miraculous, but it is hard to believe that there can be any more skilful than the Aboriginals. Not only can they recognize immediately the kind of animal that has made a track well-nigh invisible to untutored eyes, but they can also tell the creature's age and sex, its size and whether it is wounded or healthy. Even more astonishing, they can recognize the footprints of all the close members of their tribe and are quick to detect the tracks of any stranger intruding, uninvited, into their country.

One of the Europeans at Yuendumu told us of an old man who, out walking in the bush, saw a faint footprint in the sand. He recognized it as that of his brother whom he had not seen for many years. Judging from the track, it must have been several days before that his brother had passed that way, but nonetheless the old man decided immediately to follow the spoor. For five days he trailed it, until at last, in the evening, he caught up with his brother camping by a waterhole. The two men sat there talking for two nights and a day. Then the old man walked for five days back to Yuendumu.

Our hunters soon found kangaroo spoor. As silence was imperative, they conversed with one another, as they tracked several hundred yards apart, like tic-tac men, with an eloquent language of hand signs. Soon they were out of sight. Within an hour, all three of them were back, each carrying over his shoulder a kangaroo. One they decided to cook immediately. Making a fire with a wommera in the same way as Charlie had done, they heaped it with branches. After cutting out some of the entrails, taking great care not to puncture the gall bladder, they threw the body of the kangaroo, unskinned, into the flames. As the fire burnt down, they heaped ashes over the carcass and went to sleep in the shade of a tree. Half an hour later, the kangaroo was cooked, juicy and tender.

So the Walbiri showed us that they, through skills and

knowledge developed by necessity and evolved through generations, could survive in country that has killed many a man of another race, who did not understand it as they did. Now, at Yuendumu they were being taught different skills. The men on the station were being trained to become stockmen and shown how to care for cattle, roping them, branding them, mustering and following up strays. Gangs laboured at erecting fences across the desert to prevent the herds from wandering. Those who were particularly skilled went out to work as stockmen on the nearby cattle stations, but they still returned regularly to their people at Yuendumu. The women were taught dressmaking, laundry work and cooking. A Baptist missionary had laboured there for many years. Two school teachers held classes for the children every day, and twice a week the Superintendent gathered together the older men into a council to discuss the work and progress of the station. When I attended they were talking about the siting of a new block of houses that the government was soon to erect for them, and there was a long debate about who should be the first occupants. The Superintendent listened with great patience. By his side, acting as interpreter, sat a young Walbiri boy who, being orphaned when a baby, had been brought up by the missionary and spoke perfect English.

He seemed nervous, and with good cause. The responsibilities on his shoulders, the strains and pressures to which he was subjected, were immense. On the one hand his foster parents and the rest of the white community expected him to behave according to the morality and custom of his Christian upbringing. Yet he could never feel really at ease in a gathering of whites, never be unaware that he was of a very different race. On the other hand, his blood relations, old tough warriors, and his contemporaries who had served a savage apprenticeship in the desert, knew that he had not truly qualified to be a Walbiri man, for he had not undergone the initiations and ceremonies that they had. His body was unmarked by ritual scars. Only recently there had been a crisis. The Superintendent, anxious to fathom some of the older men's objections to one of his plans, had asked the lad to interpret. The elders objected. They were discussing matters that could not be revealed to an uninitiated man. A compromise was agreed upon. The boy was to be taken and the nail of his thumb engraved with a ritual symbol. But it was not a full initiation and whether it would really solve the problem seemed doubtful. I did not envy the boy.

One day, we noticed a group of men sitting some distance from the encampment. I walked over towards them and stopped some hundred yards away. Most of the people were cattlemen in long trousers and broad-brimmed hats, but among them I recognized Charlie Djagamara. He beckoned, inviting me over. The men were painting wooden shields with totemic designs. 'What for they paint 'im?' I asked Charlie.

'Soon – young boys – they cut 'im,' Charlie said.

'When they do it?'

'Dunno,' he answered. 'This not my dreamin'. I no boss man 'long 'ere. Tomorrow time, I make business. You like come along – I show you.'

We kept Charlie to his word and the next day he took us down to a different part of the scrub where a dozen men were sitting in the shade of a tree. Most of them were elders. Several were naked except for a small pubic tassel. There was an atmosphere of great good humour, the men laughing and joking among themselves. Then one man started to sing and another struck two boomerangs together, beating time. They began to smear themselves with red ochre, mixed with kangaroo fat.

Then, they began decorating another man. He was to be the chief actor in the ceremony. Around his head a helper was constructing a mushroom-shaped hat of grass, binding it together with yards of human hair string. As he worked, he shrieked, fluttering his hand, fingers outstretched, in front of his mouth so that his call became a high-pitched chilling vibrato. From rusty cans, helpers took handfuls of fluffy cottony seeds, some white, some reddish brown, and stuck them to the actor's body. Slowly, a swirling totemic design, red-brown on a field of white, took shape on the actor's back. He was becoming a snake. As he was being decorated the snake man shook his shoulders and twitched as though shudders were running through his body. Down was stuck to his chest and his back, to his headdress and eventually all over his face so that his features became invisible behind an amorphous mask. It dripped from his nose, overhung his eyes and concealed his mouth, like moss.

In many ways, the beliefs underlying this ceremonial markedly resembled those held by Magani and his people in Arnhem Land. The Walbiri say that the world and everything in it was created during the Dreamtime, by creatures and objects that travelled across the land, making the rocks and the waterholes and performing ceremonies. During these rituals, the Dreamtime beings shook their bodies and the down with which they were covered was flung off, just as the down of the snake dancer had been, and impregnated the surroundings. These particles, *guruwari*, give life to all living things. The *guruwari* of the ancestral kangaroo is that which gives life to present-day kangaroos, so that, in a sense, the Dreamtime exists within them. Similarly, it is *guruwari* that enters the womb of a woman. The exact tracks followed by all the Dreamtime beings as they moved across the country are well known, so a woman knows to what totem her child belongs by recalling where she was when she conceived. As a result, brothers may not always belong to the same totem, and men of quite different clans may have a kinship because they were conceived on different parts of a track made by the same ancestral spirit.

But although the Dreamtime was in the past, it is also coexistent with the present, and a man, by performing the rituals, can become one with his 'dreaming' and experience eternity. It is to seek this mystical union that the men enact the ceremonies. But the performances also serve other purposes. By them men cherish the *guruwari* and so ensure the continued abundance of their totemic animal. Sometimes newly initiated men are brought to watch the ceremonies so that they may learn the songs and witness the mysteries. Sometimes, as on the occasion we had seen, no novices are present and the ritual is performed to re-affirm the clan's unity with their totem and as a mutual demonstration of their brotherhood. By taking part together in these mysteries, by sharing and cooperating in the preparations and performance, they strengthen the bonds of fellowship that unite them.

It was at the snake ceremony that we met Tim. He was one of the youngest men present. After the performance, we talked together. Tim knew a great deal about the world beyond his desert. During the war, he had got a job with the Army driving a truck, one of the few Walbiri to do so. Several times, he had travelled the length of the bitumen. He knew Alice Springs and he had visited Darwin. He had even flown in an aeroplane. Now he was the driver of the settlement's lorry. He knew well the ways of the white man. But nothing of what he had seen had weakened his allegiance to his ancient gods. He talked passionately about the ceremony, anxious to convince us of its importance and potency. It was he who urged us to come with him and see the sacred rock where the snake had first emerged on to the earth.

We went out in our truck. Charlie and two of the other old men who had taken part in the ceremony came with us. We drove, with Tim directing us, to a lonely valley. One side of it was formed by a long overhanging cliff face, painted all over with animals, symbols and people. Tim pointed to it. 'This dreaming place.'

Tim showed me around, pointing out the different designs, and telling me what they meant to his people. While we talked, Charlie and the other old men had gone to the other end of the rock. Charlie had taken a tin of white ochre from behind a boulder and was painting yet another design on the cliff face.

Our journey was at an end, our return to London overdue. By the time we had driven back to Alice Springs, our car could go no further. Racked and pounded by the desert, it could not tackle another thousand miles back to Darwin without a major overhaul and large-scale repairs. We left it in a garage to be sent back to Darwin on a land train.

We ourselves had to fly back. Below us lay the Northern Territory, the Stuart Highway a thin line scratched on its surface. Men had given their lives trying to explore this country. Planters and pastoralists had tried to dominate it and had failed. Prospectors had died trying to extract minerals from it. Jack Mulholland and the other men at Borroloola had come to hide themselves in its loneliness. But only the Aboriginals living in their traditional manner can survive in it unaided. Unlike the white man, they make no attempt to dominate it. They do not try to tame its animals or to cultivate its sands, but to them it yields enough to keep a man's soul in his body. In return, the Aboriginals worship it. Its rocks and its waterholes are the creations of their gods and their walkabouts through it become pilgrimages. Perhaps no one else can ever understand it as they do, accepting equally its beauty and brutality.

Soon, even the Stuart Highway was invisible. There was nothing now but empty arid desert, freckled with bush stretching monotonously to the horizon.

About the Author

———

Sir David Attenborough is a broadcaster and naturalist whose television career is now in its seventh decade. After studying Natural Sciences at Cambridge and a brief stint in publishing, he joined the BBC in 1952 and spent ten years making documentary programmes of all kinds, including the *Zoo Quest* series. In 1965, he was appointed Controller of a new network, BBC2, and then, after four years became editorially responsible for both BBC1 and BBC2.

After eight years of administration, he returned to programme-making to write and present a thirteen-part series, *Life on Earth*, which surveyed the evolutionary history of animals and plants. This was followed by many other series which, between them, surveyed almost every aspect of life on the planet.

Discover the first adventures of

Sir David Attenborough

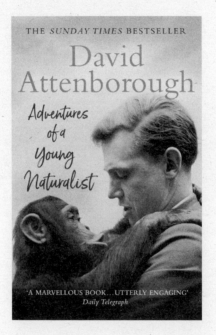

Available in paperback and eBook